A DAYTRIPPER'S
GUIDE TO MANITOBA

EXPLORING CANADA'S
UNDISCOVERED PROVINCE

BARTLEY KIVES

D0882102

GREAT PLAINS
PUBLICATIONS

Great Plains Publications
420 – 70 Arthur Street
Winnipeg, MB R3B 1G7
www.greatplains.mb.ca

Great Plains Publications gratefully acknowledges the financial support provided for its publishing program by the Government of Canada through the Book Publishing Industry Development Program (BPIDP); the Canada Council for the Arts; as well as the Manitoba Department of Culture, Heritage and Tourism; and the Manitoba Arts Council.

Design & Typography by Relish Design Studio Inc.
Printed in Canada by Friesens

CANADIAN CATALOGUING IN PUBLICATION DATA

Main entry under title:

Kives, Bartley
    A daytripper's guide to Manitoba : exploring Canada's Undiscovered province / Bartley Kives.

Includes index.
ISBN 1-894283-64-3

    1. Manitoba—Guidebooks   I. Title.

FC3357.K58   2006   917.2704'4   C2006-900501-X

*To Aba, whose journey continues
despite the end of his travels.*

CONTENTS

PREFACE

The licence plate says "Friendly." It should also say "Undervisited," "Underappreciated," and "Undiscovered," even by the people who live within its borders.

Manitoba, in the minds of most Canadians, is a land of endless grain fields populated by parka-wearing bumpkins with a fondness for snowmobiles and ice fishing. Or at least that's what Canadians would think if they even stopped to consider Manitoba for a nanosecond.

This province – locked away in a mid-continental netherworld between Nunavut and North Dakota – defies simple categorization. Manitoba is neither Eastern nor Western, refusing to identify with either urbane Ontario or antagonistic Alberta and – wrongly, perhaps – turning up its nose at simple Saskatchewan. It's also neither urban nor rural, as its 1.2 million souls are divided between quirky metropolitan Winnipeg and the rest of this 650,000 square kilometre coffee-pot. And it's not even a real Prairie province, as fertile farmland only covers a southwestern triangle hemmed in by boreal forests, some of the largest lakes in the nation, and the rugged Canadian Shield.

Manitoba is a place few travellers really know, whether they live in Winnipeg, the rest of Manitoba, or anywhere else. The pages in your hands constitute the first general-purpose guidebook to the province, which is amazing, considering the number of travel tomes on the market. It's also amazing considering the attractions Manitoba has to offer, including beaches without crowds, more lakes than non-mathematicians can quantify, a mix of urban culture and unspoiled wilderness, and a multifaceted ethnic mosaic that should be the envy of the modern world.

But the mission behind *A Daytripper's Guide to Manitoba* is not to proselytize the masses who've never visited before. Obviously, Thompson isn't Tahiti, Dauphin will never be Disneyland, and the Giant Golfball of Gilbert Plains isn't destined to outshine the Great Wall of China any time soon.

Most Manitoba tourists actually live inside the province. Many more just happen to be passing through, either for business or as part of a cross-country jaunt along the Trans-Canada Highway. Others come here specifically to fish, shop, paddle, or head north to the province's sole well-developed tourist attraction, the ecotourism

The author braving the wilds of Wolseley on a portage to the Assiniboine River.

Mecca of Churchill. This guidebook is intended to serve all Manitoba travellers, from ecotourists to culture vultures. Don't be fooled by the title – this *Daytripper's Guide* is meant for long-term visitors and locals, too.

In the following chapters, you'll get the basic goods about natural and cultural attractions in every region of Manitoba. The vast majority of these places can be reached within a day's drive of Winnipeg, although others warrant longer excursions.

On that note, if you want to see much of Manitoba, you're going to need a car. You're also going to need an energetic set of limbs, a sharp pair of eyes, and an adventurous palate. As flat as the land may seem, this is no place for the sedentary or the soft.

Just one word of warning, which is standard for any guidebook: It never hurts to inquire further about any destination you're thinking of visiting. This guidebook was completed in early 2006. After this date, prices are bound to go up, restaurants are bound to close, and some undiscovered attractions are bound to be trampled by visitors, possibly because of this very book.

If you find any inaccuracies – or wish to add more information for a possible future edition – please e-mail info@greatplains.mb.ca.

Thanks in advance. Enjoy Manitoba!

And if you happen to be a parka-wearing grain farmer who drives a snowmobile to the local ice-fishing hole, my apologies. Thanks for buying the book, anyway.

Bartley Kives
Winnipeg, 2006

Katarina Kupca

A BRIEF HISTORY OF MANITOBA

The Earliest Inhabitants

Compared to almost any other chunk of earthbound real estate, Manitoba is one of the newest places on the planet. As recently as 13,000 years ago, a massive sheet of ice covered every square centimetre of the province. Plants, animals, and people only moved in after the glaciers melted, which means every single creature in Manitoba – every fish, mosquito, rodent, and corporate lawyer – is a recent arrival, in the grand geological scheme of things.

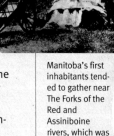

PAM

Manitoba's first inhabitants tended to gather near The Forks of the Red and Assiniboine rivers, which was an historical trading route for First Nations throughout the region.

The great glaciers didn't melt all at once, but in a series of hiccups and spasms that allowed life to move first into the southwest corner of the province, eventually spreading northeast. The earliest humans arrived not long after the ice receded, likely following big game and offers of cheap real estate. Artifacts found near Boissevain, a town south of Brandon, suggest the first Manitobans moved in sometime between 12,000 and 10,000 BC and hunted mastodons and long-horned bison, both of which are now extinct.

Over the next 10,000 years, wave after wave of Aboriginal peoples migrated into the province and sometimes out again, as the climate fluctuated between temperate and mind-numbingly cold. From around 5,000 BC to around 200 BC, more technologically advanced toolmakers hunted elk and caribou but also fished, foraged for wild vegetables and berries, and began to cultivate wild rice. Then, from around 200 BC to AD 1100, a series of increasingly sophisticated semi-nomadic cultures developed seasonal but permanent villages throughout southern Manitoba, as well a complex network of trade routes with distant Aboriginal groups.

Opposite: Thousands of seasonal workers, mainly from Ontario, would take the train to Manitoba for work during the fall harvest.

Four distinct groups – the Dene, Cree, Dakota Sioux, and Ojibway – were firmly established in the province by the time Europeans arrived *en masse* to cause trouble for the locals.

The Dene and Cree have been in Manitoba for centuries, if not millennia. The Dene are Athapaskan-speaking hunter-gatherers whose numbers are now greater in Nunavut and the Northwest Territories. They once followed caribou across northwestern Manitoba, but are now largely confined to two remote communities: Tadoule Lake and Lac Brochet.

The Cree, whose language is in the Algonkian family, are the most populous indigenous group in Manitoba. The Cree fished and hunted along boreal forests, rivers, and lakes from Hudson Bay right down to the bottom of Lake Winnipeg. Forced to move west or settle, Cree communities are present in every part of the province, with the exception of the extreme north and southwest.

The Ojibway are another Algonkian-speaking group, who may prefer to be called Anishinabe. They are the most recent arrivals. Ojibway moved into Manitoba from Ontario in the 1700s, after leaving their traditional lands east of Lake Superior, where they came into conflict with the Iroquois as well as settlers from England and France. Today, Ojibway communities are concentrated in Manitoba's southeastern quadrant.

The Dakota, the northernmost branch of the mostly American Sioux, are most commonly associated with Manitoba's southwestern plains, though Siouan-speaking Assiniboine – traditional allies with the Cree – used to hunt and fish as far north as the Saskatchewan River. That said, most of the Dakota who live in Manitoba moved into the southwest corner of the province from the United States, either to avoid conflict with the incoming Ojibway in the late 1700s, or fleeing from the US military in the late 1800s. Today, Manitoba's Dakota communities remain concentrated in a ribbon of land from Portage la Prairie to the Saskatchewan border.

Before the arrival of Europeans, indigenous peoples lived tough but independent lives, surviving the harsh climate by living off the land in relative harmony with nature. To describe the First Nations experience after 1492 as anything less than cultural genocide would be an irresponsible understatement. To many indigenous people, the entire continent of North America is a war crimes site – and Manitoba is no different, despite the fact roughly one in ten people in the province can still claim some Aboriginal ancestry.

The sad tale of indigenous/European contact in Manitoba is too involved to recount here. Generally speaking, Manitoba's mostly nomadic First Nations were forced to settle on isolated reserves of marginal economic value as Canada's federal government pursued a policy of forced assimilation. That failed, as a resilient Aboriginal population survived a brutal period from 1850 to 1990 with its identity intact, albeit tenuously, in a handful of the more remote communities.

Over the past 15 years, a cultural reawakening has coincided with an improvement in living standards, though Manitoba's indigenous people continue to be less healthy, wealthy, and gainfully employed than the provincial norm. But the future only bodes well, as a fast-growing Aboriginal population is uniquely positioned to take advantage of the province's stable economy and chronic shortage of skilled workers.

New Kids on the Block

The first white guy to see Manitoba was British seaman Thomas Button, who sailed into Hudson Bay and visited the mouth of the Nelson River in 1612. But the first European to really explore the

PAM

province was Englishman Henry Kelsey, who paddled up the Churchill and Saskatchewan rivers and reached the edge of the Prairies as early as 1670, the same year the London, England-based Hudson's Bay Company was established to speed the flow of furs from the Canadian backwoods to the hat shops and coat racks of Europe.

Over the next century, British explorers and fur traders fanned out from forts at York Factory and later Churchill to make contact with Cree and Assiniboine trappers. At the beginning, trade was conducted by canoe. Eventually, much larger York boats were used to schlep European goods like gunpowder, flour, and booze up the Hayes River and down the length of Lake Winnipeg, eventually arriving at forts where furs would be collected for the return trip to Hudson Bay.

As the English explored from the north, the French moved in from the east. The first French Canadian to make his mark on Manitoba was Sieur Pierre Gaultier de la Vérendrye, a Quebec-born explorer who spent most of his life searching for a passage to the Pacific Ocean. After hearing tales of a great inland sea, he paddled west from Montreal, wound up in Lake Winnipeg, and got his feet muddy at the future site of the Manitoba capital in 1738. La Vérendrye established forts across southern Manitoba and northwestern Ontario. But the gig wasn't easy – he often ran out of provisions and became embroiled in a conflict between the Ojibway and Sioux.

Both factors contributed to the death of his son Jean-Baptiste, who was slaughtered in a Sioux ambush on Lake of the Woods while paddling east for supplies. The elder La Vérendrye eventually made it as far west as the Missouri River near the North Dakota/Montana border, but died without ever glimpsing the West Coast.

Following in La Vérendrye's footsteps, the French-Canadian voyageurs of the Montreal-based North West Company – the Hudson's Bay Company's bitter rival – plied small waterways from the east, paddling big-assed cargo canoes along a lake-and-river route now defined by the Ontario/Minnesota border. By 1810, the two fur-trading empires had erected 180 forts across what's now Manitoba, including rival posts at the forks of the Red and Assiniboine rivers. The intense competition finally ended with the amalgamation of the North West Company into the HBC in 1821.

By this time, the French and British in southern Manitoba co-existed with Scottish immigrants – who had established a settlement in the Red River Valley – and the semi-nomadic, bison-hunting Métis, people of mixed French and Aboriginal descent. Tensions between the newcomers and locals – especially the increasingly dispossessed Métis – eventually led to the creation of Manitoba.

The Seven Oaks Massacre occurred in 1816 when a simmering rivalry between fur trading companies erupted into violence at what is now West Kildonan, Winnipeg.

Manitoba's Violent Birth

The first European settlers in the Red River Valley quickly learned it wasn't the greatest idea to build their new homes on a floodplain. Early Red River communities were nearly destroyed by massive floods in 1826 and 1852.

But southern Manitoba was also wracked by periodic bloodshed, as territorial squabbles between the Métis and others erupted into battles. The Métis fought Scottish settlers at Seven Oaks – now in the West Kildonan area of Winnipeg – in 1816, and then the Sioux several times during buffalo hunts in southern Manitoba.

In the late 1860s, it was uncertain whether southern Manitoba would join an expansionist United States or become part of the newly established Dominion of Canada. Ontario-born Anglophones moving West favoured ties with Ottawa, but French-speaking Métis feared the loss of their already tenuous land rights. The matter came to a head in 1869, when the Hudson's Bay Company turned over its remaining lands to Canada and Ottawa sent land surveyors to the Red River region. That enraged the Métis, who had already begun to settle down on the same land.

Led by charismatic St. Boniface–born preacher Louis Riel, the Métis set up a provisional government, seized control of Upper Fort Garry, and petitioned Ottawa to negotiate Manitoba's entry into confederation.

But Riel's efforts were doomed by ethno-religious politics. Canadian Prime Minister Sir John A. Macdonald broke off negotiations in 1870 when he learned the French-speaking Catholic ordered the execution of English-speaking Protestant rabble-rouser Thomas Scott.

Riel was charged with Scott's death and forced to flee in advance of an approaching Canadian army. But a tiny, "postage-stamp" sized Manitoba surrounding the Red River was granted provincehood, complete with language and religious rights for Francophones.

Remaining popular with local French-speakers, Riel went on to be elected to Parliament but was never allowed to sit. He spent years in exile in Montana before leading Saskatchewan Métis into one last military adventure: the Northwest Rebellion, which ended in defeat at Batoche, Saskatchewan, in 1885. Riel was captured, convicted of treason, and hanged.

It was only in the late twentieth century that Riel was recognized as a defender of indigenous rights and acknowledged as the founder of Manitoba, although the federal Parliament has still refused to grant Riel a posthumous pardon. His remains are buried on the grounds of the Basilica in St. Boniface (see *St. Boniface* in the *Winnipeg* chapter).

Boom, Bust, and Decline

The creation of Manitoba was soon followed by the 1874 founding of Winnipeg, the gateway for the settlement of western Canada. The century-long trickle of immigrants soon turned into a flood, as the completion of rail links to Minnesota and Ontario aided Ottawa's mission to populate the Canadian prairies with immigrants from across Europe.

Russian Mennonites arrived in southern Manitoba in 1874 and Icelandic settlers established a colony along Lake Winnipeg near Gimli in 1875 (see *Western Beaches* and *New Iceland* in the *Beaches and the Interlake*). Over the next four decades, they were followed by Ukrainians, Poles, Germans, Jews, and other Eastern Europeans, who helped swell Manitoba's population from about 25,000 in 1870 to almost 500,000 by the time the province's current boundaries were adopted in 1912.

While farming communities sprouted up all over southern Manitoba, many immigrants filtered back into Winnipeg, a roaring boomtown with colourful saloons, theatres, whorehouses, and a class of *nouveau riche* merchants who made massive profits in real estate and warehousing.

From 1905 to 1912, Winnipeg was the fastest-growing city in North America outside Chicago, its railway-rich US counterpart. But the 1914 completion of the Panama Canal suddenly made shipping cheaper than rail transport, effectively ending Winnipeg's boom and setting the city down a long course of relative decline that continued into the 1990s. Once Canada's third-largest city, Winnipeg now ranks eighth.

In 1919, Winnipeg was further pummelled by a general strike, the only workers' revolt ever to seize a Canadian or US city. Again, ethnic politics played a role, as English Protestant city leaders blamed the civil unrest on supposedly Bolshevik immigrants from Eastern Europe, though there was broad support for the strike among workers of many backgrounds.

As in Chicago, Winnipeg's arrested development in the '20s and '30s ironically protected the character of the city, as heritage buildings that might otherwise have been torn down still stand. A stunning collection of warehouse and office buildings constructed between 1880 and 1920 in downtown Winnipeg's Exchange District has been designated a National Historic Site (See *The Exchange* in the *Winnipeg* chapter).

After the advent of European immigration, Manitoba soon became the bread basket of Canada, exporting more wheat than any other province in the country.

PAM

But even through the Depression and into the postwar period, Winnipeg remained the economic engine for the rest of Manitoba and retained the finest cultural and intellectual life on the Prairies. Winnipeg established western Canada's first art gallery in 1912; the entire nation's first professional ballet company in 1939; and a symphony orchestra in 1946.

And as World War II loomed, the city cemented its reputation for independent thought when the *Winnipeg Free Press* was the lone Canadian voice editorializing against the growing Nazi threat and warning about the perils of appeasing Hitler.

Modern Manitoba

The latter half of the twentieth century saw Manitoba develop a stable and diverse economy based on a mix of agriculture, manufacturing, and services. There are grain farms and seed companies, hog barns and meat packers, aerospace and bus manufacturers, and insurance and investment companies. Much of the province's economic activity is centred in Winnipeg, with the notable exception of massive hydroelectric projects in the north and enormous hog barns all across the south.

PAM

Flooding has characterized much of southern Manitoba's history, especially in Winnipeg, which was ill-advisedly built on the Red River floodplain.

However, the biggest postwar undertaking had nothing to do with pigs or power. In 1950, after another Red River flood devastated much of Winnipeg, Premier Duff Roblin ordered the creation of the Red River Floodway, a massive trench dug around the eastern side of Winnipeg. Originally, "Duff's Ditch" spawned ridicule. Yet nobody laughed in 1997 when the floodway allowed Winnipeg to escape the devastation of the Flood of the Century, which all but destroyed downtown Grand Forks, ND, and displaced 30,000 people in southern Manitoba.

The Floodway did not, however, protect farms and towns in the Red River Valley just south of the city, leading rural residents to charge that their homes were sacrificed for the well being of Winnipeg. The aftermath of the '97 flood only served to highlight the divide between the Manitoba capital and the rest of the province.

With roughly 700,000 souls, metropolitan Winnipeg's population dominates a province of 1.2 million people. But there's a huge political and cultural chasm between the people who live inside and outside the Perimeter Highway that defines the city's limits.

Rural and small-town Manitoba retains a self-reliant spirit left over from the pioneer days. Farming is in decline, but other rural pursuits such as hunting, fishing, and snowmobiling remain a way of life. Rural voters typically support the Conservatives in provincial elections and at the federal level.

Winnipeggers, on the other hand, generally try to live the same suburban dream as residents of any mid-sized city in North America. But as an industrial town, Winnipeg's large number of unionized workers and diverse ethnic makeup typically leads to support for the centrist federal Liberals and the centre-left provincial NDP. Winnipeg voters are also a cosmopolitan lot, twice electing the openly gay Glen Murray to the mayor's office before welcoming his successor, Sam Katz, the city's first Jewish mayor, in 2004.

During the postwar period, the province experienced a second wave of immigration, as Italians, Greeks, Portuguese, Chinese, Filipinos, and Caribbean peoples joined Eastern Europeans on the move to Canada in the 1950s and '60s. Later waves of immigration echoed political strife around the world, as Manitoba welcomed an influx of Chileans and Vietnamese in the 1970s, Salvadorans in the '80s, Ethiopians and Somalis in the '90s, and Sudanese in the early twenty-first century. Most of the immigrants settled in Winnipeg to join growing numbers of Cree and Ojibway migrating south from reserves. The city's multiculturalism has become a source of pride to the locals and a pleasant surprise to visitors, who now encounter more noodle shops ladling out coconut-lemongrass soup and East Indian cafés featuring spicy tandoori chicken.

But there's no disguising Manitoba's challenges: slow population growth, a shortage of skilled labour, and a capital city marred by urban decay that likely began with the completion of the Panama Canal more than 90 years ago. The hope for the future lies with downtown Winnipeg's ongoing revitalization, the rising fortunes of the fast-growing First Nations population, and the promise of future hydroelectric development. Just don't expect to encounter this optimism in the form of unbridled boosterism. Manitobans are just as friendly as the slogan on the licence plate suggests, but also a tad more cynical than your average North American.

Remember, this is the only Canadian province founded in an act of rebellion, while its capital is the only city in the US or Canada to witness a mass workers' uprising. Meanwhile, much of the Aboriginal community – 10 per cent of the overall population – doesn't really recognize federal authority. Mistrust of power runs deep here, arguably deeper than in any other part of Canada.

But again, that rarely translates into personal mistrust, as Manitobans are incredibly helpful to people in need. Charitable donations exceed the national norm here, while few Manitoba motorists make it through a winter without a boost or a push from a fellow driver, usually a stranger.

If your car breaks down on the highway, this is the place you want to be. And hopefully, I'm going to encourage you to be out on the highway a lot – with a working vehicle, anyway.

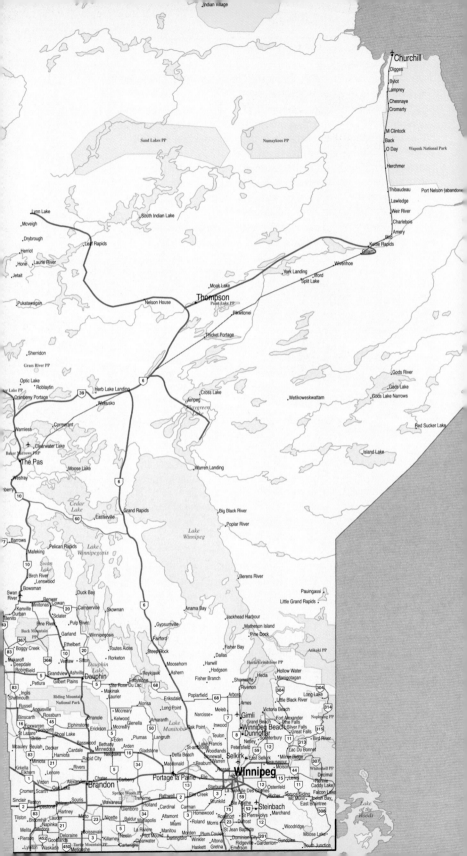

GETTING YOUR BEARINGS

2

The Geography of Manitoba

Drive down the Trans-Canada Highway and you might just believe
Manitoba really is an endless expanse of grain fields punctuated
by farmhouses and the occasional cow. But if you get off that ribbon
of boredom, you'll find less than a third of the province conforms to
the pancake-flat stereotype.

Most of Manitoba is a lush, wet, and surprisingly wild
landscape of forests, rivers, and some of the largest lakes in the
world. The diverse scenery ranges from treeless, sub-Arctic tundra
along the coast of Hudson Bay to desert-like sand dunes in Spruce
Woods Provincial Park at the opposite end of the province. There are
dense coniferous forests in the rugged Canadian Shield to the east,
spectacular stretches of rolling prairie and aspen parkland in the
west, sprawling wetlands all over the province, and even a few
places where endangered tall grasses continue to grow on the
remarkably rich, black prairie soil.

Rivers can be slow, meandering prairie ribbons, frenetic
pool-and-drop whitewater routes, or massive hydroelectric-generat-
ing monsters like the Churchill and Nelson in the north. There are
also more than 100,000 lakes, ranging from marshy, drainage-
devoid Whitewater Lake, to deep, meteor-created West Hawk, to
the massive but shallow inland oceans in the centre of the province:
lakes Winnipeg, Winnipegosis, and Manitoba, the 11th, 26th, and
30th-largest freshwater bodies in the world.

All of these features are a legacy of the glaciers that once
covered the province and the water and debris left behind when the
ice retreated. Simply put, Manitoba would not look anything like it
does if it wasn't for the Ice Age.

Manitoba's Icy Origins

According to First Nations belief, water once covered the Earth.
North America only emerged when a turtle – or, some nations say,
a beaver – dove below the surface and brought back a wad of mud.

Some Jewish and Christian cosmologists peg the planet's age
at about 6,000 years. Modern science contends it's a little longer –
more like 4.6 billion years. But anything that took place in Manitoba
before 12,000 BC is all but irrelevant, as there was nothing here but

As shown in this series of maps, prehistoric Manitoba was shaped and defined by waters from the retreating glaciers of the last Ice Age, which explains Manitoba's reputation as the "Land of 100,000 Lakes.".

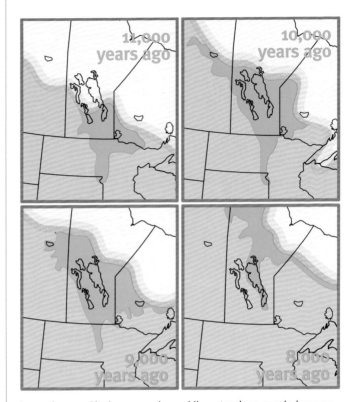

ice and snow. Glaciers more than a kilometre deep crawled across every square centimetre of the province, scraping soil and bedrock off the north and east regions and burying portions of the south and west in sediment known as glacial till. Only southwestern Manitoba failed to be completely flattened by the ice, thanks to the Manitoba Escarpment, a deposit of relatively hard shale. Today, the escarpment's steep face runs southwest from the Porcupine Hills, across the eastern face of Duck and Riding mountains, and eventually down to the US border southwest of Winnipeg.

When the glaciers retreated, generally from southwest to northeast, the meltwater at first drained to the east through what's now Lake Superior. Most of it pooled into Lake Agassiz, a glacial lake that covered Manitoba before eventually draining into Hudson Bay when the rest of the ice sheet finally melted.

Manitoba's "great lakes" – Winnipeg, Manitoba, Winnipegosis, Cedar, and Dauphin – are the most obvious legacy of ancient Agassiz. But you can also find remnants of its sandy beaches in Spruce Woods, Sandilands Provincial Forest, and the Lauder Hills.

Long glacial-deposited ridges called end moraines mark places where the ice stopped moving forward and deposited all the debris it was carrying along a wide curve. One of the largest in the province begins as an isthmus between Lake Winnipegosis and Cedar Lake and extends east into Lake Winnipeg as Long Point. Other glacial ridges called eskers mark places where sand and gravel was carried along channels in the melting ice. Birds Hill Park, just northeast of Winnipeg, is a good example.

The retreating ice also deposited massive boulders called glacial erratics, many of which can still be spotted in farmers' fields or along the southeast shore of Lake Winnipeg. Mighty torrents of glacial meltwater also carved out the Assiniboine, Shell, and Pembina valleys – wide spillways that dwarf the small rivers that now meander through the valley bottoms.

When the last of the ice melted, Manitoba was so compressed that the north side of the province – where the glaciers were thickest and heaviest – actually began to bounce back. In a process known as glacial-isotatic lift, rocks around the Hudson Bay shoreline have been rebounding at an average rate of roughly 1.3 metres per century. You can actually see this rebound in action during a visit to Churchill, as docking rings pounded into the rock to moor fur trade-era ships now sit many metres south of the waterfront.

The retreating ice also gave plants and animals a chance to colonize an empty territory and create one of the newest ecosystems on earth. Again, this process took place from the southwest to the northeast, so it's no surprise there's less biodiversity in the northeastern lowlands than there is in the southwestern grasslands.

Today, Manitoba can be divided up into five loosely defined geographic regions: the Canadian Shield, the Manitoba Lowlands, the south-central prairies, the southwestern highlands, and a small strip of tundra along Hudson Bay.

The Regions of Manitoba

The Canadian Shield

The largest region of Manitoba, the Canadian Shield covers most of the northern half of the province as well as the eastern third. Coniferous forests, granite ridges, and thousands of cool, clear lakes and rivers of various sizes and lengths dominate this vast, sparsely populated area. The same bumpy, uneven landscape can be found in northeastern Alberta, northern Saskatchewan, northern Ontario, and western Quebec.

The Shield, named after the billion-year-old Precambrian rock

Charles Shilliday

Spring thaw near Dorothy Lake in Whiteshell Provincial Park.

uncovered by glaciers, is home to most of Manitoba's logging, mining, and trapping. Major centres include the nickel-mining city of Thompson (pop. 13,256) in the centre of the province and the copper-and-zinc town of Flin Flon (pop. 8,100, with Creighton, Sask.) along the Saskatchewan border.

Twenty Cree and two Dene communities are also scattered across the northern Shield, including some accessible only by winter ice road and by air. Unemployment is a major problem facing these remote communities, although some are negotiating for a piece of the profits from future hydroelectric projects.

The most significant rivers in the northern Shield are the high-volume but heavily dammed Churchill and Nelson rivers, and two heritage rivers, the Seal and the Hayes. All four drain east into Hudson Bay.

Rivers in the southeastern Shield, meanwhile, drain west into Lake Winnipeg. The Pigeon, Berens, and Bloodvein, prized by canoeists and kayakers, are protected by Atikaki Provincial Wilderness Park. The less-remote Manigotagan River flows from Nopiming Provincial Park through a new provincial-park river corridor established in 2004. The southernmost – and most-developed – protected area in the Shield is Whiteshell Provincial Park, home to thousands of cottage lots and dozens of lodges and resorts. The heaviest concentrations are at Falcon and West Hawk lakes.

The most common trees in the Shield are spruce, jack pine, and fir. Large birds include bald eagles, great blue herons, osprey, great grey owls, and white pelicans, while wolves, moose, beavers, white-tailed deer, and black bears are common mammals. Less common are elk, wolves, woodland caribou, river otters, mink, lynxes, and wolverines, the latter only found in remote areas.

Manitoba Lowlands

On a big map, Manitoba's most dominant features are the wide, shallow "Great Lakes" that rank as some of the biggest puddles on the planet. Lakes Winnipeg, Manitoba, and Winnipegosis, and their smaller cousins, Dauphin and Cedar lakes – all remnants of glacial Lake Agassiz – sit in a completely flat basin in the centre of the province, surrounding an equally level expanse of boreal forest and wetlands known as the Interlake.

Bartley Kives

No, it's not the Mediterranean: Limestone cliffs at Steep Rock, on the east side of Lake Manitoba.

The main difference between the Lowlands and the Canadian Shield is geology. Instead of hard, Precambrian granite, Lowland bedrock is relatively soft, porous limestone, a sedimentary rock formed from the remains of ancient sea creatures. Erosion of this limestone leads to stunning natural features, like the cliffs at Sturgeon Gill Point on Lake Winnipeg and Steep Rock on Lake Manitoba, underground snake pits at Narcisse and a spring jetting out of the rock in Grass River Provincial Park. But much of the Lowlands is relatively featureless – and undeveloped, as human settlement is inhibited by poor drainage.

The chief economic activities in the Lowlands are tourism, logging, and commercial fishing. Lake Winnipeg's southern basin is lined by beaches and cottage communities, which serve as summer getaways for Winnipeggers. Lake Manitoba is the destination of choice for residents of Portage la Prairie.

Both lakes support large fisheries for pickerel, a tasty, white-fleshed fish the rest of the world calls walleye. Other frequently

Charles Shilliday

caught species include whitefish, cisco (locally called "tulibee"), sauger, and sometimes mullet (usually sold as "sucker") and carp. Lake Winnipeg goldeye, a delicacy when smoked, has lately become something of a rarity.

There are few large communities in the Lowlands, but plenty of small towns and First Nations. The largest centres in the Interlake are Gimli, a Lake Winnipeg fishing community and resort town founded by Icelandic immigrants, and Peguis, a series of Cree and Ojibway towns that together comprise one of the largest reserves in Manitoba. Both communities are home to approximately 5,000 people, though much of Peguis's population lives off-reserve.

The largest community in the Lowlands is paper-mill town The Pas and neighbouring Opaskwayak Cree Nation in the northwestern corner of the region. The twin communities on the Saskatchewan River have a combined population of about 8,300.

Harvest time west of La Rivière, in Manitoba's Pembina Valley.

The Prairies

In strict geographical terms, Manitoba's Prairies are a southern extension of the Lowlands – the land is just as flat and the bedrock equally soft and porous. But 200 years of human settlement have seen most of the wetlands drained and replaced with farms, towns, and cities, the largest being Winnipeg (pop. 706,000); the sister cities of Morden and Winkler (combined pop. 14,100); Portage la Prairie (pop. 13,000); Steinbach (pop. 9,227); and the steel-producing city of Selkirk (pop. 9,752).

As the most densely populated region of Manitoba, the Prairies – located in the south-central portion of the province – have been altered to the point where little of the indigenous flora and fauna remains. Tall grasses and wildflowers that once covered the region have been all but eradicated. Only a handful of tall-grass prairie preserves near tiny Vita and Stuartburn protect rare plants such as the Western Fringed Prairie Orchid, which is unique to Manitoba, at least in Canada. Large predators like the plains grizzly were hunted out centuries ago, the passenger pigeon was shot to extinction by the 1920s and the indigenous mule deer have disappeared. Even the once-numerous plains bison is now restricted to captive populations on ranches and inside parks and nature reserves.

Surviving prairie fauna include coyotes, many species of hawks, and the remarkable great grey owl, Manitoba's provincial bird and one of the largest in the world. But the white-tailed deer thriving in record numbers across the prairies are actually recent invaders from the east. Like rabbits in Australia, they seem to thrive off human settlement, living off farm stubble and even congregating around the big-box stores of southwestern Winnipeg.

Common crops in the Prairies include wheat, canola, barley, corn, and sunflowers, the latter most visible on farms near the US border in Manitoba's "Bible belt" – the fast-growing, mostly Mennonite communities of Altona, Winkler, and Morden. Marijuana grown both indoors and outside is believed to be one the province's biggest cash crops, much to the chagrin of local Mounties.

Along with the flat terrain, the most prominent feature of southern Manitoba is the gentle curve of meandering rivers like the eastward-flowing Assiniboine; the flood-prone, north-flowing Red; and the narrow Seine, which flows northwest from Sandilands Provincial Forest, one of the last remaining wooded areas on the Prairies and home to a large black bear population.

If you don't count Lakes Winnipeg and Manitoba, important bodies of water in the region include the boggy Whitemouth Lake, a prized fishing hole in the middle of Sandilands, and Buffalo Bay, a small corner of Lake of the Woods.

Birders and waterfowl hunters, meanwhile, cherish wetlands at Delta Marsh north of Portage la Prairie, Oak Hammock Marsh northwest of Winnipeg, and Netley Marsh at the bottom of Lake Winnipeg.

Southwestern Highlands

The southwest corner of Manitoba rises subtly over the rest of the province, though you can only get a sense of the elevation if you stand right on the edge of the Manitoba Escarpment and look east. The Porcupine Hills, Duck Mountain Provincial Park, Riding Mountain National Park, and Spruce Woods Provincial Park mark the eastern edge of Manitoba's very modest highlands, which also include islands of elevation such as Tiger Hills, Brandon Hills, and Turtle Mountain Provincial Park.

Prairie autumn sunset.

Charles Shilliday

Aspen forests and open meadows within the parks protect habitat for moose, elk, beavers, deer, and, in Spruce Woods, Manitoba's only lizard, the northern prairie skink. But outside the parks, Manitoba's highlands look a lot like a western extension of the Prairies, with grainfields and cattle pastures dominating the undulating landscape.

The largest communities in the southwest are Brandon (pop. 40,000), Manitoba's second-largest city, and Dauphin (pop. 8,100), which sits just north of Riding Mountain. The dominant rivers are the Assiniboine, Little Saskatchewan, Souris, and Pembina, which look like narrow ribbons compared to the massive glacial-meltwater-created valleys they follow throughout most of the region. Lakes are less prevalent here than elsewhere in Manitoba. The most notable are Clear Lake, inside Riding Mountain; the dam-created Lake of the Prairies in Asessippi Provincial Park; and Pelican Lake, a narrow ribbon near the Pembina River Valley. Whitewater Lake is also an important birding area.

The Southwest was settled following the earliest retreat of the glaciers. Arrowheads found near Boissevain date back 12,000 years and are believed to have been made by the Clovis people, some of North America's earliest inhabitants.

Northern Tundra

A narrow strip of tundra curves around the extreme northeast corner of the province at Hudson Bay, from Nunavut toward the Ontario border. This is a land of ice, snow, lichen, and permafrost, where trees are stunted or non-existent, and the frigid ground melts into impassable bogs during a brief but spectacular summer. It's also home to Manitoba's most famous ambassador – the polar bear – and, not coincidentally, the top ecotourist destination in the province, Churchill (pop. 963), the only settlement of any size in the region.

This may look and *feel* like the Arctic, but this is too warm to be a true Arctic environment. Still, you can experience a semblance of a Nunavut experience, given the spectacular Northern Lights, 22 hours of darkness in December (and corresponding daylight in June), and Churchill, a town that feels like an outpost on the edge of the world.

Vegetation in the extreme northeastern fringe of this region is restricted to lichen, sedge, grasses, dwarfish one-sided trees and wildflowers that bloom brilliantly during the summer. The fauna includes ptarmigans, tundra swans, Arctic foxes, wolves, barren-ground caribou, and a resident population of roughly 1,200 polar bears, who spend all summer on land before venturing out on Hudson Bay ice to hunt for harbour seals during the winter. The bears' summer denning grounds are protected by Wapusk National Park, which is mostly off-limits to visitors. Beluga whales, meanwhile, congregate by the thousands each summer at the mouth of the Churchill River.

Between the tundra and the boreal forests of the Canadian Shield lies a transition zone known as the taiga, characterized by a mix of lichen, muskeg, and stunted stands of black spruce. Other than fly-in fishing camps and wilderness rivers, the taiga is too tough to reach to attract tourists.

Almost Arctic: the rocky shore of Hudson Bay at Churchill.

Bartley Kives

Manitoba's Climate

Rummage through a Manitoban's closet and you'll find an unusual diversity of clothes. The province boasts a climate of extremes, as bitterly cold winters, warm, muggy summers, and bouts of sogginess during the spring and fall means everyone must own a parka, bathing suit, and every conceivable garment in between.

The only place in the world with more extreme temperature swings than the Canadian Prairies is the Gobi Desert in Mongolia. In Winnipeg, there's an 89-degree spread between the all-time record high temperature, 41°C in 1949, and the record low of −45°C in 1960.

While those extremes are freakish, even a normal year in southern Manitoba usually sees a couple of 32°C days in July and a handful of February nights when the mercury dips below −35°C. Factor in the windchill − the effect of wind on exposed flesh in cold temperatures − and Manitoba can be a chilly place, indeed. Winnipeg is one of the coldest cities in the world in mid-winter, as the average January day peaks at −13°C and bottoms out at −23°C at night.

But averages fail to tell the entire climactic story. Winnipeg also has a slightly longer frost-free period than supposedly milder Calgary − the temperature stays above zero for 170 days a year in the Manitoba capital, vs. 169 in its oil-rich Alberta rival.

So what allows Winnipeg to be a tiny bit less frosty than Calgary, where Chinooks frequently cause mid-January thaws? The answer has to do with Manitoba's balmy summers.

July days in Winnipeg typically max out at 26°C and usually stay above 13 C at night, which is four to five degrees warmer than almost any town in Alberta.

Most of southern Manitoba experiences very similar weather, though areas around the big lakes tend to be more unpredictable. Generally speaking, Southern Manitoba is a tiny bit warmer and wetter as you move from west to east. The U.S. border town of Gretna and the southeast hamlet of Sprague are often Canadian hotspots during the summer.

Moving up into the Parkland, the Riding Mountain resort town of Wasagaming is usually colder than the rest of the region, partly due to its greater elevation. But just east of the national park sits the town of McCreary, which usually enjoys warmer temperatures than its neighbours because of air compression on the Manitoba Escarpment.

Northern Manitoba shivers through an even colder climate, as remote communities like Lynn Lake and Thompson experience extremely bitter winters. But late in the fall, even more remote Churchill may seem relatively mild, as the waters of Hudson Bay act as a moderating influence until they freeze. Precipitation varies much more than temperature from year to year. Over the past 25 years, southern Manitoba has experienced both flood and drought conditions.

Two blizzards during the winter of 1996-97 led to the Flood of the Century, which engorged the Red River and temporarily displaced 30,000 people. Overland flooding during the rainy spring and summer of 2005 submerged farmland from Portage la Prairie to Brandon. But the mild, dry winter of 1987-88 saw Winnipeg get less than three months of snowcover instead of the usual five. And the winter of 2002-03 was so dry across the province that Manitoba Hydro lost profits due to low water levels, which reduced generating capacity.

So how do you prepare for a trip to Manitoba? Basically, expect everything Mother Nature can throw at you. Summers are usually warm and winters are usually cold, but any day in the spring or fall could mean sun, rain, snow, or any combination of the above. In other words, expect the best but plan for the worst.

The following Environment Canada weather data will help you prepare for typical conditions – as long as you realize there isn't anything typical about Prairie weather.

JULY CONDITIONS

WINNIPEG
Average high: 26°C
Average low: 13°C
Monthly precipitation: 71 mm

BRANDON
Average high: 26°C
Average low: 12°C
Monthly precipitation: 73 mm

KENORA, ONT.
Average high: 24°C
Average low: 15°C
Monthly precipitation: 95 mm

WASAGAMING
Average high: 24°C
Average low: 9°C
Monthly precipitation: 75 mm

THOMPSON
Average high: 23°C
Average low: 9°C
Monthly precipitation: 86 mm

CHURCHILL
Average high: 17°C
Average low: 7°C
Monthly precipitation: 56 mm

JANUARY CONDITIONS

WINNIPEG
Average high: −13°C
Average low: −23°C
Monthly precipitation: 20 mm

BRANDON
Average high: −12°C
Average low: −24°C
Monthly precipitation: 19 mm

KENORA, ONT.
Average high: −13°C
Average low: −22°C
Monthly precipitation: 26 mm

WASAGAMING
Average high: −13°C
Average low: −26°C
Monthly precipitation: 18 mm

THOMPSON
Average high: −19°C
Average low: −31°C
Monthly precipitation: 18 mm

CHURCHILL
Average high: −23°C
Average low: −31°C
Monthly precipitation: 17 mm

Driving Distances

Selected approximate driving distances from Winnipeg, in kilometres, from the Perimeter Highway (1 mi. = 1.6 km; 1 km = 0.62 mi.):

Altona – 98
Angle Inlet, Minn. – 185
Asessippi Provincial Park – 362
Baldy Mountain – 389
Beausejour – 46
Bemidji, Minn. – 380
Birds Hill Provincial Park – 15
Bismarck, ND – 650
Boissevain – 241
Brandon – 197
Calgary, Alb. – 1,340
Carman – 62
Chicago, Ill. – 1,400
Dauphin – 304
Denver, Col. – 2,235
Edmonton, Alb. – 1,360
Emerson – 96
Estevan, Sask. – 471
Falcon Lake – 126
Fargo, ND – 355
Flin Flon – 750
Fort Frances, Ont. – 399
Gillam – 1,034
Gimli – 76
Grand Beach – 87
Grand Forks, ND – 233
Grand Rapids – 408
Gull Harbour – 168
International Peace Gardens – 309
Itasca State Park, Minn. – 384
Kansas City, Mo. – 1,315
Kenora, Ont. – 205
Lac du Bonnet – 91
Lynn Lake – 1,066
Madison, Wisc. – 1,170
Melita – 310
Manigotagan – 182
Mantario Trail (north trailhead) – 149
Mantario Trail (south trailhead) – 141
Minaki, Ont. – 250
Minneapolis–St. Paul, Minn. – 730
Minnedosa – 203
Minot, ND – 469

Montréal, Qué. – 2,410
Morden –104
Morris – 52
Narcisse snake pits – 98
Neepawa – 175
Nopiming Provincial Park (south entrance) – 160
Oak Hammock Marsh – 27
Ottawa, Ont. – 2,220
Patricia Beach – 66
Pierre, SD – 975
Pine Falls – 111
Pisew Falls – 635
Portage la Prairie – 70
Regina, Sask. – 570
Russell – 338
Saskatoon, Sask. – 830
Sault Ste. Marie, Ont. – 1,285
Selkirk – 21
Sioux City, Iowa – 870
Souris – 226
Spruce Woods Provincial Park (Spirit Sands trailhead) – 177
Steep Rock – 217
Steinbach – 48
Stonewall – 24
Swan River – 476
The Pas – 602
Theodore Roosevelt National Park, ND (North Unit) – 699
Thompson – 738
Thunder Bay, Ont. – 700
Toronto, Ont. – 2100
Turtle Mountain Provincial Park (east entrance) – 306
Vancouver, BC – 2,150
Virden – 277
Wasagaming – 253
West Hawk Lake – 140
Winkler – 102
Winnipeg Beach – 66
Yorkton, Sask. – 440

Hucking the Jambusters: A Glossary of Manitoban English

Anishinabe(k), Anish *noun or adjective* Ojibway.

Autopac *noun* Public auto insurance, or a place that sells it.

back lane *noun* Alleyway.

bear box *noun* Bear-proof storage device for food or garbage, usually metal.

beer bash *noun* An afternoon social at a university campus. See social.

boosters *noun* Jumper cables.

booter *noun* The act of stepping through lake or river ice and getting your boots wet.

but it's a dry cold *retort* A commonly uttered lie.

DEET *noun* Acronym for pesticide N, n diethyl-m-toluamide, the most effective means of keeping mosquitoes off your skin.

fall supper *noun* A public dinner in a rural community or small town, usually in September and October. Originally "fowl supper," as the main course was goose, duck, or passenger pigeon, during the pioneer days.

flying rats *noun* Canada geese, to farmers; herring gulls, to fishers.

Giv 'er *imperative command* Enthusiatic form of encouragement to try something, as in "Giv 'er some juice and see if she starts."

goldeye *noun* Smoked freshwater fish, Hiodon alosoides, found only in and around Manitoba.

Halloween apples *exclamation* Halloween greeting used in Manitoba instead of "Trick or treat."

huck *tr. verb* Throw or toss, usually without great regard for accuracy.

Hurry hard! *exclamation* Curling-rink version of give'er.

jambuster *noun* Jelly doughnut, usually covered in icing sugar.

jam (out) *verb* To back out or otherwise renege on a commitment.

jammer (also jam tart) *noun* One who jams out.

Jeanne's Cake *noun (proprietary)* A bland but addictive layer cake with a cookie bottom.

LC *noun* Government-owned liquor store, short for Manitoba Liquor Control Commission.

loogan *noun* Hooligan or rowdy person. Supposedly a Chicago term brought to Manitoba during Prohibition.

meegwetch *greeting* Literally, "Thank you" in Ojibway.

megabarn *noun* Uncomplimentary term for industrial-sized hog operations.

monkey trail *noun* Trails (esp. unpaved) for mountain-biking, etc.

muskie *noun* The muskellunge (*Esox masquinongy*), a large, aggressive freshwater fish similar to the northern pike.

nip *noun* A hamburger, usually but not exclusively at Salisbury House restaurants.

Old Dutch *noun (proprietary)* A brand of potato chips found only on the Canadian and US prairies.

out East *noun, adverb* Toronto, southern Ontario, or any part of Canada east of Thunder Bay, Ont.

'Peg City (or The 'Peg) *noun* Winnipeg.

perogies *noun (pl.)* Flour dumplings stuffed usu. with potato, cheddar, cottage cheese, or sauerkraut.

Perimeter vision *noun* Inability of Winnipeggers to see or understand the rest of Manitoba outside the Perimeter Highway.

pickerel *noun* Western Canadian term for a fish known elsewhere as walleye.

Sal's *noun* A Salisbury House restaurant.

Sev *noun* A convenience store, usually 7-Eleven.

schmoo torte *noun* A light, nut-flecked cake topped with whipping cream and caramel sauce.

smokie *noun* A fat, barbecue-friendly sausage.

social *noun* Boozy, informal fundraising party for charities, non-profit organizations, or couples trying to finance a wedding.

soft drinks *noun (pl.)* Soda pop. Considered quaint or archaic elsewhere.

tansi *greeting* Cree equivalent of "Hi, how are you?"

'Toban *noun or adjective* Northwestern Ontario term for a Manitoban tourist, sometimes considered derogatory.

townie *noun* Year-round resident of summer vacation community. Antonym of "cottager."

Uke *adjective or noun* Ukrainian.

vendor *noun* A privately owned beer store attached to or adjacent a hotel (as opposed to an LC).

wrenijke (or varenikes/vareniki) *noun (pl.)* Mennonite/Russian variants of perogies.

STUFF TO SEE
AND DO

3

Exploring Manitoba can be a yin-yang experience, as Winnipeg offers big-city culture while the rest of the province offers natural wonders and small-town charm.

First-time visitors to Winnipeg often marvel at the low cost of visiting art galleries and museums, taking in live theatre, or sitting down to a decent meal. The multitude of affordable cultural attractions is something Winnipeggers take for granted, as, unlike tourists, they expect their institutions to be cheap.

Winnipeg has never done a great job of trumpeting its many assets, most of which don't translate well into the language of travel marketing. But the rest of Manitoba does an equally uneven job, and not just because the province fails to rival Hawaii and California as a holiday destination.

The deal is, most Manitoba tourists come from elsewhere in the province and often visit the same destination each year. Winnipeggers in particular are notorious for hitting the same provincial-park campground every July, August, and Labour Day long weekend, stubbornly refusing to try anywhere new. As a result, people who work in the fields of tourism and hospitality – from waiters and hotel clerks all the way to park rangers – sometimes assume a degree of familiarity on the part of their visitors.

And small towns with no obvious tourist attractions fail to promote the things that do make them interesting. For example, the southeastern Manitoba hamlet of Piney, where some of the world's best mineral water is bottled, makes no effort to show off or sell its product to thirsty motorists zipping up and down Highway 12.

I'm not advocating that Manitoba become as tacky as South Florida, where every second trailer park offers phoney Indian souvenirs and gasoline-powered airboat rides. But the absence of independent travel info is the main reason I've compiled this guidebook – and likely the only reason you decided to buy it.

So without any further ranting, here's what's great about Manitoba:

- Sandy, secluded beaches that rarely see more than several dozen visitors on summer weekdays.
- More lakes and rivers than you could ever hope to fish or paddle.

Opposite: All Canadian circulation coinage, plus coins from around the world, is produced in the Royal Canadian Mint in St. Boniface – a signature building designed by Étienne Gaboury.

- Thousands of square kilometres of mostly unvisited natural areas inside national and provincial parks, as well as on Crown land.
- At least 382 species of birds frequenting more than 300,000 square kilometres of undeveloped forests and wetlands.
- The world's largest concentrations of polar bears and red-sided garter snakes, and some of the last forests where wolves and caribou still thrive.
- Four distinct seasons, including a winter with enough snow to actually look and feel like winter.
- Small towns that come alive each summer with an array of idiosyncratic celebrations.
- A large and increasingly vibrant Aboriginal population that's never forgotten its traditions.
- North America's second-largest fringe-theatre festival and one of its best folk-music festivals.
- And Winnipeg, arguably the most culturally rich small city in North America that doesn't go by the name of Austin, Texas.

Manitoba's attractions vary from region to region. Most but not all cultural attractions are concentrated within Winnipeg, while the rest of Manitoba is the place to get outdoors. Here is a sample of what you can see and do – you'll find more detail in each chapter of this guidebook.

Cultural Attractions

Galleries

Charles Shilliday

The Winnipeg Art Gallery is renowned for its collection of Inuit art – the largest in the world.

While few Inuit live in Manitoba, the province's location below the middle of Nunavut means you can find spectacular art from the Arctic in private and public galleries around the province. The Winnipeg Art Gallery boasts the world's largest collection of Inuit art, but you can also see and usually buy soapstone and whalebone carvings at private galleries elsewhere in Winnipeg and up in Churchill. Just beware of soapstone trinkets sold at tourist traps – they may have no more connection to Inuit culture than an Eskimo Pie. When in doubt, inquire about the artist.

Cree and Ojibway art is just as stunning and even more widely available, especially in northern Manitoba towns. In Winnipeg, you can find a wide selection of Aboriginal art – from Inuit soapstone carvings to contemporary works – at galleries such as Wah-Sa, Northern Images, Nunavut, Bayat, and Urban Shaman, to name a few.

The Manitoba capital is also home to a wide array of conventional and contemporary art galleries, concentrated most heavily in the city's Exchange District. Within a couple of blocks of McDermot Avenue, you can take in an abstract installation at the trail-blazing, artist-run Plug In Gallery, marvel at the stratospheric sticker prices at Mayberry, or pick up an affordable print at the Warehouse Artworks.

Winnipeg Free Press

Museums

Nearly every town in Manitoba operates some kind of museum. Set up inside abandoned rail stations, former churches, or old one-room schoolhouses, these usually document the pioneer history of the community in question, which is great, if you're fascinated by 100-year-old agricultural implements.

While even the most mundane small-town museum can provide a quirky diversion during a long drive, there are some genuine gems in rural Manitoba. If you're interested in early Aboriginal history, the best $2 you'll ever spend will be on the Moncur Gallery, a collection of archeological artifacts located in the basement of a public library in Boissevain. Dinosaur fans should check out the Mesozoic-era marine reptile skeletons at the Canadian Fossil Discovery Centre in Morden. And World War II history buffs will enjoy a visit to Brandon's Commonwealth Air Training Plan Museum, which chronicles the training of Allied flyers from around the English-speaking world.

As the provincial capital, larger Winnipeg offers bigger and better-funded museums, such as the popular Children's Museum at The Forks, the St. Boniface Museum, and the Manitoba Museum, a sort of history-of-everything that includes a life-size replica of a transatlantic sailing ship used during the time of the fur trade.

A small museum with teeth: the modest Canadian Fossil Discovery Centre in Morden.

Sun-baked neo-hippies shake their patchouli-scented behinds at the Winnipeg Folk Festival. More than 80 acts from around the planet play the four-day, outdoor event in Birds Hill Park, arguably the finest of its kind in North America.

Festivals and Fairs

Bottled up indoors most of the winter, Manitobans let loose in the summer with a flurry of festivals packed into the short stretch of balmy weather between Victoria Day and Labour Day. These range in nature from relatively quaint summer fairs like Frog Follies in St. Pierre-Jolys (yes, they actually race frogs) and Morden's Corn and Apple Festival to big-budget music festivals attracting more than 10,000 fans, most notably Dauphin's Countryfest and the Winnipeg Folk Festival in Birds Hill Park. Other major rural events include Canada's National Ukrainian Festival at Dauphin; Gimli's Icelandic-themed Islendingadagurinn; and the Morris Stampede, the second-largest rodeo in western Canada.

In Winnipeg, the big three summer festivals are downtown's Jazz Winnipeg Festival, the Exchange-based Winnipeg Fringe Theatre Festival, and Folkorama, a city-wide celebration of multiculturalism. Wintertime events, meanwhile, include the Winnipeg Symphony Orchestra's New Music Festival; the Northern Manitoba Trappers'

Festival in The Pas; and St. Boniface's Festival du Voyageur, commemorating the Francophone community's roots in the seventeenth-century fur trade.

Flip to page 48 for a list of Manitoba festivals and the weekends on which they normally occur, keeping in mind some events move around from year to year.

Live Music

It isn't quite Manchester or Seattle, but Manitoba enjoys a reputation for producing a disproportionate number of quality recording artists. Generally speaking, there's substance behind the hype.

Bartley Kives

Back in the '60s, acts like Neil Young and The Guess Who got their start playing Winnipeg community centres, paving the way for made-in-Manitoba success stories like rock bands Crash Test Dummies, The Watchmen, Propagandhi, and The Weakerthans, solo artists Loreena McKennitt, Chantal Kreviazuk, and Remy Shand, and classical stars Tracy Dahl and James Ehnes.

Few of these performers still live in Manitoba, but the music scene based in Winnipeg remains vibrant. At the grassroots level, up-and-coming local

A love-hate relationship with Winnipeg: Literate indie-rock quartet The Weakerthans defined the cultural paradox at the heart of the city's psyche early in the decade.

acts play small clubs like the West End Cultural Centre, Pyramid, Royal Albert Arms, The Zoo, and Times Change(d) High & Lonesome Club. But in recent years, there's been a significant increase in the number of major touring acts visiting the city, thanks to a strong Canadian dollar, an improved Winnipeg economy, and the 2004 completion of downtown's MTS Centre, one of the twenty-five-busiest concert venues in the world in 2005.

Other significant Winnipeg concert venues include the Centennial Concert Hall and two fully restored heritage theatres, the Burton Cummings Theatre and the Pantages Playhouse. Live music venues in the rest of Manitoba include Brandon's Keystone Centre and the tiny but unusual Manitou Opera House in the heart of the Pembina Valley.

The best way to find out who's playing where in Winnipeg is to pick up the *Winnipeg Free Press* on Thursdays and flip to the listings in *The Tab*.

Performing Arts

Winnipeg's claim to fame as a cultural centre is due to presence of bricks-and-mortar institutions like the Winnipeg Symphony Orchestra, the Royal Winnipeg Ballet, Manitoba Opera, Winnipeg's Contemporary Dancers, and several professional theatre companies, most notably the Manitoba Theatre Centre, Prairie Theatre Exchange, Rainbow Stage, Shakespeare in the Ruins, and the Francophone Cercle Molière.

The WSO, RWB, and Manitoba Opera all perform at the Centennial Concert Hall but occasionally tour the rest of the province during the fall-to-spring performance season.

The MTC stages big dramatic productions at its Mainstage as well as an edgier series of plays in its smaller Warehouse Theatre. PTE focuses on made-in-Manitoba productions, while the summertime Rainbow Stage concentrates on popular musicals, and SIR adapts the Bard's works to indoor and outdoor settings in Assiniboine Park.

Aboriginal Culture

Compared to secretive First Nations like the Hopi of northeastern Arizona, Manitoba's Aboriginal communities are extremely outgoing. Visitors with an interest in First Nations culture are usually welcome at annual gatherings called powwows, though it's a good idea to check ahead: ceremonies differ from community to community.

You can also get a sense of Manitoba's lengthy Aboriginal history by visiting sacred sites like the petroforms of Whiteshell Provincial Park, and – if you're determined – petroglyphs at Tramping Lake near Snow Lake, Paimusk Creek east of Norway House, and along the Bloodvein River.

Made-in-Manitoba Food

To me, the most rewarding aspect of travelling is tasting food unique to a particular region. No matter where you are, you can always discover regional delicacies if you resist the temptation of eating at fast-food franchises and corporate-owned restaurant chains, which specialize in serving up big, huge plates of humdrum.

Manitoba's Eastern European heritage means perogies pop up frequently, served as a main course, side dish, or even breakfast item. When you have a choice, always order the potato-and-cheese-filled dumplings boiled or pan-fried – the deep-fried variety should only be consumed at a roadside stand in a Lake Winnipeg beach community, and even then, only when you've been drinking.

Unfortunately for foodies, ethnic culinary traditions unique to Manitoba rarely make their way out of the home kitchen. If you're lucky, you might be able to sniff out hearty Mennonite fare like *kielke* (noodles in cream gravy), dive into a traditional

Winnipeg Free Press

Winnipeg music is not just punk rock and The Guess Who: Former conductor Andrey Boreyko leads the 67-member Winnipeg Symphony Orchestra, which plays host to challenging works by living composers each winter during its New Music Festival.

Barbecue in Manitoba (left) is a decidedly seasonal affair, but make sure you try the increasingly rare Winnipeg goldeye (right), a delicate smoked freshwater fish, whenever – or if – you find it on a local menu.

Charles Shilliday   Joe Bryksa/Winnipeg Free Press

31

Franco-Manitoban tourtière – a baked pie of ground beef, pork, and (rarely!) venison – or chew a thick wad of bannock, the Canadian term for the Aboriginal staple the Americans call frybread.

Compared to cooking styles, made-in-Manitoba ingredients are much more common on local menus. No trip to the province is complete without a taste of the sweet-fleshed freshwater pickerel. Most of it comes straight from Lake Winnipeg and is usually breaded lightly and then pan-fried.

Manitoba anglers also make fantastic smoked fish, the finest being the increasingly rare goldeye, a tiny but tasty relative of the giant arapaima of the Amazon River. Smoked goldeye's rich flavour and delicate texture – and that of the closely related mooneye – even outshines smoked trout. Never, ever pass up an opportunity to try it.

Truly wild rice, only grown in eastern Manitoba and parts of Ontario and Minnesota, is common on local menus, though many chefs still don't know how to cook it properly. It's also cheaper here than anywhere else on Earth, so consider buying a packet as a travel memento or gift.

Other Manitoba foodstuffs to sample include locally raised lamb (among the best in the world), lean bison (who can resist chowing down on the provincial symbol?), and saskatoons, blueberry-like fruit that are excellent in pies and jams. Also for dessert, try Shmoo torte, a nut-flecked white cake covered in caramel sauce.

To wash it all down, the most popular local microbrews are bottled in Winnipeg by the Fort Garry Brewery, which favours a strong hint of molasses in its darker products. Gimli is also the home of Crown Royal, Canadian whisky that comes in the fuzzy purple bag. You can also find locally made fruit wines made of saskatoons, strawberries, and even rhubarb at Manitoba Liquor Commission stores.

Many Winnipeg restaurants now feature local or regional cuisine, which includes bison, wild rice, pickerel, and saskatoons.

Restaurants

Yeah, I know – didn't we just talk about food? But there's a difference between a made-in-Manitoba cuisine and the food you actually find in restaurants.

In Winnipeg, you can chow down on almost any kind of ethnic cuisine you can possibly crave. Asian cuisine is a particular strong suit, as there are dozens of Vietnamese, Japanese, Indian, Lao, Thai, Filipino, and Korean joints to rival the usual mix of roadhouses, pizza parlours, and Chinese-American restaurants you'll find anywhere in North America. Africa and the Middle East are represented by Ethiopian, Eritrean, Somali, Lebanese, and Israeli kitchens.

Charles Shilliday

Europe and the Americas can be sampled at Portuguese, Greek, German, French, Caribbean, Mexican, and Salvadoran establishments.

High-end dining is on the upswing, as the *prix fixe* tasting menu has made its way west from Toronto. At the other end of the scale, Winnipeg offers a huge number of homegrown burger joints that make life difficult for McDonald's and Wendy's. There are also restaurant chains unique to the Canadian Prairies.

Salisbury House (locally called "Sal's"), partly owned by Guess Who lead singer Burton Cummings, offers burgers called "nips," old-school breakfasts, and gloriously untrendy filter-drip coffee in a cafeteria-style atmosphere. Earls, a more high-end chain, is like Hooters for white-collar men: The waitresses look like fashion models and the food is lighter and more contemporary. The Fyxx, meanwhile, is a locally owned coffee chain with four Winnipeg locations to rival the likes of Starbucks and Second Cup.

Outside Winnipeg, your restaurant options are more limited, as small towns offer the basics, and the quality of highway diners can be hit-and-miss. While there are a handful of high-end establishments in bedroom communities around Winnipeg, most rural fare tends to fall into the category of "more is better," with huge portions of short orders like perogies and hamburger steaks served up at reasonable prices.

When in doubt, ask a local for advice – or eat wherever you see a lot of cars on a Sunday evening.

Christopher Pike/Winnipeg Free Press

Playing out of downtown Winnipeg's MTS Centre, the Manitoba Moose fill a massive crater created in the local hockey landscape when the NHL's Winnipeg Jets took off for browner pastures in Arizona.

Spectator Sports

When the National Hockey League's Winnipeg Jets left for Phoenix in 1996, some observers mourned the death of professional sport in Winnipeg.

All the moaning and groaning was nonsense, as the Canadian Football League's Winnipeg Blue Bombers, American Hockey League's Manitoba Moose, and Northern League of Baseball's Winnipeg Goldeyes do a fantastic job of quenching the local thirst for competitive sport.

The CFL Bombers are among the oldest clubs in professional sports, having turned 75 in 2005. They play in aging Canad Inns Stadium, which seats 32,000 but is expanded to approximately 50,000 when the city hosts the Grey Cup (as it will in 2006).

The AHL Moose usually play before crowds of about 8,000 at MTS Centre, which has a capacity of 15,000. Independent baseball's Goldeyes, meanwhile, usually come close to selling out downtown Winnipeg's 7,500-seat CanWest Global Park, a gorgeous ball diamond located next to the Forks and owned by Winnipeg Mayor Sam Katz.

Outside Winnipeg, the biggest sporting draw is the Western Hockey League's junior-aged Brandon Wheat Kings, who play at the 5,000-seat Keystone Centre. The OCN Blizzard of the Manitoba Junior Hockey League also has a rabid following up in The Pas and neighbouring Opaskwayak Cree Nation.

But for the ultimate Manitoba sporting experience, forgo hockey for a curling bonspiel, which can make national stars out of ordinary Janets and Joes. A surprisingly difficult game to master, curling is a religion on the Canadian prairies, partly because the players on the ice don't look much different than the hosers in the stands.

Shopping

A stereotypical list of Manitoba mementos would include Aboriginal art, handmade crafts, and non-perishable foodstuffs like wild rice and saskatoon berry jam.

All this stuff is great, but you'll probably have more fun if you forget about knick-knacks and focus instead on vintage clothing, antiques, and second-hand books and music. Thanks to the relatively low population density, there's more great junk on the Prairies than anywhere else in Canada.

While Winnipeg boasts an abundance of vintage clothing boutiques, small towns are often the best place to find the most interesting items, as university students in the city are notoriously quick to snap up all the best clothing and furniture in non-boutique stores like Value Village. The smaller the community, the better the chance of finding something weird, unique, or possibly even valuable. Just make sure you know what you're doing before you spend big bucks on a supposed antique.

If new consumer goods are what you're after, Winnipeg offers the same array of shopping-mall retail franchises you'll find anywhere else in Canada. Winnipeg's three largest malls are Polo Park in the west, St. Vital Centre in the southeast and downtown's Portage Place. Higher-end new clothing and consumer goods can be found in shops scattered along Winnipeg's Academy Road, Corydon Avenue, Osborne Street, and in the Exchange District, in descending order of price.

Of course, not everyone wants to drop big bucks on designer clothing. If you prefer cheap tourist crap – and be honest, you probably do – the biggest concentration of useless doodads can be found at The Forks.

OUTDOOR ACTIVITIES: Non-winter

Beaches

Given Manitoba's reputation for chilliness, the variety and quality of beaches in the province is nothing less than shocking. Though the sunbathing season is short, there are excellent strips of sand along many of the province's lakes, a legacy of glacial Lake Agassiz and 10,000 subsequent years of wind and wave action. The most popular beaches include Grand, Victoria, Winnipeg, and Gimli beaches on Lake Winnipeg, and Twin Lakes on Lake Manitoba. Cooler waters may

be found at Wasagaming Beach in Riding Mountain Park and West Hawk Lake and Falcon Lake beaches in Whiteshell Provincial Park, while inexplicably popular artificial beaches exist at Birds Hill and St. Malo provincial parks.

Beaches abound in the sub-Arctic: The three-km-long beach at Grand Beach Provincial Park, where crowds number in the tens of thousands on summer weekends.

If you prefer more solitude, Patricia and Beaconia beaches afford more privacy and tolerate nudists. But there are even more secluded beaches accessible only from the water – Lake Winnipeg alone has hundreds of kilometres of sand visited only by the occasional kayak, sailboat, or motorboat.

Canoeing and Kayaking

If you'll excuse the brutal pun, Manitoba is a paddler's wet dream. Raging rapids in the Canadian Shield beckon whitewater paddlers; flatwater canoeists can find solitude on more than 100,000 lakes; and sea kayakers who can't afford to hit Baja California can keep their skills sharp on wide-open Lake Winnipeg or take on the life-threatening tidal challenges of frigid, polar-bear-frequented Hudson Bay.

The remote Seal River, the historic Hayes, and the relatively accessible Bloodvein all belong on the life list of any serious paddler. But few people have the time or experience to take on monumental trips.

Visiting Manitoba without getting on the water is like going to Memphis without visiting Graceland. Here, the author plies a placid Canadian Shield waterway.

Experienced guides and out-fitters can take you practically any-where, for the right price. But if you're a novice, it's better to start with a day paddle on a placid Prairie river like the Assiniboine or La Salle. Or if you have a little wilderness experience, consider a

Jason Sorby

weekend trip in Whiteshell or Nopiming provincial park, both blessed with established flatwater routes and well-marked portages.

Even-more-experienced canoeists consider the Crown land east of Lake of the Woods in very northern Ontario as one of the best flatwater-paddling areas in North America. A large portion of this region is known as the Experimental Lakes Area, where University of Manitoba biologists conduct environmental research.

Kayakers, meanwhile, prefer the portage-free maze of islands in Lake of the Woods itself, or head on to Lake Winnipeg to explore the islands of Hecla-Grindstone Provincial Park and the Kasakeemeemisekak Archipelago. Playboaters, on the other hand, congregate at easily accessible rapids on the Whitemouth River near Elma, or Sturgeon Falls on the Winnipeg River in Whiteshell Provincial Park.

If you're serious about a wilderness paddling trip, it's a good idea to flip through guidebooks like John Buchanan's *Canoeing Manitoba Rivers*, Hap Wilson and Stephanie Aykroyd's *Wilderness Rivers of Manitoba*, or the *Routes* page on Paddle Manitoba's website, www.paddle.mb.ca.

If you're interested in day paddles, you can rent a canoe, kayak, or playboat at most busy beaches during the summer, or at The Forks in downtown Winnipeg. Longer-term rentals are available from Winnipeg retailers Wilderness Supply Company, Wave Track, and Mountain Equipment Co-op, or outfitters such as Clearwater Canoe Outfitters in The Pas or Northern Soul Wilderness Adventures in Winnipeg.

Hiking and Backpacking

Given the absence of mountains, Manitoba is no place for hikers who thrive on high altitude and get off on the long, lingering lactic-acid burn that comes with serious climbs. But there are many places in the province where the scenery makes a walk worthwhile, if not always challenging.

Whiteshell Provincial Park offers eight day-hikes through the rugged Canadian Shield landscape, the most popular being the 8.2-kilometre Pine Point Rapids trail. There's a little more elevation on the east face of Riding Mountain National Park, which rises 350 metres from the surrounding prairie.

Spruce Woods Provincial Park offers the most celebrated day-hike in the province in the Spirit Sands, a small patch of active sand dunes crisscrossed by a 10-kilometre trail system. Other short trails can be found in almost every other provincial park, including Birds Hill, located just 20 kilometres northeast of Winnipeg.

Backpacking options are a little more limited, as most parks lack trails of any considerable distance. Riding Mountain has an extensive trail system, but the wide, flat former roads are better suited to cyclists and horseback riders. The two best backpacking trails are the easy, 22-kilometre overnight to northern Manitoba's Kwasitchewan Falls, the province's highest at 15 metres; and the biggest walk of them all – Mantario Trail, a relatively strenuous,

63-kilometre north-south jaunt across the wildest section of the Whiteshell, traversible in three to five days.

It's also possible to cross the entire width of the province on Manitoba's 1,200-kilometre portion of the Trans Canada Trail (www.tctrail.ca), but I wouldn't advise it: Much of the route follows gravel roads, which doesn't make for the greatest hiking.

Just outside Manitoba, the best backpacking trail within a day's drive of Winnipeg is the Achenbach Trail in the north unit of North Dakota's Theodore Roosevelt National Park. This 29-kilometre loop, one of the best overnight hikes in North America, descends into the spectacular Little Missouri River badlands.

For more ideas about rural walks, pick up *Manitoba Walks*, a guidebook published by the Prairie Pathfinders, a non-profit walking club.

Cycling and Mountain Biking

On paper, flat land should translate into easy cycling. But high winds rarely make it easy for long-distance riders anywhere in southern Manitoba.

Cyclists who consider crossing the province should start at Saskatchewan and head east, as the prevailing winds blow from the west. On the Trans-Canada Highway, semi-trailers are a constant menace. East-west Highways 2, 3, and 23 are a lot less busy and more scenic.

Serious road cyclists looking for a shorter spin may be frustrated by riding in Winnipeg, where there's little in the way of dedicated trails beyond the Assiniboine River Parkway and riverside roads. The best advice can be found in the *Cyclists Map of Winnipeg*, on sale at most Winnipeg bike shops (see *Gear Retailers* in the *Things To Know* chapter) as well as at McNally Robinson bookstores. Bikes may also be rented at some sporting-good retailers.

Charles Shilliday

Cycling through Beaudry Provincial Heritage Park, a small protected area just west of Winnipeg.

Popular paved routes across the province include the Riverwalk in Brandon, the seven-kilometre Pine Ridge Bicycle Trail in Birds Hill Provincial Park, and the 13-kilometre South Whiteshell Trail, which runs from Falcon Lake to West Hawk Lake in Whiteshell Provincial Park. For other road cycling options, visit the Manitoba Cycling Association (MCA) at www.cycling.mb.ca.

Offroad cyclists have a few more options, thanks to cross-country ski trails that double as mountain-bike routes during the warmer months. Trail systems at Birds Hill Provincial Park, Sandilands Provincial Forest, and Grand Beach Provincial Park are suitable for novice mountain bikers, while the Brandon Hills, Birch Ski Area (open to MCA members only), and other areas of the Manitoba Escarpment offer more-challenging terrain. Both Turtle Mountain and Spruce Woods Provincial Parks offer the opportunity to ride a little longer on loops maxing out around 40 kilometres. One of the best daytrips in the province is the Epinette Creek-Newfoundland trail in Spruce Woods, a 42-kilometre single-track loop featuring many small hills but also enough sandy soil to cushion any spill.

To my knowledge, Riding Mountain National Park is the only place where you can ride off-road for days without encountering a vehicle. In dry conditions, the 67-kilometre Central Trail, which bisects the west side of the park, makes for a challenging overnight or leisurely long weekend. Just watch out for moose, bears, deer, and especially elk during the fall mating season.

Other off-road cycling destinations include sections of the Trans-Canada Trail around Asessippi Provincial Park and Inglis; the Ontario border town of Ingolf; and the exposed greenstone up in Flin Flon, which the locals liken to the slickrock in Moab, Utah.

Horse Trails and Ranch Vacations

Riding Mountain National Park got its name for a reason: Early traders ditched their canoes to cross Manitoba's modest highlands on horseback.

Charles Shilliday

Today, the best way to see wildlife in southern Manitoba's only national park is up in the saddle, which allows you to see above grasses and shrubs. The park has dozens of day-riding routes, plus equestrian campsites for longer rides. Other popular riding areas include Birds Hill, Spruce Woods, and Turtle Mountain provincial parks.

For a list of equestrian campsites and horse-friendly B&Bs – plus rural and farm vacation ideas – visit www.countryvacations.mb.ca.

Ranchers in southwestern Manitoba sometimes still rely on cowboy techniques to round up livestock.

Climbing

The highest point in Manitoba is Baldy Mountain, which stands a not-very-staggering 831 metres above sea level. It takes all of about 30 seconds to reach the summit from a parking lot just off the main road running through Duck Mountain Provincial Park. There is no actual climbing here. For real rock-climbing, head east to the exposed granite of the Canadian Shield. There are at least nine established, road-accessible climbing areas north of Kenora, Ont., as well as numerous canoe-accessible rock faces in the Experimental Lakes Area to the southeast. Many of these are described by the Manitoba Section of the Alpine Club of Canada at www.alpine-club.mb.ca.

Needless to say, you better know what you're doing before you go rock climbing in the middle of the bush. In Winnipeg, you can climb in a more controlled environment on indoor walls at Vertical Adventures (77 Paramount Rd., 632-5001) and Mountain Equipment Co-op (303 Portage Ave, 943-4202).

Top Ten Manitoba Attractions

MOST EXCITING URBAN NEIGHBOURHOOD: Winnipeg's Exchange District

The draw: Cut-stone and terra cotta warehouse buildings dating back to the late nineteenth century, the province's heaviest concentration of art galleries and vintage clothing boutiques, three concert halls, a dozen nightspots, and the Manitoba Museum.

The duration: However long you like. Take a one-hour walking tour or explore the neighbourhood for days.

The damage: Free for window-shoppers on foot. Throw in museum admission, a concert, and dinner, and you might be able to spend $120 a day.

Winnipeg's Exchange District, filled with turn-of-the-twentieth-century architecture, often features in Hollywood films as a stand-in for American cities like Chicago or Kansas City. Many Winnipeggers credit our city fathers for maintaining this neighbourhood's heritage, but in fact, stagnation through most of the twentieth century allowed the city to protect the buildings.

BEST WILDLIFE-WATCHING SPOT: Churchill and the Hudson Bay coast

The draw: The world's largest congregation of polar bears in the fall, amazing wildflowers in the spring, beluga whales and birds during the summer, and northern lights in midwinter.

The duration: Allow yourself at least two full days to explore everything Churchill has to offer, especially since it takes a long time to get here – 36 hours by train from Winnipeg, or 13 hours from Thompson following a seven-hour drive from Winnipeg. Flights from Winnipeg take two hours.

The damage: Anywhere from $700 to more than $4,000 a head, depending on your choice of transportation, accommodations, and tours.

BEST SMALL-TOWN MUSEUM:
Moncur Gallery, Boissevain

The draw: An extensive collection of pre-contact Aboriginal artifacts dating back to the earliest retreat of the glaciers, some 12,000 years ago. Don't be fooled by the tiny room.

The duration: It only takes 45 minutes to an hour to take the self-guiding tour.

The damage: $2. No, I'm not kidding.

BEST EASY DAY HIKE: Spirit Sands,
Spruce Woods Provincial Park

The draw: A very unusual, 10-kilometre trail system encompassing active sand dunes that resemble desert, open meadows, aspen forest, and a rare colour-shifting pond called the Devil's Punchbowl.

The duration: Two to four hours, depending on how far you walk. Allow Another 3.5 hours to drive from Winnipeg and back.

The damage: $5 per vehicle, or free with a $20 annual Manitoba provincial park pass.

BEST BACKPACKING ROUTE:
Mantario Trail, Whiteshell Provincial Park

The draw: At 63 kilometres, Manitoba's longest and most rugged hiking trail, traversing granite ridges, wetlands, and lakes in a protected area of the Canadian Shield.

The duration: Three to five days.

The damage: Amazingly, there are no trail fees. Vehicles parked at trailheads require a park pass. Spend whatever you like on food, which you must buy ahead of time – unlike BC's Pacific Coast Trail, Mantario doesn't have any hot dog stands or restaurants.

BEST PLACE TO RIDE:
Riding Mountain National Park

The draw: The longest cycling and horseback-riding trails in the province, no motor vehicles, and a sprawling aspen-dominated wilderness supporting large populations of elk, moose, deer, and black bears – which you can see above the brush, thanks to your perch on a bike or horse.

The duration: Race down the eastern face on a one-hour ride, or traverse the width of the 67-kilometre Central Trail over two or three days.

The damage: $6 per adult or $15 per group per day, plus $9 per head per night for backcountry camping.

BEST PLACE TO VEGETATE: Patricia Beach Provincial Park and Beaconia Beach, Lake Winnipeg

The draw: Kilometres of very fine sand and minimal crowds; even on summer weekends, both families and the musclehead/bikini crowd prefer Grand Beach and Winnipeg Beach.

The duration: One long, lazy day.

The damage: Half a tank of gas. You need a Manitoba parks pass for Patricia Beach, but diddlysquat for Beaconia.

BEST SUMMER FESTIVAL: Winnipeg Folk Festival, Birds Hill Provincial Park

The draw: World-class folk, roots, and global music on seven outdoor stages, a glorious natural setting, and a wild campground resembling a miniature Burning Man Festival, all during the warmest weekend of the year.

The duration: Four days, if you can handle the stimulation.

The damage: Up to $60 for a day pass, $150 for a weekend pass, and $30 for camping, with discounts offered for early-bird purchasers.

BEST WHITEWATER RIVER: The Bloodvein, Atikaki Provincial Wilderness Park

The draw: Clear, well-maintained portages around class I-IV rapids on this ribbon of Canadian Shield beauty – accessible by portage or floatplane only – suit wilderness trippers of all skill levels. Bald eagles, river otters, and pre-European petroglyphs only sweeten the pot on this classic pool-and-drop river.

The duration: Seven to twelve days, depending how far east you start.

The damage: Nothing if you portage in, but flying in on a floatplane can set you back hundreds of loonies per person. Fully outfitted trips will put you over $1,000.

BEST RESORT TOWN: Wasagaming, Riding Mountain National Park

The draw: Rustic wooden buildings in the National Park style, the beach and marina at Clear Lake, a massive summer campground, and easy access to wilderness attractions throughout Riding Mountain, Manitoba's only road-accessible national park. Nearby Onanole, outside the park, gives you everything the Parks Canada does not allow.

The duration: A night or two in town, and perhaps longer in the backcountry.

The damage: Expect to pay $110 per night for accommodations alone.

Mike Deale

Wildlife Watching

Every October, up to 1,200 polar bears congregate on the Hudson Bay coast just east of Churchill, waiting for the ice to freeze. This unusual concentration of gigantic predators brings tourists from around the world to this northern Manitoba outpost, swelling both the town's population and the price of hotel rooms until the bears finally leave in early November.

Most of Churchill's visitors come to see the bears from safe vantage points in oversized vehicles called tundra buggies. But the town is also worth a visit during the summer, when milk-white beluga whales and their charcoal-grey babies gather in amazing numbers in the Churchill River estuary.

Visitors to Manitoba are often suprised to see large flocks of white pellicans, which congregate all summer in regular feeding and breeding spots such as Lockport, on the Red River north of Winnipeg.

Churchill is Manitoba's top ecotourist destination, but certainly not the only one. Riding Mountain National Park brings in visitors every fall to hear the elk bugle. Wolf fans head to the Whiteshell during full moons in the hopes of hearing howls. You also stand a decent chance of seeing moose, coyotes, black bear, and snapping turtles in a variety of parks.

If you're fascinated by cold-blooded creatures, about 70,000 red-sided garter snakes gather at limestone pits in the Narcisse Wildlife Management Area every spring and fall in the largest congregation of reptiles anywhere on Earth.

And if you have an interest in birds, you can spend a lifetime observing up to 382 species that either breed in Manitoba or pass through the province on annual migrations. Birding hotspots include Oak Hammock Marsh northwest of Winnipeg, Delta Marsh at the south end of Lake Manitoba, and Whitewater Lake just north of Turtle Mountain. But it's easy to spot some sort of interesting avian species anywhere there's a river, marsh, or lake – which is just about everywhere. Manitoba has large populations of dramatic species like white pelicans, cormorants, bald eagles, osprey, great grey owls, loons, great blue herons, and all manner of ducks, songbirds, and raptors. If you're lucky, you may also see sandhill cranes, ruby-throated hummingbirds, and snowy egrets.

Patience is required for any wildlife-watching excursion, so put in plenty of trail time, and don't set unrealistic expectations. If you're hell-bent on seeing elusive creatures like wolverines, forget about the bush and head straight to Winnipeg's Assiniboine Park Zoo.

That said, it is disturbingly easy to observe certain types of wildlife. At dusk and dawn, white-tailed deer pose a serious threat on Manitoba highways. During the spring and fall, Canada geese flock in such large numbers, light sleepers reach for earplugs. And anywhere towns encroach on forest, you could encounter human-habituated black bears, so it's extremely important to keep campsites and cottage areas clean.

For more ideas about wildlife watching, pick up Catherine Senecal's *Pelicans to Polar Bears* or Bill Stillwell's *Scenic Secrets Of Manitoba*. The definitive birdwatching bible is the Manitoba Naturalist Society's massive and remarkably complete *Birds of Manitoba*, but it's easier to tote around Andy Bezener and Ken De Smet's paperback field guide *Manitoba Birds*.

Fishing

The biggest fish ever caught in Manitoba was a 185-kilogram lake sturgeon pulled out of the Roseau River in 1903. These ancient monsters have all but disappeared from Manitoban waterways, but the province continues to teem with wonderfully tasty walleye – although we call them pickerel – as well as northern pike, lake trout, and massive channel catfish.

It might sound like a boast, but there really is nowhere in Manitoba where the fishing is genuinely lousy. There are more than 100,000 lakes in the province and an unquantifiable number of rivers and streams. Even the muddy, mildly polluted Red River supports a world-class catch-and-release catfish hotspot north of Lockport.

In total, Manitoba's inland waterways are home to 95 fish species, 83 of which are native to province. For more information about where to find them, peruse the fantastic *Freshwater Fishes of Manitoba*, an ichthyological tour-de-force by Kenneth Stewart and Douglas Watkinson.

Windsurfing and Sailing

Near-constant winds and open waters make Manitoba's big lakes ideal for racing around on windsurfers, kitesurfers, and sailboats. But extended touring is not as popular as you might guess, as lakes Winnipeg and Manitoba don't have enough ports of call to sustain the kind of sailing culture that flourishes in Lake Ontario, for example.

Sailboats frequently launch from marinas at Gimli and Gull Harbour on Lake Winnipeg. There are far more yachts plying the

Charles Shilliday

Kite surfing on Lake Winnipeg near Gimli.

deeper waters of Lake of the Woods, where there's a multitude of islands as well as wealthy cottage-owners. Kenora, Ont. has an extensive marina.

Boating and Cruises

Boating and fishing usually go hand-in-hand on most Manitoba lakes, but powerboats and other small pleasure craft are not uncommon summer sights, especially on the Red River near Winnipeg and on Lake of the Woods, in northwestern Ontario. Very few Manitoba lakes are off-limits to motorized craft. The main exceptions are designated wilderness areas inside provincial and national parks.

But you don't have to own a boat to hit the water. You can take day or evening cruises on Clear Lake in Riding Mountain National Park, on the Red River in Winnipeg, and the Souris River in Souris.

Lake of the Woods has even more of a marine culture. You can rent or charter houseboats, powerboats, sailboats, powered yachts, and even tugs out of Kenora, Sioux Narrows, and Nestor Falls, Ont.

Hunting

One of Manitoba's most lucrative tourist draws is bear hunting, as it remains legal to bait the beasts in this province. While I personally

Charles Shilliday

find the practice repugnant, it provides a healthy income for outfitters in economically depressed rural areas. As well, Manitoba's black bear population is large enough to withstand the limited pressure of controlled hunting.

In southern Manitoba, there are bear-hunting seasons in the spring and fall. There are also seasons for white-tailed deer, moose, elk, wolves, ducks, geese, and upland birds, although seasons vary, and non-residents may be subject to restrictions. Woodland caribou, mule deer, polar bear, and all birds of prey are among species protected from hunting.

For more information about opportunities for killing all manner of furry and feathered things, pick up a copy of Manitoba Conservation's *Hunting Guide* at a local hardware or sporting store, or visit www.gov.mb.ca/conservation/wildlife/huntingg/index.html.

Hunting for Giant Canada geese (*Branta canadensis maxima*) near Woodlands, Manitoba.

As well, federal law governs the hunting of migratory birds, including waterfowl. Refer to the Canadian Wildlife Service website (www.cws-scf.ec.gc.ca) for details.

To American visitors, Canadian firearm regulations may appear complex and bizarre, so it's a good idea to read up ahead of time. Check out the Canadian Firearms Centre website at www.cfc-ccaf.gc.ca/ to avoid a headache – or confiscated weaponry – at the border.

OUTDOOR ACTIVITIES: Winter

Cross-country Skiing

One of the weirder ironies of a Manitoba winter is that cold doesn't always guarantee snow. While the first white stuff usually falls by the second week in November, there often isn't enough to support skinny skis until Christmas – and even then, it may take another few weeks for river ice to freeze.

As a result, the cross-country ski season in Manitoba can seem excruciatingly short for people who enjoy one of the most balanced forms of cardiovascular exercise known to humankind. Given the province's flat topography, traditional Nordic skiing remains unusually popular – in other parts of North America, it's often considered a senior citizen's pastime.

Few Manitoban cross-country ski trails are completely flat, however. Trail systems at Pinawa, Grand Beach, Falcon Lake, Birds Hill Park, Pumpkin Creek, Bittersweet and the Birch Ski Area offer enough hills to challenge novice skiers. There are also longer trails at Turtle Mountain, Spruce Woods, and Riding Mountain, the latter boasting an incredible 275 kilometres of traditional Nordic trails as well as a couple of routes groomed for skate-skiing. Frozen lakes and rivers also make for great skiing surfaces, as long as you avoid snowmobile routes. Most power-sled users are courteous to skiers, but the noise can be annoying.

For a list of Manitoba ski trails and detailed directions, visit the Cross Country Ski Association of Manitoba at www.ccski.mb.ca.

Downhill Skiing and Snowboarding

When you don't have actual mountains, you make do with what you have. That's why three of Manitoba's most popular ski-and-snowboard areas are actually holes in the ground.

Western Manitoba's Asessippi Provincial Park sits on the eroded banks of the Shell River Valley. La Rivière's Holiday Mountain runs down the Pembina Valley, while metro Winnipeg's Springhill Winter Park takes advantage of the oversized drainage ditch known as the Red River Floodway. Obviously, none of these places will ever host the Winter Olympics, but the modest elevation is just right for people learning to ski.

Other shirt downhill ski slopes can be found at Falcon Lake, Stony Mountain, Minnedosa, Thunder Hill west of Swan River, and Mystery Mountain, north of Thompson. If none of this works for you, it's time to save up for that trip to Whistler, BC.

Snowshoeing

Forget about those horrible childhood memories of lashing complex leather bindings to heavy wooden snowshoes and walking bow-legged through deep powder until your groin muscles ache. Modern,

Charles Shilliday

Spring Hill Winter Park, on the outskirts of Winnipeg, makes use of an artificial trench dug for the Red River Floodway.

Bartley Kives

Don't be afraid of a little snow. While there is an element of risk in winter camping, a pair of snowshoes can make almost any trail traversible all year – even the frozen surface of Lake Winnipeg.

aluminum-frame snowshoes are light and ridiculously easy to use – if you can walk, you'll have no problem snowshoeing.

Along with a pair of winter boots, deerskin mukluks, or waterproof, insulated hikers, snowshoes allow you to hit any hiking trail you like, no matter how deep the snow, and probably wind up with the trail all to yourself. And once January rolls around, you can also explore frozen rivers and streams.

Riding Mountain National Park offers three dedicated trails, but you can snowshoe almost anywhere you like in the province, provided you don't mess up cross-country ski trails.

Snowshoes are also great for winter camping, either as the primary means of moving along the trail, or in combination with cross-country skis. Some hikers also take a small pair along during late-season backpacking trips, just in case.

Winter Camping

As crazy as it sounds, winter camping in frigid Manitoba can be an amazing experience, provided you take the right gear and precautions.

On a still winter day, leafless forests and frozen lakes seem almost magically quiet. And in wilderness areas, the snow cover provides a record of all the wildlife in the area – snow makes it easy to identify the footprints of animals that leave no trace of their passage during the summer.

Winter kite surfing on Lake Winnipeg near Gimli – compare it to kite surfing on page 43!

Charles Shilliday

If the idea of sleeping in a tent in the middle of the winter still seems insane, there are back-country cabins in Spruce Woods and Riding Mountain. You can also rent heated yurts at Minaki Yurt Adventures, north of Kenora, Ont.

If that still seems too rustic, you can always rent a cabin. Year-round accommodations ranging from rustic huts to luxury lodges are concentrated in Whiteshell Provincial Park and, in western Manitoba, near Riding Mountain.

Ice Fishing

To people who make a living off pickerel, ice fishing is a way of life. For thousands of other Manitobans, it offers a chance to build elaborate temporary structures on lake and river ice and consume copious quantities of alcohol as long as the frigid weather holds.

The most lavish ice fishing huts are decked out with portable heaters, couches, generators, stereos, and satellite TV. Hand augers have been replaced by gasoline-powered drills, which easily poke holes through any lake or river ice. If you've ever been to a sports bar on NFL Sunday, you pretty much know the atmosphere.

Still, it would be unwise to turn down an invitation to go ice fishing, as there are few more definitively Manitoban experiences. You just better be able to hold your rye, as heated Portapotties are never around when you need them.

Dog Sledding

In mid-January, "mush" refers to more than what happens to your brain when you're exposed to a northern Manitoba winter. Outfitters in Churchill and Thompson offer dog sled rides and sometimes even instruction.

In southern Manitoba, the Manitoba Dog Sledding Association maintains trails in Birds Hill Provincial Park, Mars Hills Wildlife Management Area, and Agassiz Provincial Forest.

Snowmobiling

An essential means of transportation for hunters and trappers up north, snowmobiles are extremely popular recreational vehicles in southern Manitoba. A 10,000-kilometre network of volunteer-maintained snowmobile trails criss-cross the province, making it possible to ride from town to town without having to use roadways.

Snowmobiles are noisy, but do a lot less damage to the environment than ATVs, as most riders stick to established trails. A map of Manitoba's snowmobile routes, as well as rules and regulations, is online at the Snowmobilers of Manitoba website at www.snoman.mb.ca.

In a nutshell, every snowmobile must be registered and insured, while drivers must wear helmets and pony up $100 for an annual Snopass from Snoman (Snowmobilers of Manitoba), which helps pay for trail maintenance. Tourists can buy a seven-day pass for $40.

Holiday and Festival Calendar

January

New Year's Day (Nationwide, Jan. 1): All retailers, government offices and banks, as well as most restaurants and many cultural attractions are closed.

Winnipeg Symphony Orchestra New Music Festival (Centennial Concert Hall, Winnipeg, late January or early February): Ten days of works by current and twentieth-century composers.

February

Festival du Voyageur (St. Boniface, Winnipeg, mid-February): Western Canada's largest winter festival: celebration of Francophone community and fur-trade-era history, with live music and snow sculptures.

Trappers Festival (The Pas and Opaskwayak Cree Nation, mid-February): Winter festival, with dog-sled races and skills competitions.

March

National Screen Institute Film Exchange (Winnipeg, first week of March): Independent film festival.

Royal Manitoba Winter Fair (Keystone Centre, Brandon, late March and early April): Week-long agricultural expo.

April

CBC Winnipeg Comedy Festival (Winnipeg, late March or early April): Week-long stand-up comedy festival.

Good Friday (Province-wide, late March or early April): Banks and government offices are closed.

Sugaring-Off Festival (St.-Pierre-Jolys, mid-April): Maple-syrup-tapping festival.

May

Delta Marsh Birding Festival (Delta Marsh, second weekend in May): Bird-watching festival.

Victoria Day (Nationwide, third weekend in May): Commonwealth-inspired holiday that amounts to the first long weekend of the summer, with fireworks held in most Manitoba communities on the Sunday or Monday night. Government offices, banks and most retailers are closed.

June

Back 40 Festival (Morden, first weekend in June): Folk and roots music.

Manitoba Paddlefest (Fort Whyte Centre, first weekend in June): Canoeing and kayaking expo.

Winnipeg International Children's Festival (The Forks, Winnipeg, second week in June): Children's performers and activities.

Winnipeg International Film Festival (Winnipeg, second weekend in June): Independent film festival.

Jazz Winnipeg Festival (Downtown Winnipeg, mid-June): Ten-day jazz, pop, and urban-music festival. Free outdoor and ticketed indoor performances.

National Aboriginal Day (Manitoba-wide, June 21): First Nations, Métis, and Inuit celebrations on summer solstice, including a powwow at The Forks in Winnipeg.

Brandon Summer Fair (Brandon, third week of June): Gut-wrenching rides, carnival food, and a circus.

Red River Exhibition (Exhibition Park, Winnipeg, late June): Two-week carnival with midway rides and free performances.

Nickel Days (Thompson, late June): Town fair.

July

Canada Day (Nationwide, July 1): National holiday, akin to US Fourth of July. Free performances and fireworks in most Manitoba communities. Banks, government offices and most retailers are closed.

Trout Festival (Flin Flon, Canada Day weekend): Fishing derby/ fishfest.

Dauphin's Countryfest (Selo Ukraina Site, Dauphin, first weekend in July): Four-day country and country-rock festival with major international headliners; three outdoor stages, four campgrounds.

Manitoba Highland Gathering (Selkirk, first Saturday in July): Scottish cultural festival.

Winnipeg Folk Festival (Birds Hill Park, second weekend in July): Four-day folk, roots, rock, and world-music festival, considered among North America's best; seven outdoor stages, two campgrounds.

Pioneer Days (Killarney, second weekend in July): Town fair.

Manitoba Stampede and Exhibition (Morris, mid-July): Manitoba's largest rodeo.

Carman Country Fair (Carman, mid-July): Town fair.

Gathering of Nations (Pilot Mound region, mid-July): Regional multicultural festival.

Prairie's Edge Bluegrass Festival (Beausejour, mid-July): Bluegrass and gospel music in an outdoor setting.

Strawberry Festival (Portage la Prairie, mid-July): Town fair and strawberry harvest.

Winnipeg Fringe Theatre Festival (Exchange District, Winnipeg, late July): Short plays, sketch comedy, and experimental theatre in twenty small venues; it's the third-largest festival of its kind in the world.

Brandon Folk Music and Art Festival (Keystone Centre Grounds, late July): Two-day folk festival.

Neepawa and Area Lily Festival (Neepawa, late July): Town fair and lily exhibition.

Sunflower Festival (Altona, late July): town fair.

Turtle Island Festival (Boissevain, last weekend in July): Town fair, with turtle races.

Thresherman's Reunion and Stampede (Austin, last weekend in July): Agricultural festival, rodeo, and dance.

August

Civic Holiday (Province-wide): Usually first Monday in August. Banks and government offices closed.

Norway House York Boat Days (Norway House Cree Nation, first week in August): Cree heritage celebration, with rowboat races and dances.

Islendingadagurinn (Gimli, first weekend in August): Town fair, film festival, and Icelandic cultural festival.

Canada's National Ukrainian Festival (Selo Ukraina Site, Dauphin, first weekend in August): Ukrainian musical and cultural celebration.

Manitoba Summerfest (Grand Beach Entertainment Centre, first weekend in August): Classic rock festival.

Pioneer Days (Steinbach, first weekend in August): Town fair and Mennonite cultural expo.

Frog Follies (St. Pierre-Jolys, first weekend in August): Town fair, with frog races.

Métis Days (St. Laurent, first weekend in August): Town fair and Métis cultural celebration.

Folklorama (Winnipeg, first two weeks of August): Multicultural celebration with forty-plus pavilions representing ethnic and national groups.

Great Woods Music Festival (Great Woods Park, Beausejour, early August): Blues and roots music.

Harvest Festival (Winkler, early August): Town fair.

Potato Festival (Portage la Prairie, early August): Town fair.

Opaskwayak Indian Days (Opaskwayak Cree Nation, mid-August): First Nations cultural celebration.

Quarry Days (Quarry Park, Stonewall, mid-August): Town fair.

Wild West Daze (Virden, mid-August): Indoor rodeo and town fair.

Corn And Apple Festival (Morden, final weekend in August): Three-day town fair.

Festival Chantecler (St. Pierre-Jolys, last Saturday in August): Francophone cultural expo.

Cook's Creek Heritage Day (Cook's Creek, last Sunday in August): Community fair.

September

Labour Day (Nationwide): First Monday in September. Banks, government offices and most retailers closed.

St. Malo Summer Festival (St. Malo, early September): Strongman competitions, soapbox derby, and casino.

Ashern Rodeo (Ashern, first weekend in September): Rodeo and town fair.

Pembina Valley Honey, Garlic and Maple Syrup Festival (Manitou, second weekend in September): Town fair and culinary expo.

Winnipeg International Writers Festival (Winnipeg, late September): Week-long literary festival with public readings.

Harvest Moon Festival (Clearwater, late September): Outdoor folk and rock festival.

October

Roland Pumpkin Fair (Roland, first Saturday in October): Town fair and harvest festival.

Beef and Barley Festival (Russell, early October): Town fair.

Thanksgiving (Nationwide, second Monday in October): Harvest festival, held one month earlier than in U.S. Banks, government offices and most retailers are closed.

Hoof and Holler (Ste. Rose du Lac, Thanksgiving long weekend): Cattle auction, rodeo, and dance.

November

Manitoba Livestock Expo (Brandon, early November): Music and moocows.

Remembrance Day (Nationwide, Nov. 11): Solemn memorial day for Canadian war dead, with public ceremonies at 11 a.m. Banks and government offices closed.

December

Christmas Eve (Nationwide, Dec. 24): Business as usual during the day; Retailers and most restaurants close at 6 p.m.

Christmas Day (Nationwide, Dec. 25): Banks, government offices, restaurants, retailers and some cultural attractions are closed.

New Year's Eve (Nationwide, Dec. 31): Business as usual during the day; Retailers and government liquor stores close at 6 p.m.

THINGS TO KNOW

4

Getting Around
Cars

You can live without a car in Winnipeg, but if you want to see a lot of Manitoba, you'll need a set of wheels. At 650,000 square kilometres, the province is twice the size of Norway, bigger than Ukraine, roughly the same size as Afghanistan, and slightly larger than the combined area of California and New York. While most of the population is concentrated in the south, distances between cities, towns, parks, and other attractions remain immense. If you want to set your own agenda, you'll need a vehicle to get where you want to go, as bus service is inconvenient, railway destinations are limited, and passenger flights within the province tend to be prohibitively expensive.

If you don't own a car, rental rates are a little expensive by North American standards. Expect to pay anywhere from $35 to $65, before taxes, per day for a subcompact. You'll always pay less if you reserve ahead of time, especially if you book online. While 16-year-olds can drive in Manitoba, you need to be 21 – and in possession of a valid licence – to rent a car from most agencies.

Manitoba highways are well-marked and easy to navigate. Most paved roads are in good condition, although American drivers will find more potholes and broken pavement than they're accustomed to at home. Winter conditions, however, will test the nerves of even the most experienced driver. While major highways tend to be clear of snow within hours of a heavy dump, some roads can remain slick for days, and blowing snow can reduce visibility to next to nothing, even during daylights hours. In open prairie, high winds can make it appear as if snow is falling sideways.

Even worse, the action of tires over packed snow occasionally creates an extremely slippery surface known as black ice, which is all but impossible to spot. The best thing to do in winter is simply be sensible: give yourself plenty of time to travel long distances, stay off the road in lousy weather, and keep a cellphone and warm clothes in the car in the unlikely event you spin out into a ditch and need to wait for a tow.

And at any time of year, don't get the behind the wheel when you've had a few bottles of Fort Garry ale. Manitoba has the toughest drunk-driving penalties in North America, with a variety of suspensions, fines, and vehicle seizures kicking in after your blood-alcohol percentage reaches a measly 0.05. For most people, that

Opposite: The ruins of the Trappist monastery at St. Norbert: Goth kids come at night, but the caretakers prefer that you visit by day. The monks have since relocated to Holland, Manitoba.

translates into a single drink. And yes, the laws are enforced – RCMP conduct spot checks near popular beaches on summer weekends, while Winnipeg cops randomly pull over thousands of drivers during the December holiday season.

Buses

Unglamorous but reliable Winnipeg Transit can take you anywhere you want to go in the Manitoba capital, except during the wee hours of the morning. You can find schedules and route information at the front of the MTS White Pages, online at www.winnipegtransit.com, or over the phone at 287-7433.

Three bus companies can take you around Manitoba. Greyhound Canada carries passengers from Winnipeg to hundreds of locations across the province. A full list is online at www.greyhound.ca. Sample one-way fares from Winnipeg include $36.50 to Kenora, Ont.; $27.80 to Brandon; and $91.80 to Thompson. Greyhound also travels, from Winnipeg, as far afield as Vancouver and Ottawa.

Beaver Bus Lines mostly acts as a charter service, but also operates a Winnipeg-to-Selkirk run seven days a week, up to 11 times a day. A one-way fare is $6.20, with lower fares for destinations between the two cities. Jefferson Lines, a US carrier, offers international service between Winnipeg and the North Dakota cities of Grand Forks and Fargo, going as far south as Dallas, Tex.

All three lines operate out of the downtown Winnipeg Bus Terminal at 487 Portage Ave., between Memorial Avenue and the University of Winnipeg.

Taxis, Limos, and Shuttles

For a city of 700,000, Winnipeg can be a tough place to hail a cab. The quickest way to snag one is to head to an upscale downtown hotel, one of the city's two casinos, or the front of a busy nightclub. Otherwise, call Duffy's at 775-0101, Unicity at 925-3131, Blueline at 925-8888, or Spring at 774-8294 at least 15 minutes before you need to go anywhere.

From Winnipeg International Airport, expect to pay about $20 to get downtown by taxi. Limos might make sense for larger parties, while some downtown hotels offer free rides in shuttles. For the budget traveller, Winnipeg Transit's Number 15 (Mountain/Sargent) bus takes passengers from the airport to downtown, and vice versa, for a couple of bucks a pop.

As well, Brandon Air Shuttle – a bus service – offers road transfers between Winnipeg International and Brandon up to four times a day. A one-way fare is $40. And, in 2005, a new shuttle service called the Toban Experience began offering independent travellers lifts from Winnipeg's Ivey House Hostel to seven holiday destinations in eastern Manitoba and northwestern Ontario: Falcon Lake, Kenora, Minaki, both Mantario trailheads, Lac du Bonnet, and Grand Beach. The service costs $279 per person, but allows for unlimited stays along the loop. Visit tobanexperience.com or call 1-888-358-6226 for more information.

Air Travel

If you're flying into Winnipeg from elsewhere in Canada, Air Canada and Westjet offer direct service from Vancouver, Calgary, Edmonton, Regina, Saskatoon, Thunder Bay, London, Toronto, Hamilton, Ottawa, and Montreal, with connecting service to anywhere else in Canada. There are also direct flights to Denver and Chicago via Air Canada–affiliated United Airlines, and to Minneapolis and Detroit on Northwest. Charter carrier Skyservice, which primarily flies to sun-drenched destinations in winter, may also offer limited scheduled flights within Canada. For travellers from outside Canada and the US, Air Canada is partnered with Star Alliance (www.staralliance.com), as is United. Northwest is partnered with Dutch carrier KLM.

Within Manitoba, regional carriers Bearskin Airlines, Calm Air, and First Air offer service to destinations in northern Manitoba, northern Ontario, and the Territories, including The Pas, Flin Flon, Thompson, and Churchill; Kenora and Sioux Lookout, Ontario; and Rankin Inlet, Nunavut. A handful of smaller airlines offer floatplane service to isolated First Nations, hunting and fishing lodges, or remote canoe areas. You will find a list of charter services online at www.travelmanitoba.com/huntfish/aircharters.html.

Since the cost of air travel rises and falls with the price of oil, I'm not going to bother listing sample airfares. Check www.aircanada.ca, www.westjet.com, www.travelocity.ca, or www.expedia.ca for going rates.

Trains

Go back 100 years and you could ride the rails almost anywhere in Manitoba. These days, passenger service is limited to a pair of VIA Rail routes; An east-west corridor between Ontario and Saskatchewan (part of a coast-to-coast line from Halifax to Vancouver), and a long, curving north-south jaunt between Winnipeg and Churchill.

Most tourists use the east-west route to see the rest of Canada. But with 48 hours' advance notice you can request a stop anywhere you like in Manitoba east of Winnipeg. Some savvy backpackers use VIA Rail to cut about a quarter of the distance off the Mantario Trail.

The trip up north to Churchill takes a gruelling 36 hours from Winnipeg, but many tourists take it anyway. It's much faster to drive or take a bus to Thompson and jump on the train for the final 13 hours to Hudson Bay.

Winnipeg's VIA Rail station is located in a handsome hall of a building on Main Street, just west of The Forks. VIA Rail schedules and fares are online at www.viarail.ca.

Cycling

As I mentioned earlier (see *Stuff to See and Do*), it's possible, if not particularly convenient, to see southern Manitoba by bike. Start in the west to take advantage of the prevailing winds and head east, preferably on Highway 2, 23, or 3 to minimize contact with heavy

Bartley Kives

trucks. You may also follow the partly gravel, partly off-road Trans-Canada Trail, if you have shocks on your bike and you're up to a sometimes bone-jarring challenge.

Popular bike daytrips from Winnipeg include short jaunts nearby to parks like Beaudry and Birds Hill, or to bedroom communities such as Lockport and St. François Xavier. Just make sure to keep an eye on your gear anywhere you go. While bike touring isn't big in Manitoba, bike theft is a popular sport.

Hitchhiking

True to the slogan on the licence plates, Manitobans tend to be friendly to hitchhikers. But that doesn't mean it's safe to jump in a stranger's car. Among 100 good Samaritans, there's always one nasty individual who doesn't belong behind a wheel, let alone in charge of your life. If you're broke and backpacking, there are always better transport options, like negotiating a ride with people you meet at hotels or campgrounds.

If you must hitchhike, travel in pairs for added safety and set out early in the morning to show prospective drivers you're serious about reaching a destination. And carry some kind of baggage – if you don't have any gear, it looks like you're out to steal some.

The same rules apply if you're considering giving a stranger a ride. A lone, unencumbered hitchhiker at dusk is nothing but bad news.

Finding a Crash Pad

Hotels

Winnipeg's historic Fort Garry Hotel.

In small Manitoba towns, you'll find two kinds of hotels: cheap, 1950s-style row motels along the highway, and scarier, block-like 1930s structures in the middle of what passes for downtown. The

row motels are almost always the better choice, but ask to see the room before you commit to a purchase. You can pay as little as $35 or as much as $70 for one of these spartan places, depending on the town.

In slightly bigger centres, you'll also find modern chain hotels and larger, independently owned establishments. Expect to cough up $80 to $110 to stay at the chains and $70 to $90 for the mom-and-pop motels. If you want to support a made-in-Manitoba chain, the family-friendly Canad Inns offer waterslides and all-you-can-eat buffets.

In Winnipeg, you'll find all of the above, plus a handful of more luxurious hotels with dining rooms, high-end lounges, and, in some cases, spas. The swankiest include the Fairmont, just off the corner Portage and Main; the Delta; Broadway's historic Fort Garry; and the newish Inn at The Forks. Expect to pay $150 to $250 for a room in the most-expensive Winnipeg establishments.

The best places to search for up-to-date hotel rates are the usual suspects: www.expedia.ca and www.travelocity.ca. Both sites only list the larger, more-expensive hotels, but you will save a significant amount of money if you book ahead and online.

Cabins, Lodges, and Resorts

Accommodations in parks and other wild areas range from rustic cabins to full-blown luxury lodges. Just don't get hung up on terminology, because lodges, resorts, cabins, and even hotels tend to be interchangeable terms. For instance, some fishing lodges offer gourmet meals and guided excursions, while others are just a series of cottages in the woods. Cabins for rent can be loaded with satellite TV and saunas – or lack running water and electricity altogether. Resorts, meanwhile, can refer to anything from a trailer park to a full-service hotel.

In older holiday towns, like Grand Marais and Ninette, small rustic cabins rent for as little as $300 a week. But you could easily pay $300 a night for a spacious, modern cabin in Riding Mountain or the Whiteshell. Fly-in fishing lodges in remote locations tend to be considerably more expensive.

To further confuse matters, some holiday accommodations are open year-round, while others only cater to summer crowds. Given the wide range of options, call before you book. Travel Manitoba maintains a searchable database of resorts at www.travelmanitoba.com/accommodations.

Bed and Breakfast

There are three things to consider when you opt for a bed and breakfast over a hotel room: price, personality, and privacy. B&Bs offer less of the first, more of the second, and absolutely none of the third.

Generally speaking, B&Bs offer more-interesting rooms at cheaper rates than conventional hotel chains, but there is a cost: you cannot help but interact with your hosts and fellow guests, which can be awkward if you're shy or mildly antisocial. And don't even think about having sex in a room with paper-thin walls and a four-poster bed that squeaks like a tortured rodent if you dare to get a little frisky.

That said, B&B hosts tend to be friendly and usually prove to be excellent sources of travel advice and information. In 2005, www.bedandbreakfast.mb.ca listed 21 B&Bs in Winnipeg and 79 in the rest of Manitoba.

Youth Hostels

Well, maybe make that "hostel." Manitoba has only one youth hostel, Winnipeg's Ivey House (210 Maryland St., 772-3022), located within a short bus ride (or 20-minute walk) from downtown. The 40-bed facility offers dorm accommodations ($20-$24) and private rooms ($36-$52), with cheaper rates for Hostelling International members.

They also offer nature walks, museum tours, and occasionally longer excursions, such as a nine-day Winnipeg-and-Churchill package offered in 2005 for $1,395 a head.

Campgrounds

There are two types of campgrounds in Manitoba: Government-run sites in parks, and private campgrounds usually set up along highways or near recreational facilities in the middle of small towns.

Manitoba Conservation runs 52 campgrounds in 41 different provincial parks, most open only from Victoria Day to Labour Day. There's a full list online at www.manitobaparks.com. You can reserve a spot ahead of time online or by calling 948-3333 in Winnipeg or 1-888-482-2267 elsewhere. Reservations are a good idea, as the most-popular spots typically sell out of their summer weekend spots. Expect to pay anywhere from $7 to $17 a night.

Most provincial campgrounds offer spots for tents, RVs, and campers; firewood; electricity; showers; and, in some cases, interpretive programs. What they don't offer is any semblance of a wilderness experience, as campsites are packed together tightly enough to ensure you'll get to know your neighbours. Riding Mountain National Park has six campgrounds, but only accepts advance bookings for the most-popular one, Wasagaming (1-800-707-7480).

There are also dozens of private campgrounds spread out across Manitoba, including eleven on the Trans-Canada Highway alone. Information about thirty of them is online at www.macap.ca.

Wilderness Camping

If you possess route-finding skills, you can pitch a tent anywhere you like on unregulated Crown land in Manitoba. Set up at least 100 metres away from any road, path, and waterway, practise leave-no-trace camping, and take particular care with fires.

Backcountry camping is also possible within Manitoba provincial forests and wildlife management areas, provided you check ahead with Manitoba Conservation staff at the nearest district office. Some areas may be off-limits during hunting season, closed due to logging, or simply unsafe due to bear activity.

Bartley Kives

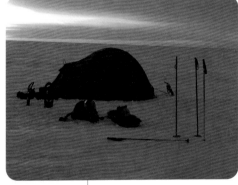

In most large provincial parks – namely Whiteshell, Nopiming, Spruce Woods, Turtle Mountain, Duck Mountain, and Paint Lake – wilderness camping is free but restricted to designated backcountry sites along established hiking and canoeing routes. You don't have to reserve sites ahead of time, but be prepared to share a camp at popular campsites on the Mantario Trail during summer weekends.

In Riding Mountain National Park, backcountry campsites cost $9 per person, per night and must be reserved ahead of time at 848-7275 or at the park office in Wasagaming. Camping in Wapusk National Park is restricted to outfitted tours where humans observe polar bears from inside an electric fence.

Places where backcountry camping is not permitted include ecological preserves, private land within parks (usually well-marked), and provincial parks near Winnipeg, most notably Birds Hill and Grand Beach, which only offer car camping.

Avoiding Headaches

Small-town Sundays

If you're thinking about a Sunday drive, don't expect to find anything open in very small towns besides gas stations and the odd Chinese restaurant. Small towns in southern Manitoba still take the Christian day of rest very seriously, so you're in for a world of disappointment if you have your heart set on visiting museums or rummaging through second-hand stores. Visit rural Manitoba on a weekday or Saturday and reserve Sundays for parks or other natural attractions instead. And remember, southern Manitoba is not Niagara or Muskoka – it takes a huge influx of wealthy Toronto daytrippers to support their networks of quaint antique shops, art galleries, and latte parlours. Genuine rural culture is a lot more rustic.

White-tailed Pylons

From April to November, white-tailed deer can be a menace on rural roads, especially in the fall, and at dusk and dawn. Manitoba's deer number about 200,000, and they live just about everywhere high-ways exist. Few drivers are killed by deer, but a collision will damage your car and very likely put you in the ditch.

Other highway obstacles include raccoons, skunks, porcupines, coyotes, and moose, the latter posing a serious threat on Highway 10 from Wasagaming to Flin Flon, and on Highway 6 from Lundar to Thompson.

Winter Driving

While I've already cautioned you about black ice and blowing snow, the warning is worth repeating: Highway driving during a Canadian winter should not be treated lightly. Always travel in a well-maintained car with enough gas and washer fluid to get from point A to B. In the event of a winter breakdown, stay in your car, where you'll remain safe and warm. This is especially important during a blizzard, as you can get completely disoriented – there's a kernel of truth behind tales about farmers who lose their way between house and barn and wind up dying from exposure.

If you're travelling any considerable distance during the winter, pack an emergency kit consisting of a candle, blanket or sleeping bag, high-carb snacks and a cellular phone. Also take a shovel, as low-clearance vehicles can get stuck in even tiny snowdrifts.

Hypothermia and Frostbite

Hardy Manitobans tend to be comfortable until the temperature dips below –15°C. You don't need to be such a hero: take a toque, gloves, and warm winter coat along for any winter excursion, even if you don't intend to be outside.

Fashion is irrelevant when it comes to staying warm. When it's extremely cold – say, below –25°C – cover every inch of exposed skin with clothing to prevent frostbite and slather your lips in balm to ward off blisters.

For outdoor winter activities like cross-country skiing, you'll also need moisture-wicking socks and long underwear, waterproof-breathable outer layers, and a daypack to stow extra layers of clothing. Staying dry is your number-one priority in the bitter cold, so peel off layers as you warm up and consider sweat your mortal enemy.

Sunburn

Manitoba is one of the few places on Earth where frostbite and sunburn pose equal threats. As counterintuitive as it sounds, you may burn more quickly in Manitoba than you would in the southern US during the summer, thanks to high ultraviolet radiation caused by our slightly thinner ozone layer.

It's easy to prevent sunburn by wearing a hat and using sunblock. SPF 30 is all you need – anything higher is a waste of cash, even if you're as white as Gwyneth Paltrow.

In June and early July, the sun rises before 6 a.m. and sets well after 10 p.m. in Winnipeg. UV levels are highest between 11 a.m. and 3 p.m.

Mosquitoes

Since much of Manitoba is wet and boggy, it's impossible to visit during the summer and not get bitten by some mosquitoes. But the nasty little critters aren't always a monstrous annoyance, as cool or dry spells during the middle of the summer tend to decimate their ranks.

In southern Manitoba, mosquitoes usually start buzzing in late May and multiply like mad until early August, when they gradually start to disappear. That's why May and September can be the best time to hike or go canoeing. On the other hand, windy summer nights can be completely bug-free, while some summers simply aren't very buggy at all.

The best way to avoid mosquito bites is to wear light-coloured long sleeves and pants on still, warm nights and apply bug spray

When to Go: Peak Seasons for Selected Activities

Beach-Hopping
Season: June through August.
Best time to go: Weekdays in July.
Rationale: The hottest sun of the summer, without the crowds.

Cross-Country Skiing
Season: Late December to mid-March.
Best time to go: Late February and early March.
Rationale: Fully frozen waterways and deep snow, but slightly longer winter days and warmer temperatures.

Festival Hopping
Season: All year.
Best time to go: Mid-June to early August.
Rationale: The biggest and best events are crammed into the early summer, including Jazz Winnipeg, Dauphin's Countryfest, the Winnipeg Folk Festival, the Winnipeg Fringe Theatre Festival, and Folklorama.

Flatwater Paddling
Season: Late May to early October.
Best time to go: Late August and early September.
Rationale: Warm water, less-crowded lakes, and fewer bugs to boot.

Hiking/Backpacking
Season: May to October.
Best time to go: Labour Day to Thanksgiving.
Rationale: Dry trails, cooler mid-day temperatures, spectacular foliage, more active wildlife, few mosquitoes, and even fewer crowds.

Mountain Biking
Season: May to October.
Best time to go: Late August and September.
Rationale: Dry trails, less oppressive heat, and, again, fewer crowds.

Performing Arts
Season: September to May.
Best time to go: September through November.
Rationale: There's more of a buzz surrounding early-season productions by the WSO, RWB, MTC, and Manitoba Opera.

Whitewater Paddling
Season: May to early September.
Peak period: Late May and early June.
Rationale: The spring melt creates big flows and submerges potential hazards.

Wildlife-Watching
Season: All year.
Best time to go: Late April and early May for garter snakes, June through August for pelicans, July for beluga whales, September for elk, late October and early November for polar bears, and winter for owls.
Rationale: You think animals have a rationale?

that contains DEET to exposed areas like your neck and the back of your hands. When you do get bit, don't sweat it – only a handful of Manitoba's 1.2 million people contract West Nile Virus each summer.

But if you're heading up north in the summer, definitely pack a bug hat, because blackflies, deerflies, and no-see-ums are vicious enough to make mosquitoes seem like cuddly little kittens.

Bears

For Manitobans and tourists alike, there's nothing more exciting than seeing a bear ... from a nice, safe distance. Up close, there's nothing cute about a 150-kilogram critter with razor-sharp claws.

Although most black bears are gentle scavengers who avoid contact with humans, they may act aggressive when cornered, surprised, or caring for their cubs. Make plenty of noise while walking along a trail in bear country to let the Yogis know you're on the way.

If you see a black bear, do not approach, no matter how cute the creature appears. Instead, back away slowly and leave the area. If the bear sees you, speak to it loudly but calmly to let it know you're a human being. Don't worry if it stands on two legs and sniffs the air – it's just trying to figure out what you are.

In the unlikely event the bear charges, hold your ground, because the advance is probably a feint. But if it actually attacks, fight back with every fibre of your being, scratching and kicking at the eyes and nose, if you can. Black bears are only interested in easy meals and will likely give up if you become too much of a challenge.

To sleep safely in bear country, never bring food or fragrant cosmetics like soap and toothpaste into your tent. Store all food, toiletries, and garbage inside a car or a metal bear-box, when available, or hang it in a drybag from a long tree limb.

Black bears can be found almost anywhere in Manitoba, except in the extreme northeast, where bigger, stronger, and more-intelligent polar bears patrol the Hudson Bay coast. If you encounter a polar bear on foot, you're probably screwed – there's no more dangerous land predator on Earth, lions, tigers, and anacondas included.

Crime

After 35 years of living in Manitoba, I've found most people polite, helpful, and considerate, if at times a little reserved. But there is a rough edge to the province that can not be ignored, as the sometimes shocking chasm between rich and poor has created an environment where theft and property crime is far more common than visitors expect.

Your personal safety is not typically a problem, even in Winnipeg's roughest neighbourhoods, despite the city's status as Canada's per-capita murder capital. Homicide is not a random crime, as the vast majority of murder victims know their assailants.

Your real concern should be the potential loss of personal property, as vehicle break-in and car-theft rates are way higher than the North American norm in Manitoba. In Winnipeg, or any populated area, lock valuables in your trunk or take them with you when you park your car. And never, ever leave bags or boxes unattended inside a vehicle – opportunistic thieves view this as an invitation to break in. I am not exaggerating the threat: Most Winnipeggers endure some kind of vehicle break-in or act of vandalism once every two years.

If you drive a minivan, pick-up truck, or SUV, consider using an anti-theft device such as a Club or kill switch. These large vehicles are often stolen for use in break-and-enter jobs and then discarded.

Other than that, the only real dangers on Winnipeg's streets are the occasional aggressive panhandler on Portage Avenue and squeegee kids who don't replace their water often enough to prevent mucking up your windshield.

Getting More Info

Tourism Info and Maps

If you need more information about any destination within Manitoba, Travel Manitoba offers year-round tourism advice at the Explore Manitoba Centre at The Forks, and runs five highway information kiosks from May to September. From east to west, they're located on Highway 1 at the Ontario border near West Hawk Lake; Highway 75 at the US border near Emerson; Highway 10 at the US border near Turtle Mountain; Highway 1 at the Saskatchewan border; and Highway 16 at the junction of Highway 83 in the town of Russell. Travel Manitoba staff also dispense advice via telephone, but only on weekdays from 8:30 a.m. to 7:00 p.m. Call 945-3777 in Winnipeg or toll-free at 1-800-665-0040.

You can also visit Travel Manitoba at www.travelmanitoba.com, while Manitoba Conservation has the lowdown on provincial parks, trail conditions (at least in theory), and fishing and hunting regulations at www.gov.mb.ca/conservation.

As well, Canadian Automobile Association and AAA members can obtain maps and travel advice from CAA travel centres in Winnipeg (870 Empress, 2211 McPhillips, or 501 St. Anne's), Brandon (61 2nd Ave. NE), or Altona (1300 18th).

There are also municipal tourist information centres in almost every city and town. Winnipeg has two such places: Destination Winnipeg dispenses advice at 259 Portage and at the Winnipeg International Airport. You can also reach this agency by phone at 1-800-665-0204, or peruse www.destinationwinnipeg.ca.

Backcountry campers seeking topographical maps should head straight to Manitoba Conservation's Winnipeg Map Sales office (1007 Century), which also sells a variety of guidebooks.

Media

Some travellers avoid newspapers, radio, and TV while on holidays to immerse themselves fully in a vacation experience. It's a nice idea, but potentially stupid, as only local media can provide you with up-to-date information about festivals and other attractions and alert you to perils like blizzards, floods, and forest fires.

Manitoba is served by five daily newspapers: the *Winnipeg Free Press, Winnipeg Sun, Brandon Sun, Portage la Prairie Daily Graphic,* and *Flin Flon Reminder.* The *Free Press* is the largest and most widely available. The Thursday edition includes the most complete entertainment listings in Winnipeg, while the outdoor column that inspired this guidebook appears on Saturdays.

Winnipeg is also served by weekly street paper *Uptown* and the monthly *Where* magazine, the latter geared to tourists and available at higher-end hotels. *Where* also maintains excellent online retail, restaurant, and tourist-attraction listings at www.where.ca/winnipeg. Don't even waste your time visiting its nearest competitor, MyWinnipeg.com, whose listings are nowhere near as readable or complete.

You can tune into 20 radio stations in Winnipeg, the most useful being news-talk stations CJOB (680 AM) and CBC Radio One (990 AM), both of which broadcast news and weather on the hour. You can hear CJOB all over southern Manitoba, while CBC Radio One covers most of the province. Also scan the FM dial for NCI Radio (105.5 in Winnipeg, 91.5 in Western Manitoba), a folksy, Aboriginal-run country music network based in Winnipeg but heard all over the province. NCI also is the only station that provides weather forecasts for remote First Nations.

For TV news, tune into one of four English-language Winnipeg newscasts: CTV affiliate CKY (Cable 5, 6 p.m. and 11:30 p.m. daily); Global Winnipeg (Cable 12, 5:30 and 10:30 p.m. weekdays, 5:30 p.m. weekends); CBC Winnipeg (Cable 2, 6 p.m. weekdays) and City (Cable 8, 6 p.m. and 11:30 p.m. Sunday through Friday, 6 and 11 p.m. Saturdays).

There are two sources of TV weather information – Environment Canada (available from some TV providers) and The Weather Network.

Gear Retailers

If you've just arrived in Manitoba and you don't have camping or travel gear, Winnipeg is the best place to pick up essential items – and as a bonus, to acquire intelligence about specific destinations. Most people who work at outdoor retailers are serious trippers and may offer invaluable advice.

Unlike in Vancouver or Calgary, Winnipeg's gear outlets are not concentrated in any specific neighbourhood. Mountain Equipment Co-op (303 Portage), geared exclusively to wilderness travellers, is the best for reasonably priced outdoor clothing, sleeping bags, and assorted gadgets. Locally owned SIR (1300 Ellice), which also caters to the hunting and fishing crowd, sports an even wider selection of tents, knives, binoculars, and other big-ticket items. Wilderness Supply (623 Ferry) specializes in canoe camping, while the staff at Backcountry Magic (1857 Portage) and Wave Track (42 Speers) know their stuff as well. Army Surplus (460 Portage) also carries a wide selection of gear – sometimes at impressively low prices – but you're less likely to obtain solid advice here.

For bike and ski gear and advice, try Lifesport (411 Pembina and 1117 Henderson), Olympia Cycle & Ski (1813 Portage, 661 Pembina, 241 Henderson, and 326 St. Mary's), Sampson's (525 Pembina), Woodcock (157 St. Anne's), or Gooch's (185 Sherbrook).

Dollars and sense

If you've never visited Canada before, make sure your pockets don't have holes – you're bound to carry around lots of loonies and toonies.

No, the whole country is not obsessed with animation. Loonies are gold $1 coins adorned with an image of a loon, while bicoloured $2 toonies depict polar bears.

Other Canadian coins are just like American currency: There are quarters, dimes, nickels and practically useless pennies. Canadian paper currency comes in denominations of $5, $10, $20, and upwards, but many retail establishments will be annoyed if you present them with a $50 bill and downright pissy if your try to pass them a C-note. To avoid getting attitude, use credit cards (VISA use is ubiquitous, while most restaurants and retailers accept Mastercard and American Express) or Interac-compatible bank cards to pay for large purchases.

Interac use is more common than paper money almost every-where but donut shops and high-traffic, mom 'n' pop diners. At Tim Hortons franchises and popular Winnipeg eateries such as The Falafel Place and VJ's, you have no choice but to pay cash.

Bank machines are easy to find, as almost every gas station and bar in the province sports some kind of ATM. Typical fees range from $1.50 to $2, on top of your regular bank card. ATMs at actual banks are always cheaper to use. Use common sense when making withdrawals, especially in Winnipeg – withdrawing large sums of money can make you a target for getting rolled, if you fail to observe your surroundings.

Tipping, meanwhile, tends to be on the cheap side in Manitoba: 15 per cent is standard in restaurants, while cabbies will be thrilled with a flat $5 on a longer ride.

Finally, public payphones cost 25 cents if you use coins or $1 if you pay with a calling card. The area code for all of Manitoba is 204, but you'll only have to use it if you call long-distance.

WINNIPEG

5

Whether you're from outside the Perimeter or a visitor to Manitoba, it would be a crime not to visit Winnipeg, an unusually artsy industrial town correctly identified by the *New York Times*, the *Los Angeles Times,* and *Utne Reader* as one of North America's best-kept cultural secrets. No other mid-sized Canadian city has so much going for it – but so little clue how to sell itself.

On one hand, Winnipeg is a quirky and creative place, where the cheap cost of living nurtures a vibrant visual arts community, excellent performing arts, and the most-celebrated music scene on the Canadian Prairies. First-time visitors marvel at the downtown architecture, rave about the food, and get taken aback by the summertime greenery. They need not be surprised, as the metro area of roughly 700,000 is large enough to boast most of the attractions of a major city, but folksy enough to remain uncrowded and to ensure the cost of doing just about anything remains modest.

On the other hand, 'Peg City suffers from a nasty reputation in the rest of Canada and a self-defeating inferiority complex at home. Winters are long and bitterly cold. Mosquitoes swarm by the trillions during the summer, industrial areas are immense, and socio-economic disparity gives the city many of the "urban doughnut" problems that plagued large American centres during the '70s, not to mention the dubious title of Canada's per capita murder capital.

But neither creativity nor ugliness is the city's defining feature. The real key to Winnipeg is a psychology of isolation, as the nearest larger centre, Minneapolis–St. Paul, is eight hours and a border crossing away. When you have 700,000 people surrounded by nothing, you end up with an extremely strong sense of regional identity. Locals often lament this as parochialism, but visitors will be delighted – you normally have to visit an outpost like St. John's, Nfld., or Iqaluit, Nunavut, to encounter such an idiosyncratic civic culture.

In other words, Winnipeg is weird, in the best possible way.

Opposite: Winnipeg's Portage Avenue, drained of life by unfettered suburban development, is now undergoing an urban renewal similar to that experienced in other North American cities.

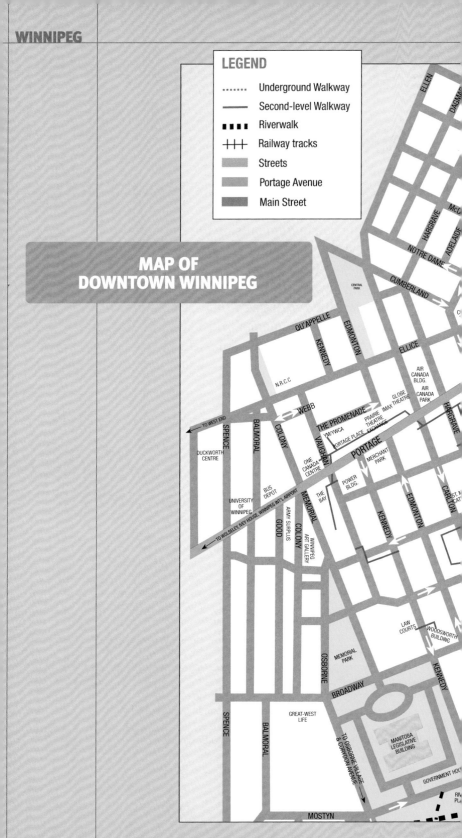

LEGEND

- .... Underground Walkway
- —— Second-level Walkway
- ■■■■ Riverwalk
- +++ Railway tracks
- Streets
- Portage Avenue
- Main Street

MAP OF
DOWNTOWN WINNIPEG

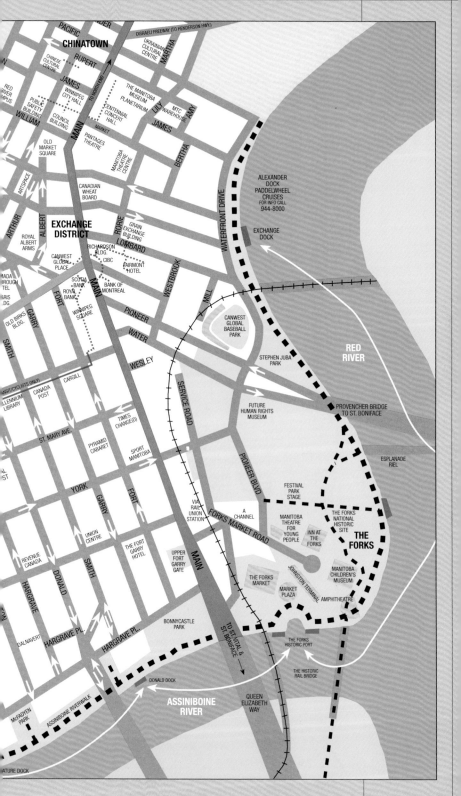

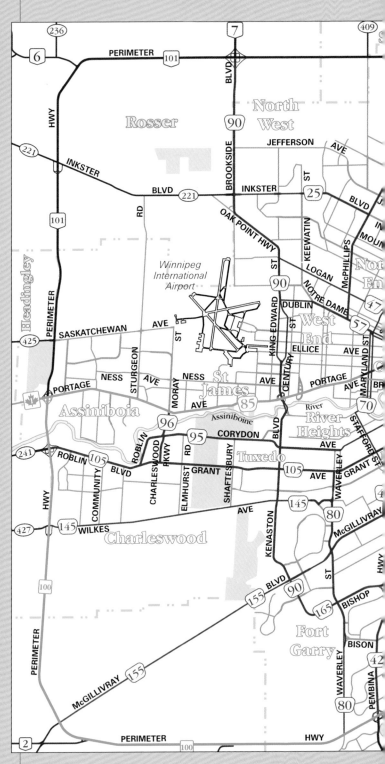

Map©2006 Sherlock Publishing Ltd.

MAP OF WINNIPEG

A Little History

For centuries, Cree and other indigenous peoples had the confluence of the Red and Assiniboine Rivers to themselves. This situation ended in 1738, when Quebec explorer La Vérendrye was the first of many Europeans to find his way here to (a) sell useless stuff to Aboriginal people, (b) colonize their land, and (c) find out the joke was on them the first time a spring flood deluged their brand-new homesteads and spawned an armada of mosquitoes.

Thousands of ethnic British, French, Scandinavians, and Métis lived in the area by the time the City of Winnipeg was founded in 1874. They were joined by hundreds of thousands of Eastern European settlers as the Canadian Pacific Railway opened up the Prairies.

At the turn of the twentieth century, Winnipeg was a boomtown, a fast-growing transport-and-warehousing centre rivalled in North America only by Chicago. This period saw the construction of the stunning cut-stone and terra cotta buildings that still stand in the Exchange District and other parts of downtown.

The exponential growth ended in 1914, when the completion of the Panama Canal killed the railway boom. Five years later, the only general strike ever undertaken in Canada and the US seemed to hasten the Depression. In the aftermath, Winnipeg would grapple with a perceived feeling of decline for the rest of the century. The city went from being Canada's third-largest metropolitan area in the 1950s – after Toronto and Montreal – to the eighth today, after Vancouver, Ottawa, Edmonton, Calgary, and Quebec City. But the long decline was more a matter of perception than reality: Winnipeg simply took a long time to accept its status as a slow-growth city, which is not such a bad thing.

This self-consciousness ended in the mid-1990s, when the city began to grow comfortable within its own idiosyncratic, creative-but-gritty skin. It's safe to say Winnipeg is more confident today than at any other time since 1914.

Winnipeg's Main Street, looking north, ca. 1875, before the advent of paved streets.

Getting Around

If you're only spending a few days in Winnipeg and don't plan to leave the inner city, you don't need a car. Most bus routes converge downtown, and most places of interest are within walking distance. But if you have time to explore the entire city or plan to see the rest of Manitoba, you definitely need a vehicle.

Cabs are expensive and difficult to hail if you're not in front of a major hotel. Winnipeg Transit buses, while cheap at $2 a ride, are inconvenient for cross-town travel, especially during off-peak hours (schedules: www.winnipegtransit.com or 287-7433).

Downtown Winnipeg skyline, as seen from Esplanade Riel.

In the summer, the Splash Dash Water Bus (see *The Forks*) is a fun way to cruise between downtown, Osborne Village, and the Corydon area, but service is sporadic due to fluctuating water levels on the Red and Assiniboine rivers.

If you drive, make sure you nab a city map. Hastily planned in what seems like 11 minutes in 1905, the city lacks any semblance of a grid pattern. Streets that abut each other at 45-degree angles and wind around the curves of meandering creeks and rivers occasionally confuse even lifelong Winnipeggers. Even worse, some long streets change names every couple of blocks. The most annoying is a single, heinous route that starts off in the north as Salter Street before becoming Isabel, Balmoral, Colony, Memorial, Osborne, Dunkirk, and finally Dakota before it dead-ends at the Red River Floodway.

Still, finding your way around is nowhere near as difficult as navigating a European capital. Winnipeg's wide major arteries, which used to be muddy ox-cart trails back in the settler days, loosely parallel the north-south Red River and the east-west Assiniboine, which converge downtown. The busiest east-west routes are Portage Avenue, Nairn/Regent, and Roblin/Grant, while Main Street, Henderson Highway, Pembina Highway, and St. Mary's Road are the primary north-south streets. A ring road called the Perimeter Highway encircles the city.

Other major features of the city include the massive Canadian Pacific Railway yard that divides downtown from the North End; the Seine River in the southeast; the Assiniboine Park and Forest in the southwest; and the International Airport, precariously situated right next to a residential area called St. James as well as the city's busiest shopping area, a big-box wasteland informally known as the Polo Park area.

Luckily, it's easy to land a plane on the flat prairie.

WHERE TO GO

The Forks

First-time visitors to Winnipeg usually head straight for **The Forks**, a riverside shopping-and-dining complex credited with helping revitalize the inner city. But you don't need to devote an entire afternoon to the place. If you've visited Vancouver's Granville Island, you'll get a sense of déjà vu.

Located at the confluence of the Red and the Assiniboine, The Forks is the most convenient place to pick up souvenirs and tourism brochures, the latter at the **Explore Manitoba Centre**. Once a sprawling green space, the increasingly crowded site features restaurants, shops, an indoor market and multi-ethnic food court, outdoor patios facing the Assiniboine, and a marina where you can rent canoes and – when the rivers aren't bulging over their banks – catch a ride on the **Splash Dash Water Bus**, a river taxi that stops at eight inner-city docks and doubles as a sight-seeing cruiseboat. One-way water bus fares are $2.50, while thirty-minute tours are $9.

The best place to chow down at The Forks is the cheap, multicultural food court in the **Forks Market**, where Caribbean stall **Bindy's** slaps together excellent roti and **Tall Grass Prairie**, a satellite of a fantastic Wolseley-area bakery, offers organic breads, amazing cinnamon buns, and Folk Fest cookies. At most of the sit-down

MUST SEE:
The Forks
Touristy gift shops and restaurants at the confluence of the Red and Assiniboine rivers.

Canada Day at the Forks.

Charles Shilliday

restaurants, you're paying for the view – **Muddy Waters Smokehouse**, **Finn McCue's pub**, and the **Old Spaghetti Factory** are all run by WOW! Hospitality Concepts, a local corporation that cares more about their concepts than their food. Some diners rave about the ambitious prix fixe menu at **Sydney's**, the priciest restaurant in the development, but I personally find their culinary reach exceeds their grasp.

During the summer, interpretive programs at The **Forks National Historic Site** and **Oodena Celebration Circle** drive home the point that people have been meeting at The Forks for millennia. In the winter, you can skate, cross-country ski, snowshoe, or stroll on the river ice, which is usually (but not always) safe to traverse by January. When the ice is solid, you can walk or skate along groomed river paths all the way to Osborne Village and the Corydon area.

Other Forks attractions include the **Manitoba Children's Museum** (9:30 a.m. to 4:30 p.m., Sunday to Thursday; 9:30 a.m. to 8 p.m. Fridays and Saturdays; admission $6), **Manitoba Theatre For Young People** (tickets and schedules: www.mtyp.ca or 942-8898), and three outdoor stages, although the largest is rarely used now that the PA system points directly at **Inn at The Forks** ($125-$150 for a room), the only hotel on the site and one of the newest in the city.

At the north end of the site, a striking pedestrian bridge called **Esplanade Riel** connects The Forks to St. Boniface. Halfway across the span, a **Salisbury House** restaurant offers south-facing views of the Red River. In the summer, expect to wait up to an hour for a table. Again, the main feast is for your eyeballs, not your tastebuds.

Still farther north, you'll find **CanWest Global Park**, a 7,300-seat ballpark used by the Northern League of Baseball's **Winnipeg Goldeyes** from May through August. Winnipeg Mayor Sam Katz owns both the team and stadium, arguably one of the nicest in minor-league ball, with civilized concessions and fully stocked bars. Tickets range from $4 to $15 at 780-3333 or www.ticketmaster.ca.

While some Winnipeggers grumble The Forks is already too developed, at least one more massive project looms on the horizon. One of the city's wealthiest clans – the Asper family, controllers of the CanWest Global media empire – is spearheading a plan to build a $200-million monolith called the **Canadian Museum for Human Rights** at the north end of the site. Their vision calls for a 2.25-hectare (5.5-acre) museum with architecture as distinct as the Guggenheim Museum in Bilbao, Spain, or Jerusalem's Yad Vashem Holocaust memorial. As of early 2006, plans for the museum were still coming together.

Once you've had your fill of The Forks, you can make your way on foot to four interesting neighbourhoods: The Exchange District to the north, Downtown to the west, old St. Boniface across the Red River to the east, and Osborne Village, accessible by strolling west along the river walk past the Legislature then taking the Osborne Bridge south across the Assiniboine.

Although controversial during construction, striking pedestrian bridge Esplanade Riel is now the most popular symbol of Winnipeg's slowly revitalizing downtown. The bridge connects The Forks with St. Boniface

The Exchange District

The most visually stunning stretch of downtown Winnipeg is **the Exchange**, where a very-cool collection of late-nineteenth and early-twentieth-century warehouse buildings escaped the wrecking ball throughout the twentieth century. The area is now protected as a National Historic Site – economic stagnation has its benefits!

The buildings demand a **walking tour**, either of the formal variety ($6 guided walks leave Old Market Square at 10 a.m. and 2 p.m. daily from June 1 to Sept. 5) or informally, as urbanites will dig the assortment of curio shops, vintage clothing boutiques, used music/bookstores, and especially art galleries concentrated within two blocks of the corner of McDermot Avenue and Albert Street. The galleries alone are worth the trip, as you can check out the avant-garde **Plug In Gallery** (286 McDermot), upscale **Mayberry Fine Art** (212 McDermot), affordable **Warehouse Artworks** (222 McDermot), Aboriginal-centred **Urban Shaman** (233 McDermot), and community-oriented **Site** (55 Arthur) and **Ace Art** (290 McDermot) within a couple of hours.

The streets with the most impressive architecture, meanwhile, are Princess, King, and Main, the latter featuring a collection of majestic former financial institutions like the recently restored **Millennium Centre** (389 Main), **Bank of Hamilton** (395 Main), **Confederation Life Building** (457 Main), and the **Royal Bank Building** (Main and William), the oldest surviving skyscraper in western Canada.

The Exchange is also home to many of Manitoba's big cultural institutions. Sprawling along Main Street across from the Soviet-style, concrete-encrusted **City Hall**, the **Manitoba Museum**, **Planetarium**, and **Science Gallery** occupy a complex connected to the west side of the Exchange by an underground tunnel. The museum has natural-history exhibits and galleries representing all of Manitoba's ecosystems and a life-sized recreation of the Nonsuch, an ocean-going fur trade sailing ship. A bargain at $8, the museum is open 10 a.m. to 4 p.m. Tuesday to Friday and 11 a.m. to 4 p.m. weekends and holidays.

MUST SEE:
The Exchange District
Early-twentieth-century architecture, performing arts, funky vintage retailers, and the highest concentration of art galleries anywhere in Manitoba.

MUST SEE:
Manitoba Museum
A life-size replica of an HBC sailing vessel, prehistoric fossils, and recent artifacts illustrate the natural and human history of Manitoba.

Early-twentieth-century architecture on Main Street. Neoclassical columns define the building style of what was once the financial centre of western Canada.

Charles Shilliday

Charles Shilliday

The Planetarium, located below the museum, offers old-school astronomy shows on weekends ($6.50) and live rock bands and electronic artists on the first Saturday night of every month ($7.50). The Science Gallery ($6.50), however, is a little dated. For show and temporary exhibit into, visit www.manitobamuseum.mb.ca.

Next to the Museum sits the **Centennial Concert Hall**, a 2,300-seat theatre that serves as a home for three performing arts institutions: the **Royal Winnipeg Ballet**, **Manitoba Opera**, and the **Winnipeg Symphony Orchestra**.

The heart of the Exchange District is at the funky corner of McDermot and Albert.

The Royal Winnipeg Ballet, Canada's first professional ballet company, usually presents four productions during the fall-to-spring season. You can purchase tickets at 956-2792 or www.rwb.org. In 2006, they range between $22 and $68 a pop.

Manitoba Opera (www.manitobaopera.mb.ca or 942-7479) presents two full productions and one concert each season, with individual seats ranging for $29 to $84 (Ticketmaster Artsline, 253-2787).

And the 67-member Winnipeg Symphony Orchestra presents a bewildering array of concerts from September to May, offering up a fantastic, challenging midwinter **New Music Festival** (late January or early February) and serious classical music all season – but also symphonic arrangements of classic rock for the mullet-wearing crowd, and artistically suspect pops concerts aimed at blue-hairs. For better and for worse, this is an orchestra for all tastes: Check out the lineup at www.wso.mb.ca or 949-3950. Tickets range from $16 to $62 at 949-3999, while the New Music Festival is much cheaper.

The other big cultural institution in the Exchange is the **Manitoba Theatre Centre**, which presents six sometimes-stodgy plays per season at its Market Avenue Mainstage ($16 to $54 a seat) and four edgier offerings at the smaller **Warehouse Theatre** on Rupert Avenue ($12 to $40). You can buy tickets and check out the program at 942-6537 or www.mtc.mb.ca.

MTC also runs the city's most exciting summer festival, the **Winnipeg Fringe Theatre Festival**, which completely energizes the Exchange in late July. For 12 days, you can check out more than 100 short plays and comedy sketches in dozens of small, mostly makeshift venues, all within walking distance of Old Market Square, rarely paying more than $8. You'll need to drop $5 on a Fringe program to navigate your way through the selection, or pick up the *Winnipeg Free Press's* daily Fringe Guide – anything that gets four or more stars is bound to sell out.

In June, Old Market Square also serves as a base for free performances during the 10-day **Jazz Winnipeg Festival**

MUST SEE:
Winnipeg Fringe Theatre Festival
Avant-garde theatre and improv and sketch comedy at North America's second-largest fringe festival.

(www.jazzwinnipeg.com), which also runs jazz, rock, and electronic concerts in a dozen downtown locales. The square is also the site of sporadic weekday concerts and a Sunday-morning market all summer. Directly to the south, rep theatre **Cinematheque** (www.winnipegfilmgroup.com), in the Artspace Building, offers experimental and art-house flicks all year for $5 ($3.50 for members).

The Exchange also boasts two fully restored heritage theatres that date back to the Vaudeville era. The 1,640-seat **Burton Cummings Theatre**, named after the mustachioed and still quite alive Guess Who singer, is the venue of choice for rock concerts. Snag a seat on the floor, because the view from the upper balcony will induce vertigo. The 1,400-seat **Pantages Playhouse Theatre** is more often used for folk and middle-of-the-road performers. Both theatres were used as backdrops for the Brad Pitt film *The Assassination of Jesse James*.

The northwest side of the Exchange also houses a small **Chinatown** that stretches toward Higgins Avenue. The best and biggest dim sum parlour is **Kum Koon Gardens** (257 King), where you're guaranteed to wait in line on weekends, while **Maxim Bakery** (285 Alexander) is the place to load up on Chinese pastries on weekday mornings.

Other excellent Exchange eateries include the upscale-Italian **Tre Visi** (173 McDermot), authentic French bistro **Mirlycourtois** (188 Princess, upstairs), Mediterranean-inspired **Allora** (Lombard at Waterfront Drive), and the casual Underground Café (70 Arthur, in the basement), famous for its veggie burgers. Quaff coffee at **The Fyxx** (93 Albert) or neighbouring **Mondragon** (91 Albert), a co-operatively run, all-vegan restaurant and leftie bookstore.

The Exchange is also home to a dozen-odd nightclubs, including gritty punk-rock landmark **Royal Albert Arms** (48 Albert), tall-ceilinged danceteria/pick-up joint **Empire Cabaret** (436 Main), and the two-level **King's Head** (120 King), an ostensibly private British pub where $5 will gain you a lifetime membership.

Roaming around this neighbourhood with a belly full of liquor is not dangerous, but you should stick to the more heavily populated southern parts of the Exchange. Areas to the north of City Hall are a little dodgier at night, and should be avoided on foot during the wee hours by people who consider themselves less than streetwise.

To the northeast, meanwhile, condos are sprouting up along an as-yet-underdeveloped **Waterfront Drive**. At the unassuming looking Alexander Docks, **Paddlewheel River Rouge Tours** (944-8000, www.paddlewheelcruises.com) offers afternoon sight-seeing cruises (May to October, $14.75), sunset dinner-dance cruises (May to October, $15.75), and night-time cruises (summer weekends, $15.75) along the Red River, plus longer jaunts down to Lower Fort Garry (see Central Plains and Valleys). These are sedate trips, but several times a summer, Winnipeg hip-hop DJs Hunnicutt and Co-op turn one of the ships into a floating **Funk Boat** (check www.djcoop.com for dates). In July and August, Paddlewheel also offers morning bus tours that stop at places like The Forks, the Manitoba Legislature, and Assiniboine Park ($22), and also offer a combined morning bus/afternoon cruise package ($34.50). In May, June, and some-times even in July, high water levels may prevent the Paddlewheel and Splash Dash boats from operating.

Also on the northeast side of the Exchange, amid a string of scuzzy hotels and run-down buildings, you'll find more cultural gems like Ukrainian art gallery **Oseredok** (184 Alexander East), an Aboriginal spiritual centre called the **Circle Of Life Thunderbird House** (Higgins & Main) with adjoining teepees, and the **Canadian Plains Gallery**, in the basement of the Aboriginal Centre (181 Higgins).

Downtown

Just west of The Forks and south of the Exchange, Winnipeg's sprawl-ing downtown is starting to recover from a century of incompetent planning and uninspired civic leadership.

Toward the end of the railway boom, when most of the inner city's economic activity was concentrated along Main Street, hubris-afflicted retailers Eaton's and The Bay had the bright idea of erecting massive department stores on Portage Avenue, thus stretching out downtown into a needlessly large dogleg of an urban core that could easily serve a city the size of Philadelphia.

Charles Shilliday

Downtown Winnipeg, with CanWest Global Place in the centre.

Thanks to Winnipeg's slow population growth over the past 80 years, downtown has never been able to reach critical mass. Generations of entrepreneurs and politicians have tried to "save" downtown with megaprojects like The Forks, the Manitoba Museum/Centennial Concert Hall complex, Portage Place mall, and hockey arena MTS Centre.

Today, there are many signs of life in the city's core, though visitors still complain of feeling unsafe due to empty streets and aggressive panhandlers. Their beefs are legitimate, but let's get a grip – downtown Winnipeg is a Garden of Eden compared to Vancouver's heroin-ravaged East Side or the inner core of practically any midwestern American city.

The first place Canadian tourists head is the corner of **Portage and Main**, arguably Canada's most famous intersection and easily one of the windiest in North America. Unfortunately, there's nothing to see here beyond the majestic Corinthian columns of the **Bank of Montreal building** – pedestrians have not been allowed to cross Portage and Main since 1976, when an underground walkway was built to speed the traffic flow.

If you insist on visiting the intersection, take note of the two tallest office buildings, each representing the ambition of the city's most powerful families. On the northeast corner sits the **Richardson Building**, a 30-storey tower created by financiers James Richardson &

Sons, Limited. Standing 9.5 metres higher, on the northwest corner, is **CanWest Global Place**, headquarters for the Asper family's media holdings. The old-money Richardsons tend to avoid publicity; the *nouveau riche* Aspers are more flamboyant. Both families serve as Winnipeg's de facto royalty.

Compared to the Exchange District's uniformly fantastic architecture, downtown Winnipeg is a canine's croissant of post-modern monstrosities and neo-classical pretense. Arguably the ugliest structure is **Portage Place**, an otherwise useful mall that houses three attractions on its third and uppermost level: an **IMAX cinema**; three-screen rep cinema **The Globe**; and **Prairie Theatre Exchange** (www.pte.mb.ca), a Canadian-centric company that stages six productions during an October-to-April season. PTE tickets range from $18 to $32 at 942-5483.

Buildings worth visiting for the architecture alone include the newly completed **Millennium Library** at Donald and Graham, the **VIA Rail station** on Main Street, the nearby remains of Hudson's Bay Company (HBC) fur-trading post **Upper Fort Garry** – now just a single stone gate on Broadway, unfortunately – and the surprisingly stately **Manitoba Legislature**, which boasts a pair of bronze, life-sized bison at the foot of a grand staircase in the north-facing front lobby at Memorial and Broadway. The impressive interior is open to the public daily, from 8 a.m. to 8 p.m.

On the south side of the Legislature, facing the banks of the Assiniboine, stands a sterile **statue of Louis Riel**, Manitoba's controversial founder. This bland image of Riel as a dignified statesmen was installed in 1994 to replace a much more fascinating piece by Étienne Gaboury – Winnipeg's most celebrated architect – and sculptor Marcien Lemay. They cast Riel as a naked, twisted and tortured soul, but Métis leaders didn't like looking at the great man's genitals and demanded the statue switcheroo. The Gaboury/Lemay version now stands across the Red River on the grounds of St. Boniface College. Visit both to see why politicians should never be allowed to make artistic decisions.

MUST SEE:
Manitoba
Legislature
Stately neoclassical architecture, open to the public.

Strolling through Memorial Park, just north of the Manitoba Legislature.

Charles Shilliday

Charles Shilliday

On the north side of the Legislature, a green space called **Memorial Park** – home to war memorials and impromptu summer soccer games – stretches toward Portage Avenue. Keep heading north and you'll come to **the Bay** department store, one of the last vestiges of that seventeenth-century fur-trading empire, the HBC. Across Memorial, it's impossible to miss the monolithic facade of the **Winnipeg Art Gallery** – the largest gallery in the province, the oldest in western Canada, and home to the most extensive permanent collection of Inuit art in the world.

The WAG usually houses three temporary exhibits at a time (current info: www.wag.mb.ca or 789-1760). Admission is a bloody steal as $6 for adults. Hours are 11 a.m. to 5 p.m. Thursday through Sunday and Tuesday, and 11 a.m. to 9 p.m. on Wednesday. The WAG is closed on Mondays.

If you're looking to purchase Aboriginal art or handicrafts, visit downtown's **Wah-Sa Gallery** (302 Fort), Northern Images in Portage Place (second floor), or the modest **Four Directions** on the main floor of the Ramada Marlborough Hotel (Smith Street at Ellice Avenue).

As fas as Winnipeggers are concerned, the biggest downtown attraction is the city's new hockey arena, **MTS Centre**, completed in 2004 on the site of the former Eaton's department store. Originally a controversial project – despite the bankruptcy of the Eaton's chain, elderly loyalists opposed demolition – the 15,500-seat facility attracted more than a million fans during its first year in operation, when it ranked as one of the busiest concert venues in the world. Event listings are online at www.truenorthproject.mb.ca.

From mid-October to early April, MTS Centre also serves as the home of the American Hockey League's **Manitoba Moose**, the farm team for the Vancouver Canucks of the National Hockey League. In a hockey-mad city, the Moose are the biggest game in town, though Winnipeg was slow to embrace the team after the beloved NHL Jets moved to Phoenix in 1996. Tickets range from $16 to $34 at www.ticketmaster.ca.

Public walkways on the second floor of the arena act as a free museum of sorts, with old front pages of the *Winnipeg Free Press* along Hargrave Street and a statue of Eaton's founder Timothy Eaton, which used to sit on the main floor of the old department store, perched in front of a window overlooking Portage Avenue. The second-floor pedestrian area is part of an elaborate system of enclosed walkways that connects much of Winnipeg's downtown, affording protection from the winter brain freeze. The walkways run from the Richardson Building and Fairmont Hotel northeast of Portage and Main; continue underground through the Lombard

Downtown Winnipeg's MTS Centre, a hockey arena and concert venue, was built on the site of the former Eaton's department store.

MUST SEE:
Winnipeg Art Gallery
The world's largest permanent collection of Inuit art, plus contemporary exhibits.

Concourse mall; and head aboveground through the Canada Post building, the Millennium Library, and City Place mall before continuing west through MTS Centre to Portage Place and the Bay store.

On the most frigid winter days, so many pedestrians use the temperature-controlled walkways that downtown streets appear deserted. Unfortunately, you can't use this system to get around late at night, so bar-hoppers must rely on cabs and sensible clothing.

Given its size, downtown Winnipeg has relatively few nightspots. Four popular watering holes within stumbling distance of each other include original rock venue the **Pyramid Cabaret** (340 Fort), bourbon-soaked roots-rock hole-in-the-wall **Times Change(d) High & Lonesome Club** (Main at St. Mary), the lounge at **Earls on Main** (Main at York) – where the genetically gifted serving staff is a big part of the attraction – and cocktail lounge the Palm Room at the Fort Garry Hotel (222 Broadway).

If you don't want to stay at a chain hotel, the very cool **Fort Garry**, completed in 1913, has a glorious marble lobby, a spectacular Sunday brunch, a brand-new spa, and rooms that'll set you back $140-$160. The ritzier **Fairmont**, just off the corner of Portage & Main, is even pricier at $190-$230. The rest of the downtown chains vary from $90 to $150.

The best downtown restaurant offerings include Indian buffets at **East India Company** (349 York) and **Ivory** (200 Main), very traditional sushi created by the only Japanese-trained chef in Winnipeg at **Edohei** (355 Ellice), vegetarian Chinese at **Affinity** (208 Edmonton), upscale Italian at **Amici** and casual sister restaurant **Bombolini** (326 Broadway), and old-school European at **Dubrovnik** (390 Assiniboine). You can also chow down right on the corner of Portage & Main at **Hy's Steakhouse** (Richardson Building, main floor), but the main attraction here is the real estate – for $35, you can find a better slab of beef elsewhere.

If you'd rather save your money, a tiny shack called **VJs** (170 Main, across from the VIA Rail station) serves up sumptuously sloppy burgers and some of the best thick-cut fries in the known universe. You eat in your car or outside on picnic tables. Also a must for serious foodies is the most authentic diner in Manitoba: **the Wagon Wheel** (205 Hargrave) roasts turkey every morning for their amazing, massive clubhouse sandwiches and offers remarkably efficient service, even during the frenetic lunch hour rush. You can also get a pickerel lunch for an almost unbelievable $7.50, when the fish is in season. The décor has not changed since the early '60s – you sit at a lunch counter or cozy booths, listening to talk radio station CJOB during the milliseconds it takes for your lunch to arrive.

Late-night downtown grub is a little more problematic. The most dependable spot is **Ken's** (333 Ellice at Hargrave), a Chinese restaurant open on weekends until 4 a.m. The best breakfasts, aside from the $25 weekend buffet at the Fort Garry, can be found at **Don Deli** (120 Donald at Broadway), which offers Mennonite selections like crackling, farmer's sausage, and gloms kuak, a cottage-cheese pancake.

Charles Shilliday

St. Boniface

Winnipeggers are fond of claiming their city has the largest Francophone population of any Canadian city west of Ottawa. It's a nice idea, but it's complete bullshit, as Toronto, Vancouver, Calgary, and Edmonton sport larger numbers of ethnic French-Canadians, as well as more people who actually speak French, according to Statistics Canada.

What makes Winnipeg appear more Francophone is many of the city's 75,000 French speakers are concentrated in **St. Boniface**, an inner-city neighbourhood that was a proud and separate city until 1974, when Winnipeg swallowed up most of its suburbs.

On foot from The Forks, you can wander across **Esplanade Riel**, stroll down Taché Boulevard parallel to the Red River, then return to The Forks via Queen Elizabeth Way. As a diversion, you can stop in at a handful of cafés on Provencher Boulevard, but the real attraction is the stunning **St. Boniface Cathedral** at Avenue de la Cathédrale and Taché.

The surprisingly modest **grave of Manitoba founder Louis Riel** sits on the grounds of the cathedral, a very cool Étienne Gaboury structure built inside the remains of a century-old basilica partly destroyed by fire in 1968. The west-facing facade, which often appears on postcards, is stunning after dark.

A short walk east, on the Aulneau Street side of St. Boniface College, you'll find Gaboury's brilliant, tortured **statue of Riel**. To the south of the cathedral, **St. Boniface Museum** (494 Taché, hours vary) is packed with Riel artifacts, and chronicles the history of Winnipeg's Francophone community. Admission is $3.

To see real, live Franco-Manitobans, visit St. Boniface in mid-February during **Festival du Voyageur**, a 10-day celebration of Winnipeg's Francophone heritage and fur-trade history. The main festival site at Whittier Park (St. Joseph at Messager) has outdoor snow sculptures, French-Canadian folk, Celtic, and Cajun music inside heated tents; and a recreation of the Fort Gibraltar fur-trading post. More music is scattered around a dozen locations around St. Boniface – visit www.festivalvoyageur.mb.ca for current performer info. Try the taffy on snow, but don't expect fantastic Franco-Manitoban food – microwaved tourtiere just doesn't do the traditional meat pie any justice. Admission to the main festival site is $12 for adults.

To combat a general sentiment that "Le Festival" has grown a little stale, organizers tinkered with the site layout and experimented with winter camping in 2006. You read correctly: You can camp outdoors in February, albeit inside the cozy confines of a quinzhee (that is, snow dome) equipped with winter sleeping bags and bison skins. Check the festival's website or call 237-7692 for current rates.

The remains of the basilica at St. Boniface Cathedral: a majestic facade now enclosing a new church by celebrated architect Étienne Gaboury.

MUST SEE:
St. Boniface
Cathedral
The ruins of the Basilica, Louis Riel's grave, and a bold statue of Manitoba's colourful founder.

Moving to the south, there's one more St. Boniface building worth a pilgrimage for architecture buffs. **Precious Blood Church**, a conical Catholic house of worship that resembles a massive wooden teepee, stands at 200 Kenny St., southeast of old St. Boniface. Built in 1968, it, too, is a Gaboury structure. Daytime visitors are welcome, provided you don't mess with mass.

The best places to sample Franco-Manitoban cuisine are **In Ferno's** (312 Des Meurons), an extremely unpretentious and surprisingly affordable bistro; the more formal and expensive **La Vieille Gare** (630 Des Meurons); and the newest high-end French establishment in the area, **Provence Bistro** at the Niakwa Country Club (620 Niakwa). Not at all French, but also excellent – and expensive – is **Steppin' Out** (157 Provencher), which offers an ever-changing fusion menu.

At the other extreme, the Dairy Wip (383 Marion), **Mrs. Mike's** (286 Taché), and **Red Top Drive Inn** (219 St. Mary's) offer up gloriously greasy burgers and fries. **Leo's Gelati** (130 Provencher, at the foot of Esplanade Riel) is better than any Italian ice cream parlour on Corydon Avenue, while one of the best bakeries in the city is **Le Croissant** (276 Taché), which fulfills a French stereotype by giving butter, flour, and sugar the respect they deserve. New owners, straight from France, have added a café.

The only significant hotel in St. Boniface is the ho-hum **Norwood** (112 Marion), most notable for offering a cheap seafood buffet inside its dimly lit, old-school pub on Saturday afternoons. The fish is invariably overcooked, but there's something comforting about beer and a steamed lobster at the crack of noon.

Osborne Village, Corydon, and Academy

While downtown Winnipeg boasts most of the city's tourist attractions, the population density in the centre of town is pretty low. To find people on the streets, you have to head southwest.

On the south side of the Assiniboine River, **Osborne Village** is one of the few legitimate pedestrian areas in car-crazy Winnipeg, sporting a vibrant population of university students, street punks, and – paradoxically – well-heeled seniors living in high-rise condos. Dozens of funky shops, clothing retailers and restaurants are packed into a six-square-block area of the Village, concentrated around Osborne Street from River Avenue to a five-street intersection informally known **Confusion Corner**. Come during the day to shop or at night to go barhopping.

Popular spots include gritty dance club-cum-indie rock bar **Die Maschine/The Collective** (108 Osborne), the neighbouring **Toad in the Hole** pub (112 Osborne), and a very mellow faux-Mexican lounge, **Carlo's & Murphy's** (129 Osborne). Largest of all is **The Zoo**, a rock and metal bar in the Osborne Village Inn (160 Osborne).

While there are no upscale clubs in the Village, there are plenty of good restaurants, most notably the nouveau-Italian **Vivere** (433 River), fusion-themed **Fude** (99 Osborne) and *a la mode* establishment **Mise** (222 Osborne), where the inventive chef has

Charles Shilliday

had caribou-stuffed quail and buffalo wing-style frog legs on the appetizer menu.

For Asian food in the village, scarf down raw fish in funky surroundings at the dependable **Wasabi Sushi Bistro** (121 Osborne) or the subterranean **Meiji Sushi** (454 River, downstairs in the confusing Courtyard building). Or stir up a bowl of comforting bibimbap at oddball Korean teahouse **Right There** (472 Stradbrook), where the tables and benches are hewn from tree trunks and the quirky proprietor might try to talk you out of ordering some of the rare Korean spirits behind the bar.

Other popular Village spots include breakfast joint/bakery **Stella's** (166 Osborne) and brightly lit dessert café **Baked Expectations** (161 Osborne), the latter popular with suburbanites. Coffeehouses in the village, unfortunately, are restricted to the usual chains.

Canada Day in Osborne Village, one of Winnipeg's most popular pedestrian areas.

A few minutes on foot from the Village lies an even trendier pedestrian area: **Corydon Avenue**. On warm summer nights, a five-block stretch of Corydon between Daly and Wentworth streets is packed with people-watchers and patio-dwellers.

This is a typical patio-lined street, with one key Manitoban difference: In the spring, winter-weary Winnipeggers start sitting outside as soon as night-time temperatures peak above 10°C. The popular patios are crammed into a single block between Hugo and Cockburn, where you'll find **Saffron's** (681 Corydon, massive patio, lousy food), the **Red Cactus** (691 Corydon, small but always busy), and the original Corydon patio at **Bar Italia** (737 Corydon, artsy types using WiFi during the day, hip-hop kids at night).

Nominally Italian, Corydon offers gelato, cappuccino, and pizza – but also sushi, martinis, and high-end dining. Affordable sustenance may be procured at Greek café **Niko's** (740 Corydon), funky pizza joint **Café 22** (823 Corydon), and, if you don't feel like doing the European thing, **Daly Burger** (Corydon at Daly). There are also a dozen Italian joints – wander on foot and check out the menus.

The biggest wallet damage in the Corydon area happens at the excellent *prix fixe* **Gluttons** (Corydon at Lilac, attached to an upscale deli of the same name); the dependable **Café Carlo** (243 Lilac); or a little off the strip, the extremely posh steakhouse **529 Wellington** (several long blocks north at 529 Wellington Crescent), where dinner entrees average around $40 and a side of steamed broccoli will set you back $8.

At breakfast, it's also worth driving a few kilometres west down Corydon to **Falafel Place & Deli** (1670 Corydon), a lively-to-the-point-of-wacky Israeli-Canadian diner with lots of vegetarian options. Go for the yam fries, or do the authentic Middle Eastern thing and eat hummous and falafel for breakfast.

Corydon is also primo shopping territory, with dozens of gift shops, clothing boutiques, knick-knack retailers, and two Inuit art galleries, **Nunavut** (603 Corydon) and **Bayat** (a few blocks west at 163 Stafford). Most of the shops are geared to women and metrosexuals with lots of room on their credit cards.

The shopping gets even pricier on **Academy Road**, an east-west artery paralleling the Assiniboine River. Here, you'll find even more high-end retail places, salons, and a couple of spas that cater to residents of nearby Tuxedo, one of Winnipeg's wealthiest neighbourhoods. Notable Academy restaurants include **Fusion Grill** (550 Academy), which features an all-Canadian wine list and

specializes in Manitoba ingredients like boar, bison, pickerel, and Arctic char; and tiny Japanese nook **Yujiro** (580 Academy), run by the sushi chef who founded Masa on Pembina Highway.

The West End

Every great city needs a colouful immigrant neighbourhood, and the **West End** fits the bill just perfectly.

Situated to the immediate west of downtown, this gloriously multicultural 'hood is blessed with an amazing array of inexpensive ethnic groceries and restaurants. It's also cursed with prostitution, property crime, and occasional incidents of gang-related violence, including the high-profile 2005 shooting of an innocent pedestrian.

The Manitoba Legislative Building was designed by English architect Frank Worthington Simon. The "Golden Boy," which adorns the cupola – actually named *Eternal Youth* – was created by French sculptor Georges Gardet.

As a result, many suburban Winnipeggers never take a daytime stroll along Ellice or Sargent between Balmoral and Arlington – which is better for me and you. People who do visit the West End are rewarded with the chance to slurp noodles at a dozen Vietnamese noodle parlours, sample Portuguese seafood or snack on Ethiopian, Somali, Nigerian, Jamaican, Chinese, Laotian, Indian, Phillippine, Lebanese, Greek, German, Italian, and Latin American food, often at ridiculously cheap prices.

The chance of anything awful happening to you in the West End is minimal, especially during the day. Don't be afraid at night, either, though it's wise to park your car on a well-lit street. While the joy of this neighbourhood is discovering something of your own, some of the culinary highlights include the deluxe pho – that is, oxtail soup and noodles – at hole-in-the-wall **Vietnam** (555 Balmoral), fattoush salad at the Ethiopian-run **Pyramid Falafel** (510 Sargent), fresh fruit bubble tea and Vietnamese submarine sandwiches at snack joint

Asia City (519 Sargent), Portuguese egg-custard tarts and water bread at **Lisbon Bakery** (717 Sargent), perfect baba ghanouj at **Shawarma Time** (Ellice and Maryland), jerk chicken at Caribbean-run Greek restaurant **Juliana Pizza** (678 Ellice), Salvadoran pupusas at **La Fiesta** (856 Ellice) and the challenging, all-you-can eat Filipino buffet at **Artistocrat** (99 Isabel), which bravely serves up oddities like beef lung, pork stewed in blood, and whole fried mackerel. For serious foodies, this is ground freaking zero.

In addition to grub, the West End also boasts one of Canada's best live-music venues in the **West End Cultural Centre** (Ellice at Sherbrook), a non-profit folk and roots club in a former United Church. Concert listings are online at www.wecc.ca.

Just south of the West End, you'll find the only youth hostel in Manitoba, **Ivey House** (210 Maryland). See *Finding a Crash Pad* in the *Things to Know* chapter for more info.

Ivey House is situated between a gentrifying neighbourhood called **West Broadway** – home to upscale sushi joint **Wasabi On Broadway** (588 Broadway) – and a granola-crunching, already gentrified **Wolseley**, where fantastic organic baked goods can be found at **Tall Grass Bakery** (859 Westminster).

There are few tourist amenities in either West Broadway or Wolseley, though both make up part of a popular **bike-and-pedestrian route** that connects downtown to Assiniboine Park: From the Manitoba Legislature, duck under the Osborne Street bridge and head west on Mostyn, Balmoral, Furby and Wolseley to Omand Park, cross over the Assiniboine River on the pedestrian bridge to Wellington Crescent and continue west.

The North End

Go back a century, and Winnipeg's sprawling **North End** was the most vibrant immigrant community in Western Canada, a place where Ukrainian, Polish, Russian, German, and Yiddish were heard more often than English in the streets. Cut off from the rest of the city by the sprawling Canadian Pacific railyards, the North End developed a distinctive culture of its own centred around bustling Selkirk Avenue.

Unfortunately, the latter half of the twentieth century was not kind to the North End, and most of the upwardly mobile Eastern Europeans moved out. After decades of decline, the large neighbourhood is finally turning the corner, although it remains one of the largest economically depressed areas in Canada.

Happily, you can still taste the Slavic influence. And I mean that literally – the North End may be the best place in Canada to sample various varieties of Eastern European sausage, especially kubassa, the garlicky Polish-Ukrainian ham sausage.

North End butcher shops are legendary: Visit **Tenderloin** (1483 Main) for coarse-ground kubassa, **Karpaty** (536 Bannerman at McGregor) for curiously smoky barbecue sausage, and **European Meat** (533 Burrows) for gloriously hot, paprika-infused Hungarian sausage and, if your arteries can handle it, spek, a slab of smoked bacon fat.

If you're looking for smoked goldeye, **Gimli Fish** (Dufferin at McGregor) is the next best thing to driving north to the Interlake. Scarf it down with crispy lavash or bagels from **Gunn's Bakery** (247 Selkirk), a North End institution, which also makes fantastic knishes and other Jewish pastries.

For a sit-down meal, the North End boasts two legendary casual eateries, and one excellent newcomer. A local landmark since 1931, **Kelekis** (1100 Main) offers shoestring fries and delectably greasy Yaleburgers. You can sit at the lunch counter or a dining room lined with pictures of politicians, athletes and minor celebs. **Alycia's** (559 Cathedral at McGregor) is the city's most famous Ukrainian restaurant, offering up beet borscht with fluffy, Winnipeg-style rye bread and big platters of perogies (order them boiled, not fried) and cabbage rolls. And much farther to the north, just outside city limits, the **Eye Opener** diner (3132 Main) offers made-in-Manitoba breakfasts like saskatoon-berry pancakes and pickerel 'n' eggs.

Beyond the hearty food, a big attraction of the North End is its colourful past. History buffs are drawn to the **Ukrainian Labour Temple** (591 Pritchard), headquarters for Winnipeg trade unions during the 1919 General Strike, and **St. John's Cathedral** (135 Anderson), site of the first Anglican Church in western Canada and home to a graveyard first used by Red River settlers in 1812. The **Ukrainian Orthodox Cathedral** (Main and Redwood) is also worth a look-see for the architecture.

A little farther up Main, in the suburb of West Kildonan, you'll find **Kildonan Park**, which houses a modest set of gardens, an outdoor skating rink, and a covered outdoor theatre called **Rainbow Stage**, which usually produces musicals but may be closed for good by the time you read this due to financial difficulties. Avoid the park during summer evenings – there are too many muscleheads blasting lousy dance-pop out of car stereos.

Also in West Kildonan, **Seven Oaks House Museum** (115 Rupertsland) offers history about the Red River Settlement, including the 1821 Battle of Seven Oaks, which saw Métis face off against colonists. The free museum is open Victoria Day to Labour Day, 10 a.m. to 5 p.m.

The North End's Holy Trinity Ukrainian Orthodox Cathedral overlooks the Red River at Main Street and Mountain.

Polo Park

The busiest shopping district in Winnipeg is a maze of big-box stores and parking lots in a concrete no-man's land that divides the West End from residential neighbourhood St. James. The area takes its name from the **Polo Park Shopping Centre**, which in turns takes its name from an old racetrack. To reach this sprawling shopping district, drive west from downtown on Portage Avenue and take a right on either Empress or St. James.

Aside from chain retailers you can find in any major North American city, the area's chief attraction is **Canad Inns Stadium**, home of the Canadian Football League's **Winnipeg Blue Bombers**. The community-owned Blue and Gold, one of the oldest clubs in professional sport, competes in the nine-team CFL from late June to early November. Tickets range from $13 to $46 at www.ticketmaster.ca, but be careful buying inexpensive seats, as some of the cheap sections are full of drunken "loogans," which is Manitoba-speak for rowdies.

Also worth noting in the mostly ugly Polo Park area is **Westview Park**, a former landfill that's now the highest point in Winnipeg. You can drive to the top of "Garbage Hill" between dawn and dusk from a park gate at Wellington Avenue, just east of Empress Street. In the summer, park on Wellington Avenue before dawn and walk up the hill to watch the sun rise over downtown Winnipeg. In the winter, the slope at the northern part of the park makes for a great toboggan ride.

Just west of Polo Park, on the edge of **Winnipeg International Airport**, the **Western Canada Aviation Museum** (958 Ferry) offers airplane buffs the chance to check out vintage military and civilian aircraft. You really have to care about planes, however. The museum is open 10 a.m. to 4 p.m. Monday to Friday, 10 a.m. to 5 p.m. Saturday, and noon to 5 p.m. Sunday. Admission is $7.50.

Given its proximity to the airport, there are numerous hotels in the Polo Park area, with $80 to $90 the going rate for an advance reservation. The **Clarion** (1445 Portage, $110) offers theme suites, a spa, and easy access to the mall, while locally owned **Canad Inns Polo Park** (1405 St. Matthews, $90) is closest to the stadium.

Polo Park also offers two Winnipeg eateries with decades of tradition behind them. The **Original Pancake House** (now at the Clarion Hotel, ironically not the original location) is famous for its carbolicious giant apple pancakes, while **Rae & Jerry's Steakhouse** (1405 Portage) is the genuine old-school article, with red leather chairs, dark oak panelling, and properly mixed martinis. This place was retro before retro existed – take a seat in the lounge, if you're more interested in gin than giant slabs of beef.

Assiniboine Park and Forest

Occupying 440 hectares of southwest Winnipeg, **Assiniboine Park** and its wilder neighbour, **Assiniboine Forest**, make up the largest green space in the city. The park, nestled between Corydon Avenue and the Assiniboine River, is home to the **Assiniboine Park Zoo**, the

MUST SEE:
Assiniboine Park
Riverside footpaths, indoor and outdoor gardens, and the zoo.

The Pavilion in Assiniboine Park, now home to an art gallery, upscale restaurant and a painting of Winnie The Pooh, the A. A. Milne character named after Winnipeg.

Assiniboine Park Conservatory, outdoor English-style **formal gardens**, the **Leo Mol Sculpture Garden**, a duck pond, an outdoor theatre called **The Lyric**, and a Tudor-style pavilion housing the upscale **Tavern in the Park** restaurant and two floors of art exhibitions, including works by Ivan Eyre and a **painting of Winnie the Pooh**, the A. A. Milne character named after the City of Winnipeg.

The aging and dilapidated zoo, the park's biggest attraction, desperately needs to be renovated, as facilities for bears, primates, and big cats are depressingly out of date. That said, this zoo possesses one of the world's largest collections of northern and alpine mammals, most of which thrive in Winnipeg's cold climate, and also fulfills a valuable function as a breeder of endangered species such as snow leopards. It's also pretty cheap – admission is $4.25 in the summer and $3.75 during the winter.

The best time to visit is on a cool, if not utterly frigid day, when cougars, wolverines, and Arctic foxes tend to be most active. The Zoo is open 9 a.m. to 8 p.m. from Victoria Day to Labour Day, and 10 a.m. to 4 p.m. the rest of the year. It's also open on holidays.

Admission to the Assiniboine Park Conservatory, which houses native and non-native plants, is free. Beginning in 2006, the conservatory will host performances by **Shakespeare in the Ruins** (info: www.shakespeareintheruins.com), a theatre company that takes iaudiences for a stroll both inside and outside the building. The Lyric Theatre, meanwhile, offers free performances throughout the summer.

Assiniboine Park is accessible from gates at Corydon Avenue and at the end of Wellington Crescent at Park Boulevard. A footbridge over the Assiniboine River offers pedestrian access from

Portage Avenue and an ice-cream joint called **Sargent Sundae** (Portage and Overdale).

South of the park, relatively undeveloped Assiniboine Forest, one of the largest green spaces inside a Canadian city, occupies two parcels of land alongside Corydon and Grant Avenues. The northern section is bisected by a paved walkway for joggers, cyclists, and rollerbladers. The section south of Grant has eight km of wood-chip paths, plus a single, short paved walkway that provides access to a marsh. The south end of Assiniboine Forest connects to the **Harte Trail**, a flat footpath that runs west through Charleswood and across the Perimeter Highway into Headingley, eventually connecting to Beaudry Provincial Heritage Park.

St. Vital

The fast-growing southeastern suburb of **St. Vital** is just one of many examples of Winnipeg's bland suburban sprawl. Locals make the pilgrimage out here to max their credit cards at St. Vital Centre (Bishop Grandin and St. Mary's), the city's most-popular shopping mall. But the area also rates a mention for national historic site **Riel House**, Manitoba founder Louis Riel's family home at 330 River Road, open Victoria Day to Labour Day from 10 a.m. to 6 p.m. Admission is $4.

Farther east, at Fermor and Lagimodiere, you'll see the handsomely modernist, Étienne Gaboury–designed **Royal Canadian Mint** building, in which hard currency has been produced for 75 countries. Guided tours are offered seven days a week, but again, you really need to care about coins.

If you have little kids in tow, continue east down Fermor to Murdock Road, where you'll find amusement park **Tinkertown** (mid-May to mid-September, $12 for kids to ride all they want) and **Fun Mountain Waterslide Park** (mid-June to Labour Day, $13.50 for adults).

This 'burb also sports two of the city's larger parks – St. Vital and Maple Grove, both hugging the Red River.

St. Norbert

One of the few Winnipeg neighbourhoods outside the Perimeter Highway, partly Francophone St. Norbert sits at the south end of Pembina Highway, on the way to Morris, Emerson, and the US border. But this is not your typical, faceless suburb. From the end of June to Thanksgiving, **St. Norbert Farmers Market** (3514 Pembina) is the finest of its kind in the city, offering up fresh produce, preserves, baked goods, and crafts on Saturdays from 8 a.m. to 3 p.m. and Wednesdays from 1 to 7 p.m. If you need to work off what you eat, the 3.5-km **St. Norbert Dike Trail** starts just east of the market site and loops along a bend in the Red River and back through a residential neighbourhood where wild turkeys routinely wander the streets.

To the south, bald eagles, white pelicans and snapping turtles congregate at the mouth of La Salle River, which enters the Red at **St. Norbert Provincial Heritage Park**, home to a trio of restored pioneer dwellings and a one-km interpretive walking trail. And on

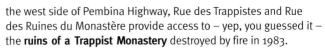

the west side of Pembina Highway, Rue des Trappistes and Rue des Ruines du Monastère provide access to – yep, you guessed it – the **ruins of a Trappist Monastery** destroyed by fire in 1983.

And, at the extreme south end of Winnipeg's city limits, at the bottom of Waverley Street, **La Barriere Park** offers canoe access to the placid La Salle River during the summer, and a network of cross-country ski trails during the winter.

Ecotourism and Trails

MUST SEE: Fort Whyte Centre
A herd of captive bison, indigenous waterfowl, and a freshwater-fish aquarium at an environmental education centre.

If you're into nature, forget about overdeveloped city parks and head straight to **Fort Whyte Centre** (www.fortwhyte.org), a non-profit environmental education centre with a herd of plains bison, several man-made lakes with year-round fishing, a small forest frequented by white-tailed deer, and an interpretive centre housing indigenous waterfowl and a freshwater-fish aquarium. Winter hours are 9 a.m. to 5 p.m. Monday to Friday, and 10 a.m. to 5 p.m. weekends and holidays, while the centre stays open later Thursday through Saturday during summer weekends. Admission is $5. To reach Fort Whyte from the inner city, take Pembina Highway south to McGillivray Boulevard, drive southwest to McCreary Road and turn right. The entrance is clearly marked 200 metres north, on the right side of the road.

The City of Winnipeg, meanwhile, runs the **Living Prairie Museum**, a tall-grass prairie preserve in St. James (2795 Ness). The 12-hectare preserve protects 160 species of indigenous grasses and other plants indigenous to the tall-grass prairie ecosystem, more than 99 percent of which has been eradicated from North America. Admission to the grounds and a small interpretive centre is free.

A fast way to get away from the city without actually leaving is to **paddle the rivers**. The Red, Assiniboine, and La Salle are naviga-ble to canoes and kayaks as soon as the ice disappears, and usually stay that way until the late fall, when water levels drop dramatically. The Seine River is usually navigable until late June, while the lower portion of Sturgeon Creek makes for good playboating during the spring snowmelt. Water levels fluctuate, so check before you head out on to the water – boat rentals are available at **Wilderness Supply** (623 Ferry, 783-9555), **Mountain Equipment Co-op** (303 Portage, 943-4202), **Wave Track** (42 Speers, 231-8226), and at the marina at The Forks.

In the winter, the Red, Assiniboine, Seine, and La Salle usually freeze solid by January, making it safe to **snowshoe and cross-country ski**. If ice conditions are good, the city also grooms an **ice-skating path** that connects St. Boniface on the Red River to The Forks and up the Assiniboine to Osborne Village.

The two best places to cross-country ski around Winnipeg include the **Windsor Park Nordic Centre** (10 Des Meurons), where the Manitoba Cross-Country Ski Association maintains eight km of trails lit for night-time skiing, and **Beaudry Provincial Heritage Park**, located just west of city on PR 241, where 16 km of trails loop around the meandering Assiniboine.

Charles Shilliday

The only place to ski downhill and snowboard is **Springhill Winter Sports Park**, located northeast of the city at Highway 59 and the Red River Floodway. Weather permitting, it's open December through March from 6:30 p.m. to 9:30 p.m. Tuesday through Friday and 9 a.m. to 4 p.m. on weekends. Visit www.springhillwinter park.com for current rates.

And while road cycling in Winnipeg can be annoying – drivers on major arteries tend to be less than courteous – designated bike routes include Scotia Street, Wolseley Avenue, and Wellington Crescent, which are closed to vehicle traffic on Sundays and holidays between Victoria Day and Thanksgiving. Assiniboine Park and Forest are also popular with cyclists and rollerbladers.

Gambling

Official Winnipeg tourism literature promotes Winnipeg's two casinos, **McPhillips Street Station** (484 McPhillips) in the North End, and **Club Regent** (1425 Regent) in Transcona, an eastern suburb. While gamblers visit by the busload, people accustomed to the glitz of Las Vegas may find these government-run ventures depressing. However, Club Regent has an interesting walk-through aquarium, and both gambling emporiums offer live entertainment, usually by fading country stars and celebrity impersonators.

A more old-school way to gamble is to visit **Assiniboia Downs** (3975 Portage, just outside the Perimeter), home to thoroughbred races from May to September. Admission is free.

You too can become a zombie: Gamble at two Winnipeg casinos, with all proceeds helping the Manitoba government pay for health care.

CENTRAL PLAINS AND VALLEYS

6

More than two thirds of Manitoba's population is concentrated in Winnipeg and the surrounding hinterland, an agricultural region dotted by dozens of towns and five cities with more than 5,000 people: Portage la Prairie, Selkirk, Steinbach, Winkler, and Morden. Aside from Winnipeg and Brandon, this is the most built-up part of the province, despite the fact the entire Red River Valley region is prone to flooding every spring – and winter commuter travel can be scarier than any amusement ride.

Many of the municipalities immediately outside Winnipeg are booming, thanks to a combination of low taxes and urban sprawl. You can also sense prosperity in Steinbach and the "Bible belt" towns of Morden, Winkler, and Altona. But the long-term downturn in the farm economy means many smaller towns are actually shrinking.

Opposite: Aerial view of Lockport, just north of Winnipeg, on the Red River.

Long before this region turned into a big bedroom community for Winnipeg, most of its natural features were eradicated. In pre-European times, the 100-km-wide Red River Valley was mostly tall-grass prairie, while areas to the east of what's now Winnipeg were heavily forested. Today, a tiny fraction of the tall-grass prairie remains, while forests have been reduced to two sizable parks: Beaudry and Birds Hill, both on the outskirts of Winnipeg. As a result, most of the attractions described in this chapter are historical and cultural as opposed to natural. And that makes them perfect for daytrips, as almost all the destinations in this chapter can be reached by an hour's drive from the provincial capital. The only exception is the western reaches of the Pembina Valley, which take up to 90 minutes to reach by car.

Red River Valley North

The banks of the Red between Winnipeg and Selkirk look a lot more like Quebec than like the rest of Manitoba. Like French colonists on the St. Lawrence River, the original Red River settlers plotted out homesteads along the water, subdividing lots into narrower and narrower strips as generations passed.

Near Edrans, MB.

Today, this slender band of land is home to some of the ritziest suburban dwellings in Manitoba, many of them *nouveau riche* monstrosities built within the past two decades. Low taxes in the rural municipalities north of Winnipeg have led to an influx of wealth, which has breathed a lot of life into this historic and once-pastoral strip.

You can meander through the area in a couple of hours along a loop from north Winnipeg. From the Perimeter, take Highway 9 – an extension of Main Street – north to River Road, also known as Provincial Road (PR) 238. Turn right and follow the scenic drive up to Lockport, detouring around flooded-out areas in the spring. Cross the Red at Highway 44 and return south along Henderson Highway, also known as PR 204.

This route also makes a great bicycle daytrip, although you will share the road with plenty of motor vehicles. You can also get a spectacular view at some of the homes in the area from the water – take a boat cruise (see *Winnipeg: The Exchange*) or paddle a canoe.

Winnipeg to Lockport

The 20-km **drive from Winnipeg to Lockport** is one of the easiest short drives in the province. If you head up the west side of the Red River, make sure you take River Road to gawk at the mammoth homes across the river and stop at a handful of historical sites.

St. Andrews Church (River Road at PR 410) is the oldest stone church in western Canada, with a graveyard that reads like a history of the settlement. The church and rectory across the way date back to 1830, and comprise a national historic site open Victoria Day to Labour Day.

Captain Kennedy House (417 River Road) is the former home of William Kennedy, a Métis entrepreneur who campaigned for Canadian annexation of the area in the 1800s. The site houses the **Maple Grove Tea Room**, open Tuesday through Sunday from May to mid-October. You don't have to be a Granny to stop in.

Henderson Highway, on the east side of the Red, doesn't offer as many views of the river. But Henderson and River Road both converge on **Lockport**, where a dam and locks span the river. The fully operational locks, completed in 1910, raise the water levels upstream on the Red and cause fish to congregate to just below, most notably massive channel catfish prized by anglers around the world.

The fish also attract flocks of white pelicans, who station themselves below the locks from late May until early September. If you can't see them at the locks, head a little north to the outflow of the Red River Floodway – it's rare to visit during the summer without seeing at least a dozen pelicans.

Two hotdog stands compete for the business of all the anglers, birders, and daytrippers who flock to the town. On the west side of the river, **Skinners** is packed with hockey memorabilia and photos dating back to the restaurant's establishment in 1929. Its east-side

Winnipeg Free Press

rival is **Half Moon**, established in 1940. For a much more upscale meal, **Rembrandt's Bistro** (Highway 44 east, inside Wellink Antiques) serves the likes of duck confit and bison meatloaf, and also offers a 12-course tasting menu if you reserve a day in advance. You'll need to reserve to get a table, anyway – visit www.rembrandtsbistro.com.

Other Lockport attractions include the **Kenosewun Visitor Centre and Museum** (Highway 44 east, Victoria Day to Labour Day), home to Aboriginal artifacts dating back 3,000 years, and just north of the town on Highway 9, **Little Britain United Church**, a Gothic structure completed in 1874.

Channel catfish are the main attraction at both Lockport and Selkirk, where anglers from around the world try their hands at catch-and-release.

Lower Fort Garry

When the great flood of 1826 turned Upper Fort Garry into an aquatic theme park, the Hudson's Bay Company decided to rebuild farther north. **Lower Fort Garry**, originally known as the Stone Fort, was a supply post in the nineteenth century, serving York boat crews heading back and forth from Hudson Bay, as well as pioneer farmers and local Métis, Cree, and Ojibway.

Today, the stone-walled fort and the buildings within are protected as a national historic site. In summer, Parks Canada interpreters don period costume in an attempt to recreate life at the tail end of the fur-trade era. This is kitschy, but worth a stop if you care about history at least a smidge.

Lower Fort Garry is located on Highway 9 between Lockport and Selkirk. It's open May 15 to Labour Day, 9 a.m. to 5 p.m. Admission is $6.50 per adult or $16.50 per family. If you're stealthy, you can wander the grounds at night – the security guard won't eject people who are just nosing around.

MUST SEE:
Lower Fort Garry and Lockport
The only fur-trading stone fort still standing on the Prairies, just north of an oddball town where pelicans and humans spend their summers trying to catch channel catfish.

Selkirk

Manitoba's fifth-largest city, **Selkirk** (pop. 9,752) takes its name from the Scottish earl who founded the Red River Settlement. Originally a river port, Selkirk now has an economy based on steel, and bills itself the "catfish capital of North America," thanks to the super-sized siluriforms that swim in the Red between Lockport and Selkirk.

Most visitors come to try to catch the cats, launching boats at the marina or building ice-fishing shacks on the Red in the middle of the winter. Winnipeggers also stop in Selkirk to buy food and supplies on the way to cottages in the Eastern Beaches and Interlake.

Chuck the Channel Cat, an 11-metre fibreglass statue, greets Main Street motorists from a perch at the front of Smitty's Restaurant – but you shouldn't eat there. Family restaurant **Barney**

Gargles (185 Main) and the **Garden on Eaton Tearoom** (205 Eaton) offer better, fresher grub.

The other chief point of interest is the outdoor **Marine Museum of Manitoba**, where six retired river and lake steamships, freighters, and tugs sit along the river at the corner of Eveline Street and Queen Avenue, near the entrance to **Selkirk Park**. The museum is open Victoria Day to Labour Day, from 9 a.m. to 5 p.m. weekdays, 10 a.m. to 5 p.m. on weekends and holidays. Admission is $5 for adults.

Selkirk also sports a **Community Arts Centre** (250 Manitoba) with a gallery and a gift shop featuring local crafts, open Tuesday through Saturday all year.

East Selkirk

If you're interested in Aboriginal history, head across the Red River to East Selkirk and then north to **St. Peter's Dynevor Anglican Church**, the centre of a formerly all-Aboriginal parish, and the final resting place of Saulteaux Chief Peguis.

Shortly before 1800, Peguis moved his people – Ojibway from the eastern shores of Lake Superior – to the Netley Marsh region at the bottom of Lake Winnipeg. After befriending the Red River settlers, he signed a treaty with Lord Selkirk and granted the land around the Red and Assiniboine rivers to the British colonists.

Peguis died a respected man in 1864, but the Canadian government repaid his generosity by forcing his descendants off their land in 1907 and relocating them to the site of the current Peguis First Nation, in the barren northern Interlake region.

To reach St. Peter's Dynevor, drive five km north of East Selkirk on PR 508 and follow the signs to the church.

Northeast of Winnipeg

Heading east from Winnipeg, there are only fifty km of farmland separating the city from the forests that mark the transition toward the Canadian Shield. This section deals with a chunk of this plain northeast of Winnipeg, between Highway 44 and the Trans-Canada Highway.

Birds Hill Provincial Park

MUST SEE:
Birds Hill
Provincial Park
Bike and ski trails
winding through
thirty-five square
km of forests and
meadows, within
a 15-minute drive
of Winnipeg.

When the flood of 1826 deluged the Red River Settlement, freaked-out pioneers dragged their oxcarts to higher ground. On the flat prairie, one of the few options was Pine Ridge, a series of sandy eskers east of riverfront land owned by a retired Hudson's Bay Company officer named James Bird.

Over the next 150 years, the modest upland subsequently known as **Birds Hill Park** would see Ukrainian, Polish, and German settlers clear land to farm rye and potatoes. Later, loggers cleared some of the pines and construction crews removed millions of tonnes of gravel and sand to build roads. But the rape of the land ended in 1964, when Birds Hill Provincial Park was established to

Bartley Kives

protect 35 square km of forest, prairie, and wetlands, creating a natural playground for nearby Winnipeg.

Today, the park's main attractions are two seasonal campgrounds, a shallow artificial lake with a pair of popular beaches, and, best of all, 16 trails for walking, cross-country skiing, horseback riding, rollerblading, and mountain-biking.

Short walking routes include the 1-km **Bur Oak** and 3.5-km **Cedar Bog trails**, both located near the park's West Gate at Highway 59, plus the 1.5-km **White-Tailed-Deer** and 2.4-km (return) **Pine Ridge trails** near the south campground and the 2-km **Nimowin trail** at the end of the road to the park's stables. You can pick up interpretive pamphlets at all five trailheads.

Pine Ridge Cemetery, the final resting place for Polish and Ukrainian settlers who cleared what's now Birds Hill Provincial Park.

The best off-road cycling route is the 14-km **Bluestem trail**, which circumnavigates the north campground, while road bikes and rollerbladers prefer the seven-km **Pine Ridge bike route**, which zips around the artificial lake.

The best cross-country ski routes are the easy **Chickadee and Aspen trails** (4 and 6.5 km, respectively) and the slightly more challenging **Esker, Lime Kiln, Tamarack**, and Bluestem trails (6, 8, 12, and 14 km, respectively). The **Hazelnut, Bridlepath**, and **Carriageway trails** are used almost exclusively by horses and horse-drawn carriages.

At the east end of the park, an artificial mound of earth called **Pope's Hill** marks the spot where Pope John Paul II held a mass in 1984. Other points of interests include the Manitoba Horse Council's **Equestrian Centre**, home to polo games during the summer, and the **Pine Ridge cemetery**, where some of the park's early settlers are buried.

Birds Hill Park also plays a starring role as the setting for Manitoba's premiere outdoor musical event, the **Winnipeg Folk Festival**, which takes over the east side of the park on the second weekend of July. About 80 folk, roots, rock, and world-music acts perform on seven outdoor stages over four days at the festival, one of the largest in North America, attracting crowds averaging around 12,000 people a day. Recent headliners have included Emmylou Harris, Ani DiFranco, Buena Vista Social Club, Buddy Guy, and Steve Earle.

About half the audience spends the weekend in the party-hardy Festival Campground, a sprawling tent city with an anarchic, Burning Man–like vibe. Attendance in this campground is capped at 5,600 people, but the more-distant Quiet Campground can hold another 1,200. The festival also sports a neo-hippie craft village, and food

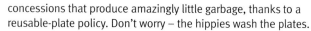

concessions that produce amazingly little garbage, thanks to a reusable-plate policy. Don't worry – the hippies wash the plates.

Weekend passes to the festival range from $70 to $150, depending on your age and how early you reserve. Visit www.winnipegfolkfestival.ca for updated ticket and camping info, a list of current performers, and a bus schedule from downtown Winnipeg. You can also order tickets by phoning 780-3333, or 1-800-655-5354 outside Winnipeg.

To reach Birds Hill Park by car, take Highway 59 northeast from Winnipeg to enter at the West Gate. To enter at the East Gate, take 59 north, head east on PR 213 – also known as Garven Road – and then turn north on PR 206 until you reach the gate.

Around Birds Hill Park

Charles Shilliday

Immediately to the south of Birds Hill Park, a destination restaurant called **Pineridge Hollow** serves Manitoba specialties like bison tenderloin, sautéed pickerel cheeks, and wild mushroom perogies. If you're inside the park, take South Drive toward the south campground and turn right at the road opposite the White-Tailed Deer trailhead and follow a footpath to the restaurant. Otherwise,

take Highway 59 to Garven Road, make a left on Pineridge Road, a right on Hillside Road, and a left on Heatherdale Road, and drive to the end, where you make one final left. Reservations: www.pineridgehollow.com or 777-3881.

Farther east, you'll find one of the most unusual structures in Manitoba, the onion-domed **Immaculate Conception Ukrainian Greek Catholic Church**, and the adjoining and quite unlikely **Grotto of Our Lady of Lourdes**. The parishioner-built church is an impressive structure on its own, but the grotto is an astonishing sight in the middle of the prairie: Two ramps and an elevated platform enclose a large artificial cave that contains plaster-cast renditions of the 12 Stations of the Cross. It's like a theme park, but the faithful take it seriously, so be respectful if you visit.

Immaculate
Conception
Ukrainian Greek
Catholic Church.

To reach the Church and Grotto, take Garven Road east to PR 212 and turn north to the Zora Road intersection. The grounds and grotto are open to the public in July and August from noon to 8 p.m. The church requests a $1 donation per visitor and also offers occasional tours.

Farther north on PR 212, in the village of Cooks Creek, the **Cooks Creek Heritage Museum** offers the usual assortment of pioneer artifacts and displays. But it's worth a visit on Cooks Creek Heritage Day, usually the last Sunday in August, when local artisans sell crafts, honey, preserves, and baked goods.

Beausejour and Vicinity

Branching off Highway 59 northeast of Birds Hill Park, Manitoba Highway 44 is the most direct route from Winnipeg to the northern Whiteshell. Stop in Garson, the first village along the way, for a meal at the **Harvest Moon Café**, a superior country diner with homemade soups, creative sandwiches, and fried pickerel. Don't be discouraged by the exterior. The small town also boasts a sport-fishing park full of trout, Arctic char, and, on warm summer evenings, teenagers going for an illicit skinny-dip.

Barely three km down the highway, the town of **Tyndall** is famous for Tyndall stone, the cream-coloured limestone used in Canada's Parliament Buildings, the Manitoba Legislature, and Lower Fort Garry – but actually quarried in Garson. You do not need to stop here at all.

Farther east on Highway 44, **Beausejour** (pop. 2,772) is best known as the home of the **Canadian Power Toboggan Championships**, a snowmobile-racing competition that usually takes place the first weekend in March. Admission to the Raceplex, which includes a 1,300-seat grandstand, is $10 for adults. Beausejour is also one of the few towns in Manitoba that allows snowmobiles and ATVs on most of its streets, albeit only in daylight hours.

Beausejour also sports the requisite **pioneer museum** (7th Street North and Gertrude, open July and August), the **remains of an old glass factory**, and an endearing greasy spoon in **Vickie's Snack Bar** (719 Park), a diner/laundromat/bus station that makes excellent shoestring french fries and serves up the most inexpensive bison burger in the province.

Northeast of Beausejour, along the Brokenhead River, **Great Woods Park and Campground** hosts two summer music festivals, the **Prairie's Edge Bluegrass Festival** in late July and the rootsy/bluesy **Great Woods Music Festival** in early August. The park is at the junction of highways 44 and 12 – if you're driving east on the 44, keep going straight until you hit the river. A lineup of performers and ticket info are online at www.greatwoodspark.com.

Dugald and Anola

Due east of Winnipeg on Highway 15, the town of Dugald is home to the **Costume Museum of Canada**, an archive of vintage clothes and fabrics. Unless you have an unusual fascination with textiles, you can zip through the main exhibit and a smaller room of archived materials in about 30 minutes. From mid-May to Labour Day, the museum is open 10 a.m. to 4:30 p.m. Monday through Saturday, and noon to 4:30 p.m. Sundays. Fall, winter, and spring hours are 10 a.m. to 4 p.m. on weekdays only. Admission is $5 for adults.

Fourteen km east, in **Anola**, the seasonal **Pumkins Pastimes Tearoom** and its two-storey gift shop caters to a similarly gentle crowd. Yes, that's a euphemism, but it's a nice euphemism.

Southeast of Winnipeg

Heading south from Winnipeg along highways 12 and 59 toward the US border, the fertile Red River Valley clay gives way to rockier soil and the beginnings of the scrubby forests that mark the transition to the Canadian Shield.

MUST SEE:
Immaculate
Conception
Ukrainian Greek
Catholic Church
A lavishly decorated
Eastern church in
the middle of the
prairies – with a
larger-than-life
outdoor re-creation
of the 12 stations
of the cross.

In the late 1800s, French-Canadian, Mennonite, and Ukrainian settlers cleared most of the land in this area, which has largely retained its ethnic character, if not its original flora and fauna. A small patchwork of ecologically rare tall-grass prairie still exists just north of the border, near the towns of Tolstoi and Stuartburn.

Steinbach

The largest city in southeast Manitoba, **Steinbach** (pop. 9,227) is also a centre of Manitoba's Mennonite community, a pacifist and famously industrious ethno-religious group with origins in Russia, Germany, and the Netherlands. The city, located 35 minutes southeast of Winnipeg on Highway 12, has a reputation for social conservatism that largely stems from a prohibition on alcohol sales that was only repealed in 2003 – by a slim vote of 51 to 49 percent.

The end of Prohibition has yet to transform this prosperous little city into a snow-swept Sodom and Gomorrah. The main attraction is the **Mennonite Heritage Village** (231 Highway 12 North), a model pioneer community with a functioning windmill, early-twentieth-century buildings, a petting zoo, and a restaurant called the **Livery Barn,** which serves up Mennonite specialties like kielke and schmondtfat (egg noodles topped with cream gravy) and plume mousse (a dessert stew made of dried fruit) from May to September.

Unlike Lower Fort Garry, the Village does not regularly employ interpreters in period costume, except on special occasions such as Canada Day (July 1) and Pioneer Days (the first weekend in August). As a result, the grounds are underwhelming compared to the Village Centre's indoor museum exhibit, which chronicles the history of the Mennonites from their origins as a persecuted religious minority in Europe to their successful colonization of the Prairies.

In July and August, Mennonite Heritage Village is open 10 a.m. to 7 p.m. Monday through Saturday and noon to 6 p.m. Sundays. May, June, and September hours are 10 a.m. to 5 p.m. Monday through Saturday, and noon to 5 p.m. on Sunday. From October to April, it's open weekdays only from 10 a.m. to 4 p.m. Admission is $8 for adults.

If you don't eat at the Livery Barn, **MJ's Kafe** (408 Main) offers Mennonite food, **The Dutch Connection** (88 Brandt, in the Dutch Connection Inn) offers more upscale meals, and the locals swear by Niakwa Pizza (23 Brandt). If you happen to be in town on a Thursday in July or August, you can find fresh munchies at the **Steinbach Farmers Market** on the grounds of Clearspring Village Mall (Highway 12 North, across from the Heritage Village).

Around Steinbach

Ste. Anne (pop. 1,513) marks the start of a nice **drive down picturesque Provincial Road 210,** which snakes southwest through at the Francophone towns of Giroux, La Broquerie, and Marchand on its way to Sandilands Provincial Forest. From mid-May to September, make a detour at PR 311 to Giroux to check out **Philip's Magical Paradise,** a museum of magic built in an old United Church.

West of Steinbach, on PR 216 near the junction of PR 311, the tiny town of **New Bothwell** is the home of **Bothwell Cheese** (61 Main), a source of the ubiquitous cheddar cubes found at Manitoba socials. The spartan factory also makes excellent cheese curds, unusually inexpensive chèvre, and 28

Winnipeg Free Press

other varieties of cheese – you can visit the attached retail store on weekdays between 8:30 a.m. and 4:30 p.m.

An example of heritage farming techniques by Mennonites near Steinbach.

Farther south on PR 216, the even tinier town of **Kleefeld** bills itself as Manitoba's honey capital. During daylight hours in the late summer, stop in at any farm along the road that advertises honey for sale.

St-Pierre-Jolys and St. Malo

About 50 km south of Winnipeg on Highway 59, the predominantly Francophone town of **St-Pierre-Jolys** (pop. 893) is the home of two extremely quaint rural festivals, the springtime **Sugaring-Off Festival**, and the **Frog Follies** in August.

The Sugaring-Off Festival is all about Manitoba maples, which taste quite different from the sugar maples found in Quebec and Vermont. As soon as temperatures allow – usually (but not always) mid-April – maple producers get busy with their taps and start boiling sap into a syrup you can try at the Sugar Shack on the grounds of the **Musée de St-Pierre-Jolys** (423 Joubert), a former convent. The museum itself is open only in July and August, Wednesday through Sunday, from 11 a.m. to 5 p.m. Admission is $2.

During the August long weekend, Frog Follies would be a run-of-the-mill rural fair if it weren't for the main attraction: frog-jumping contests usually held on the Saturday afternoon. No amphibians are harmed during the event – not even at area restaurants, which unfortunately do not offer *cuisses de grenouilles* on their menus.

Sixteen km south of St.-Pierre-Jolys, **St. Malo** (pop. 900) sports a free **pioneer museum** (July to September, 10 a.m. to 7 p.m.) and a **reproduction of the Grotto in Lourdes**. But the main attraction is **St. Malo Provincial Park**, a recreation area along a stretch of the Rat River widened by a dam and spillway. On summer weekends, the park's campgrounds and beaches are packed with families from Morris, Winnipeg, and Steinbach. Wander away from them along a 5.5-km hiking tail that arches around the northeast corner of the park. You can also rent paddleboats and canoes on the lake.

For a quick bite in this area during, stop in at the **Crow Wing Café** at **La Maison-Chapelle**, a tourism info centre on Highway 59 at the entrance to the park. You can also buy Métis handicrafts here.

The People of Manitoba

Manitoba population (2005 estimate): 1,177,600

Metro Winnipeg population (2005 estimate): 706,000

Other major centres (2001 Census): Brandon (39,716); Thompson (13,256); Portage la Prairie (12,976), Selkirk (9,752); Steinbach (9,227); Dauphin (8,085); Winkler (7,943); Flin Flon (6,267); Morden (6,142); and The Pas (5,795).

Eight most common languages at birth (2001 census): English (75 per cent); German (6 per cent); French (4 per cent); Ukrainian (2 per cent); and Filipino, Cree, Polish, and Chinese (1 per cent each).

Twelve biggest ethnic groupings (2001 census): British (56 per cent); Slavic (24 per cent); German (19 per cent); Aboriginal (15 per cent); French (14 per cent); Scandinavian (6 per cent); Dutch (5 per cent); Filipino (3 per cent); Italian (2 per cent); Jewish, Chinese, and East Indian (1 per cent each).*

Eight most common religions (2001 census): Protestant (43 per cent); Catholic (29 per cent); No religion (18 per cent); Other Christian (5 per cent); Jewish (1 per cent); Buddhist, Sikh, and Muslim (0.5 per cent each).

Politics: As of 2006, Manitoba was governed by the centre-left New Democratic Party, led by Premier Gary Doer. After the 2006 federal election, Manitoba was represented in the national House of Commons by eight Conservative members of parliament, three Liberal MPs and three NDPers.

Economy: Manufacturing (aerospace, commuter buses, farm equipment); agriculture and agribusiness (wheat, canola, hogs, dairy cattle, barley); services (retail, financial management, insurance, telecommunications); resource extraction (logging, nickel and copper mining, commercial fishing, and hydroelectric power); underground economy (marijuana production).

Sources: Statistics Canada
* Percentages don't add up to 100, due to multiple responses.

Central Daytrips

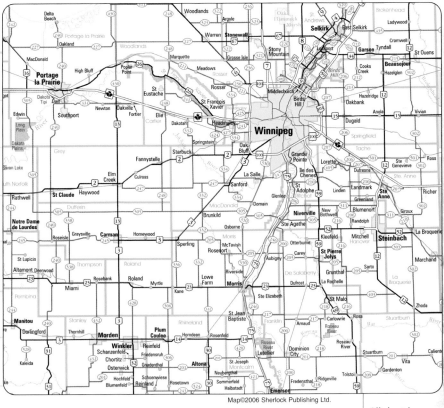

Map©2006 Sherlock Publishing Ltd.

1. River Valley North

When to go: Mid-May to Labour Day.

Prerequisites: An interest in history and some road-biking experience, if you choose to pedal the 70-kilometre loop.

Highlights: Heritage buildings and *nouveau riche* mansions along River Road, pelicans and hotdogs in Lockport, and Red River history at Lower Fort Garry at St. Peter's Dynevor.

The goods: Starting on Main Street in Winnipeg, head north on Highway 9 to PR 238, otherwise known as River Road. Make a right and drive along the Red River, stopping at St. Andrews Church before you hit Lockport to marvel at pelicans and maybe grab a hot dog at Skinners. Next, cross the river on Highway 44 to stop into the Kenosewun Visitor Centre to learn a smidgeon about the early Aboriginal history of the area.

Continue north on PR 509 through East Selkirk to St. Peter's Dynevor Church to see where Cree used to live before they were forced off their land. Flip back over the west side of the Red on Highway 4, but make the first left to PR 320. Drive south into Selkirk, gawk at the boats the Marine Museum, and

All daytrips start and end at Winnipeg.

105

head south on Highway 9 to Lower Fort Garry. Stop in, unless you've had enough Red River history, then continue south to Lockport. Cross the Red again and compare your earlier dog with the tube steaks at rival Half Moon – or sit down to a swankier meal at Rembrandt's Bistro. Return to Winnipeg along PR 204, better known as Henderson Highway. **Driving time:** 1:20.

Total time commitment: Three hours in a car; a full day on a bike.

Fees: $6.50 for Lower Fort Garry.

2. Pembina Hills and Valleys

When to go: May to Thanksgiving; it's especially nice in late August and early September.

Prerequisites: Ownership of a pair of hiking boots – there may be a couple of easy stream crossings in Pembina Valley Provincial Park.

Highlights: Rolling terrain on the Manitoba Escarpment, a decent day hike in the Pembina Valley, an ancient sea monster in Morden, and Mennonite grub in Altona.

The goods: From McGillivray Road in Winnipeg, book southwest on Highway 3 to Carman, then continue west on PR 245. Just past the community of Roseisle, turn left at the Birch Ski Area sign (Road 40 West) but immediately turn right, following a gravel road through Snow Valley to St. Lupicin, then head west to PR 244. Drive south past the massive wind-power farm, across Highway 23, then down to Manitou. Turn east on Highway 3, south on Highway 31, and then east onto gravel PR 201 to Pembina Valley Provincial Park.

Eat your lunch at the trailhead if you're starving, or hold off until you reach the bottom of the 6.5-km Pembina Rim Trail. Climb back to the top and drive east on PR 201 and then north on PR 432 into Morden. Visit the Canadian Fossil Discovery Centre, then drive east on Highways 3 and 14 to Winkler. Drive south on Highway 32 through the boomtown and head into the Mennonite heartland. Turn east on PR 243 and take a long look of the Village of Reinland. When you hit Highway 30, drive north to Altona and stop in at the South Forty for a bite. Continue north to Highway 14, then head east to Highway 75, which you can take all the way back to Winnipeg. **Driving time:** 4:45.

Total time commitment: A full day.

Fees: A Manitoba Parks Pass is required for Pembina Valley Provincial Park. Admission for the Fossil Discovery Centre is $5.

3. Red River Valley South and Tall-Grass Prairie

When to go: June and July, when the orchids are blooming.

Prerequisite: An interest in wildflowers is a good thing.

Highlights: A scenic drive along the Red, bison farms along Highway 59, a walk or two through rare tall-grass prairie habitat, and yet more Mennonite food.

The goods: From St. Mary's Road in Winnipeg, drive south on PR 200 through St. Adolphe and down to PR 305. Drive west across the Red River to visit the Flood Interpretive Centre in nearly destroyed Ste. Agathe, then double back along the 305 and drive east to Highway 59. From there, head south through St-Pierre-Jolys to St. Malo, checking out the Grotto outside the provincial park. Continue down past Roseau River to Tolstoi.

Drive east on PR 201 through the Manitoba Tall-Grass Prairie Preserve, hiking both the Prairie Shore Trail and the Agassiz Interpretive Trail, the latter located off PR 201. After that, drive east through Vita to PR 302 and head north to Highway 12, zipping up to Steinbach for dinner at MJ's or the Dutch Connection.

Leaving Steinbach, drive west on Highway 52 to PR 216, briefly zipping down to Kleefeld for craft-made honey (if it's late in the summer) or up to New Bothwell for cheese straight from the factory (if it's a weekday). Head west on PR 311 to Highway 59, and drive north to return to Winnipeg.

Driving time: 2:30.
Total time commitment: About five hours.
Fees: None.

4. Most Excellent Marshes

When to go: The spring migration in May or the fall departure in late August and early September.
Prerequisite: An appreciation for birds.
Highlights: World-class wetlands at Oak Hammock Marsh and Delta Marsh, a great sandwich in Portage la Prairie, and a trip to the Portage Sandhills Wildlife Management Area, where cars and ATVs aren't allowed.
The goods: From McPhillips Street in Winnipeg, drive north on Highway 8 to Highway 67 and turn left. Head west to the turnoff for Oak Hammock Marsh, then drive north to the Interpretive Centre. After filling your noggin with avian intelligence, go for a walk around the dike trails. Return to your car, head back to Highway 67, and drive east to Stonewall, stopping for java at Timothy Beans – or tea at McLeod House, if you're so inclined. Visit the Quarry Park Interpretive Centre if you have time, or continue west through the town of Warren to PR 248, then drive south until you reach Highway 26.

Follow this scenic drive west along the Assiniboine River to Portage la Prairie, stopping in at Fort la Reine, if you like the pioneer village thing. Go for a superior sandwich at Très Unique, then drive north on PR 248 to Delta Marsh for more world-class birding. Return along the same route but pass straight through Portage, continuing south on PR 248 until you reach Road 54 North. Turn left and drive east into the Portage Sandhills, ditching your vehicle for a twilight walk amid this fragile forest. After that, point your car east on Road 54 to Highway 13, which will take you north to the Trans-Canada Highway and then east to Winnipeg.

Driving time: 2:30.
Total time commitment: Most of a day.
Fees: $5 to visit the Oak Hammock Marsh Interpretive Centre.

MUST SEE:
Manitoba
Tall-Grass
Prairie Preserve
A rare patch of
undisturbed tall-
grass prairie, home
to endangered
plants like the
western fringed
prairie orchid and
small white lady's
slipper.

Roseau River

While most prairie rivers make for boring paddling, the **Roseau River** attracts whitewater canoeists and kayakers in April and May. A popular post-snowmelt daytrip takes paddlers down the west-flowing river from the town of Roseau River, underneath the recently repaired **Senkiw Suspension Bridge** and through Roseau Rapids at the east block of Roseau River First Nation to a takeout at PR 218. This fifteen-km trip can be extended by an additional forty km by putting in at the beginning of the Gardenton Floodway, south of the town of Vita. Do not attempt this trip if you don't have whitewater skills. Go during the spring or early summer, when high water submerges dangerous rock gardens.

Manitoba Tall-Grass Prairie Preserve

Bartley Kives

Between St. Malo and the US border, cattle ranches and forests begin to replace farmland alongside Highway 59. Thanks to the relatively poor quality of the soil in this corner of the province, more natural vegetation has been left undisturbed, most notably at a patchwork of preserves protecting thirty square km of **tall-grass prairie** between the towns of Stuartburn, Tolstoi, Gardenton, and Vita.

Orchids unfurling in the spring along the Agassiz Interpretive Trail at the Manitoba Tall-Grass Prairie Preserve.

No ecosystem in North America has been devastated more than the tall-grass prairie, which once stretched from Saskatchewan to Texas. The natural vegetation disappeared in the 1800s, when settlers ploughed up the grasses and all but killed off the bison that both lived off these plants and kept their growth in check. Today, less than one-tenth of 1 per cent of Manitoba's tall-grass habitat remains intact, though bison have bounced back from the brink of extinction as captive ranch animals.

For a double shot of tall-grass naturalism, visit both the **Prairie Shore Trail** (PR 209, about four km east of Tolstoi) in the south block of the preserve, and the newer **Agassiz Interpretive Trail** (just north of PR 201, 1.5 km east of the junction with PR 209) in the north block. The Agassiz trail is the only place in the world where you can find the endangered western fringed prairie orchid, a single-stalked plant with wispy white flowers that bloom spectacularly in July. The south block, meanwhile, is home to the almost-as-rare small white lady's slipper, which blooms briefly in May.

The entire preserve protects 300 species of plants, as well as animals like the 70-gram least weasel (which you won't see) and the awe-inspiring sandhill crane (which you can't miss, if they happen to be in the region). Between the north and south block, stop at the **Gardenton Ukrainian Museum** (Victoria Day to Labour Day, 9 a.m. to 5 p.m.), if you're interested in the cultural history of the region – there are seven Ukrainian Orthodox, Russian Orthodox, and Ukrainian Greek Orthodox churches in this corner of the province, most notably **St. Michael's** (two km west of Gardenton), completed in 1899.

Services are scarce in this area – for gas and groceries, drive east on PR 201 to Vita.

Red River Valley South

In 1997, almost the entire Red River Valley between Winnipeg and the US border turned into a temporary lake during the snowmelt-induced Flood of the Century, which swallowed up more than 1,800 square km in Canada alone. More than 25,000 people were evacuated from a dozen communities along the Red, all of which were completely surrounded – if not submerged – by frigid waters by the time the river crested in early May.

The flood devastated the Winnipeg suburb of Grande Pointe, swamped the Franco-Manitoban town of Ste. Agathe, and threatened to sneak into Winnipeg via the La Salle River before the Canadian military used bulldozers, old school buses, dirt and whatever else they could find to hastily erect a 22-km-long western barrier called the Brunkild Z-Dike.

When the waters receded, angry Red River Valley residents complained their communities and farms were sacrificed to protect Winnipeg, as the Red River Floodway acted as a sort of dam. After a nasty debate, the federal and provincial governments decided to expand the floodway to prepare for an even greater flood. (The Great Flood of 1826, for example, saw 50 per cent more water flow through the valley than the 1997 deluge had.)

Today, a ring dike surrounds every community along the Red, while many farmhouses sit on elevated mounds of earth. Not a spring goes by without Valley residents worrying about the snowmelt, despite the fact the lazy, meandering Red is placid most of the time.

The main route through the southern portion of the Red River Valley is the dull, four-lane Highway 75, on the west side of the Red. Take Provincial Roads 200 and 246, which have a lot more character.

St. Adolphe and Ste. Agathe

Heading south from Winnipeg on PR 200 – an extension of St. Mary's Road – the first settlement of any size is the pretty Francophone village of **St. Adolphe**, home of **A Maze in Corn**, a seasonal corn maze that changes configuration every year to confound regulars. Located northeast of town, the labyrinth is carved out of corn as soon as the stalks are high enough in August. It stays open through Halloween: Hours are 5 p.m. to 10 p.m. weekdays, and 11 a.m. to 10 p.m. on weekends. Admission is $7 for adults.

Continuing south on PR 200 to PR 305, cross the Red River to visit **Ste. Agathe**, a village that became the symbol for the destruction wrought by the Flood of the Century. As the Red River rose, the floodwaters made an end run around the Francophone community's dikes and rushed in from behind at Highway 75. The most enduring image of the deluge is a snapshot of the town's Catholic church, gleaming in the sunlight reflected off the floodwaters.

The church at Ste. Agathe, the only Red River Valley town to succumb to the 1997 "Flood of the Century," the town has largely recovered.

Charles Shilliday

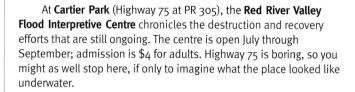

At **Cartier Park** (Highway 75 at PR 305), the **Red River Valley Flood Interpretive Centre** chronicles the destruction and recovery efforts that are still ongoing. The centre is open July through September; admission is $4 for adults. Highway 75 is boring, so you might as well stop here, if only to imagine what the place looked like underwater.

The second-largest rodeo in Canada is held annually in Morris.

Morris

An island during the Flood of the Century, **Morris** (pop. 1,673) is best known as the home of Manitoba's only professional rodeo and the second-largest rodeo in western Canada, the **Morris Stampede and Exhibition**. This event is usually held during the third weekend of July. Bull riding, steer wrestling, and other cowboy contests are held in front of a 6,000-seat grandstand. In 2005, admission was $15.

If you find yourself in town at any other time of year, you can wrestle yourself some cow at the steak pit in **Burke's Motel** (355 Main South). The usual assortment of pioneer artifacts – plus a small collection of pre-colonial First Nations arrowheads – is on display at the **Morris and District Centennial Museum** (Highway 75 at Highway 23), open June through August from 2 p.m. to 8 p.m.

Emerson

If any Red River Valley community should have been obliterated in '97, it was the border town of **Emerson** (pop. 655), whose streets were an astounding nine metres below the floodwaters when the crest of the Red lapped at the top of a ring dike, which was extended at the last minute by the Canadian Forces. Somehow, the all-but-evacuated town remained dry.

Most travellers visit Emerson as the last Canadian stop before a visit to North Dakota. The nearby US border post at Pembina, North Dakota, is open 24 hours, while a secondary crossing at Noyes, Minnesota, is open 10 a.m. to 6 p.m.

Things were a little livelier 120 years ago, when Emerson was a Prairie boomtown that profited off steamship traffic from the United States. But the town's fate was sealed when the Canadian Pacific Railway decided to cross the Red River at archrival Winnipeg instead.

Today, you can see a semblance of Emerson's boomtown past in a handful of stately nineteenth-century buildings. You can also walk a portion of the Trans-Canada Trail up the west side of the Red River. Three km up is **Fort Dufferin**, an 1872 Boundary Commission post later used as a staging ground for North West Mounted Police heading west in an attempt to tame the Canadian frontier.

Altona

Twenty km west of the river on PR 201 at Highway 30, mostly Mennonite **Altona** (pop 3,434) feels more like a Pembina Valley

Charles Shilliday

Near Altona, where the town fair celebrates the addictive sunflower seed.

town than a Red River Valley community. Low unemployment and a booming economy means this is a place to work, not to play, but that's not such a bad thing – the town, which bills itself as Canada's sunflower capital, has a reputation for being one of the safest, kindest communities in Manitoba.

Attractions in Altona are minimal, beyond a seven-storey **replica of Van Gogh's Sunflowers**. Modest **Buffalo Creek Nature Park** has a campground and a catch-and-release fishing pond. There's also a downtown **farmers' market**, operating Saturday mornings from July through September.

You can sample Mennonite food at the mid-June **Sunflower Festival**, or year-round at **South Forty Café** (22 Main), which lays out a Sunday brunch. The tearoom crowd should check out **The Jasmine Tea Room** (41 Second N.E.), located inside a craft shop. Obviously, this isn't exactly a party town.

Altona is surrounded by a dozen small Mennonite communities that make the region seem more like Germany than Manitoba. The most quaint hamlet is **Reinland**, on PR 243 near Highway 32, where families display their names on signs before their homes. And if you don't mind a straight, flat walk across farmland, a 10-km trail connects Altona to the small town of **Gretna** (pop. 563) and a US-hugging portion of the Trans-Canada Trail.

The best time to drive or walk around this area is late August, when the sunflowers are blooming. In a good year, they grow up to three metres tall, dwarfing even the most robust Mennonite farmboy.

Southwest of Winnipeg

Although the area to the immediate southwest of Winnipeg is flat and boring, daytrippers who continue west along Highways 2, 3, or 23 will be rewarded for their patience. The flatness merges into gently rolling terrain which offers some fantastic biking and cross-country skiing in the Roseisle area, decent day-hiking in the Pembina Valley, and Mennonite-flavoured culture in relatively affluent Winkler and Morden.

This diverse area is home to the southeast reaches of the Manitoba Escarpment, a very long ridge that separates the completely flat Red River Valley from higher and bumpier western Manitoba. The other dominant feature of this chunk of the province is the Pembina Valley, a wide glacial spillway that once carried the southern portion of the Assiniboine River. Technically speaking, the valley exits the province south of Morden, but the term "Pembina Valley" is commonly used to describe a 100-km-wide population corridor above the US border.

Carman

Southwest of Winnipeg on Highway 3, attractive **Carman** (pop. 2,831) sits on the Boyne River, a tributary of the Morris, which in turn spills into the Red. A five-km **footpath** circumnavigates the quiet town, and the **Walnut Street Tea Room** and Gift Shop (77 2nd) caters to the pastry set inside the stained-glass confines of a Victorian-era church. But the real attraction is actually a little higher up.

Charles Shilliday

The bridge over the Boyne River into picturesque Carman, Manitoba.

In 1975, mysterious orange lights appeared in the night sky around Carman and kept reappearing for months. The unidentified object, eventually dubbed **Charlie Redstar**, briefly made the town the "UFO Capital of the World."

But unlike Roswell, N.M., or Rachel, Nev., near Area 51, Carman doesn't try to cash in on its former fame as a UFO hotspot. Official town literature makes no mention of alien spacecraft or extraterrestrials, which probably is an oversight – Paul Bunyan isn't real, either, but he still makes a great ambassador for Bemidji, Minn. Alas, no UFOs have been spotted for decades.

Ten km west of Carman on PR 245, **Stephenfield Provincial Park** consists of a busy campground on the shore of a reservoir, with an eight-km hiking trail circling the entire small park. You'll need a Manitoba park pass for your vehicle.

Pembina Hills

Farther down PR 245, you hit the **Pembina Hills**, a gorgeous section of the Manitoba Escarpment with excellent cross-country skiing, mountain biking, and road cycling. It's also a compact place to simply drive or walk around, especially in the summer and early fall.

Just west of the small town of Roseisle, keep your eyes peeled for a sign marking the **Birch Ski Area**, home to the best mountain-bike trail system in Manitoba. Members of the Manitoba Cycling Association (annual fee: $30, available in person at the MCA's Winnipeg office at 200 Main) or any other provincial or state cycling organization have access to 40 km of terrific single track scattered among the hills, with plenty of steep ascents and a few gnarly switchbacks. You must have a helmet and an MCA-issued Birch pass, as many of the trails cut through private land. From PR 245, head south at the Birch sign for three km and make a right to the parking lot. A trail map is online at www.birchclub.com.

About 25 km of the Birch trails are open to cross-country skiers during the winter. A good nearby ski alternative is the twenty-two-km **Pumpkin Creek cross-country ski trail system**, nestled into idyllic Snow Valley. The trailhead is northwest of the Birch Ski Area – from PR 245, turn south on the Birch road, but quickly make the first right turn onto a gravel road that may be obscured following a recent snowfall. Head west past the mothballed Snow Valley ski lift until you see the trailhead on the right side of the road. The user fee is $5, which you can place into a drop-box at the Pumpkin Creek trailhead.

During the warmer months, this same gravel road through picturesque Snow Valley makes for a lovely little detour, especially during the fall. Continuing southwest for a few more km, you'll eventually reach tiny **St. Lupicin** (gravel Road 31 North at 45 West), a good place to stage a 12.5-km bike loop around the valley. Take a topographical map or a copy of *Backroads Mapbook*, if you're prone to getting lost.

About seven km northwest on PR 244, the village of **Notre Dame de Lourdes** (pop. 619) has a **pioneer museum** with a recently renovated wing celebrating the history of the Chanoinesses, an order of French nuns that moved into the area in 1895. Unlike most rural museums, Musée des Pionniers et des Chanoinesses (55 Rogers) is open year-round, weekdays from 9 a.m. to 4 p.m.

South of Notre Dame, it's impossible to miss a much grander attraction – the new **wind farm** that stretches southwest toward the village of St. Leon. In 2005, the province erected 63 windmills capable of generating 99 megawatts of electricity, which is good enough to power 35,000 homes. Utilizing wind in such a blustery corner of the world is not just a smart environmental move. The enormous turbines come with aesthetic benefits – their presence on the rolling prairie is quite dramatic. You can see the windmills from PR 244 between PR 245 and Highway 23 and also farther west along the latter road.

Another feature that stands out from the Pembina Hills is **Mount Nebo**, an odd-looking mound of bentonite clay south of Miami, a Manitoba town that bears very little resemblance to the Florida version. If you're in the area, the small hill is a worth a look-see, but don't expect an alpine climb. To reach Nebo, head south from Miami on PR 338 and turn right when the road makes a 90-degree turn to the left.

MUST SEE: Pembina Hills
Fantastic mountain-biking, great cross-country skiing, and picturesque back roads on the Manitoba Escarpment.

Charles Shilliday

Campers in the Pembina Hills.

Winkler and Morden

With a combined population of 14,000, **Winkler** and its slightly smaller neighbour **Morden** are destined to grow into a single city at some point. Superficially, Winkler is the economic engine and Morden has most of the cultural attractions – although this is not exclusively the case.

The first thing you notice about Winkler is the depth of the Mennonite influence, as even the Dairy Queen sign says "Welkommen." Mennonite immigrants, many from Paraguay and Mexico, are streaming in, to the point where Winkler's Sunny Day Products makes the best flour and corn tortillas in Manitoba. Look for them at local groceries. You can also find passable Mexican food, along with some Mennonite dishes, at **Del Rios** (44 Main).

Winkler's greatest contribution to the culinary world, however, is the skinless farmer's sausage produced en masse by Winkler Meats. This perennially popular pork product is available at groceries across Manitoba in the form of patties, finger-sized wieners, and big, phallic sausages that are perfect for the barbecue. There are imitators, but they're not as smoky-good.

Halfway between Winkler and Morden, the **Pembina Thresherman's Museum** offers a glimpse into the exciting world of vintage agricultural equipment, if you'll pardon the sarcasm. It's open May 15 to Sept. 15, 9 a.m. to 5 p.m. weekdays and 1 p.m. to 5 p.m. weekends. Admission is $3.

More-modern artifacts can found in Morden proper at the **Pembina Hills Art Gallery** (352 Stephen), a non-profit artists' co-op open seven days a week during the summer and Tuesday through Saturday in the winter. But the main attraction in Morden is the **Canadian Fossil Discovery Centre** (111-B Gilmour), a small natural-history museum in the basement of the Morden Recreation Complex. The centre seriously needs a makeover, but still sports the largest marine reptile collection in Canada, with the prized possession being Bruce, a 15-metre-long mosasaur discovered in bentonite clay outside the city. The museum is open daily from 1 p.m. to 5 p.m. Admission is a reasonable $4. The museum also offers paleontological tours to dig sites in the Pembina Hills, starting at $40 a person. For more info, check out www.discoverfossils.com.

The only place to sample Mennonite food in Morden is the **Kopper Kettle** (870 Thornhill), a family restaurant with farmer's sausage, kielke, and the fried dough known as rollekuken, tucked into the otherwise-ordinary menu. Another sustenance options include the **Rose Garden Tea Room** (577 Stephen), located inside a stone Victorian home.

Heading outdoors, **Morden Park** plays host to the **Back Forty Folk Festival** (www.back40folkfest.com) the first Sunday in June, while the entire downtown closes to cars during the last weekend in August for the **Morden Corn and Apple festival**, a town fair offering free sweet corn and apple cider.

In the summer, you can stroll the **prairie gardens** of Agriculture Canada's Morden Research Station on the east end of town, or visit

Colert Beach in Minnewasta Park ($4 for day admission) on the west side of town. A four-km spur trail connects the park to one of the nicest portions of the Trans-Canada Trail in Manitoba, which zigzags across the Pembina Hills on its way northwest to Spruce Woods Provincial Park (see *Southwestern Manitoba*).

In the winter, drive eight km west of Morden and hang a right on Road 34 West to reach the **Shannon Dale Cross Country Ski Trails**, a 22-km system. Trail-use fees are paid using the honour system – there's a drop-box for donations.

Pembina Valley Provincial Park

One of the newest parks in Manitoba, **Pembina Valley Provincial Park** protects a narrow, 1.8-square-km slice of river valley about 50 km southwest of Morden, very close to the US border. Despite its small size, the park boasts an excellent network of short day-hiking trails that descend the 100-metre-deep river valley. It really is a gorgeous little park. The most satisfying route is the 6.5-km **Pembina Rim trail**, which circumnavigates the entire park and will give your legs a chance to stretch a little. The best time to visit is late September and early October, when the leaves are turning.

To reach the trailhead, take PR 432 then 201 southwest from Morden or take PR 201 east from Highway 31. Keep your eye out for a picnic table sign – larger signage at the park entrance won't be visible until you're almost at the parking lot. There is no staff on site, so purchase a Manitoba park pass before you go.

MUST SEE:
Pembina Valley
Mennonite food in Winkler, the Canadian Fossil Discovery Centre in Morden, and an ancient glacial spillway in Pembina Valley Provincial Park.

Post-glacial torrents carved out spillways, such as the Pembina Valley, pictured here at La Rivière.

Charles Shilliday

Manitou and La Rivière

Thirty-five km west of Morden on Highway 3, diminutive **Manitou** (pop. 775) hosts the **Pembina Valley Honey, Garlic, and Maple Syrup Festival**, a foodie-friendly harvest-time event usually held during the second week of September. As well, the quaint, 385-seat **Manitou Opera House** holds biweekly coffeehouses and occasional concerts during the winter, although you'll need to scour the *Morden Times* to find out about them – the website hasn't been updated since the Chretien era. A **statue of Nellie McClung**, the former Manitou resident who led the fight for women's voting rights, stands outside the Opera House.

Another 11 km west, you hit the actual Pembina River Valley and the town of **La Rivière**. In the winter, ski hill and resort **Holiday Mountain** (www.holidaymountain.com or 242-2172) offers eleven runs down the valley, ski and snowboard instruction, and accommodations in chalets and conventional rooms. In the summer, the **Oak Valley outdoor theatre** (www.oakvalley.org or 242-3160) produces Passion plays in early July and usually holds one children's music concert in mid-August.

South of La Rivière, near the hamlet of Snowflake (junction of provincial roads 201 and 242), the **Star Mound School** makes a fascinating statement about colonial attitudes toward Manitoba's First Nations. The pioneer schoolhouse, built in 1886, was erected on sacred ground, right next to an Aboriginal burial mound shaped like a beaver. The school now serves as an interpretive museum from May to October. From **Snowflake**, drive three km west and 1.5 km north to reach the school and mound. As an added bonus, an abundance of sloughs and prairie potholes in this corner of the valley attract fantastic numbers of geese, ducks, and other waterfowl.

Although plenty of roads cross the Pembina Valley, none of them follow its meandering course. Ergo, the best way to immerse

A derelict garage near Poplar Point, near Portage la Prairie. The Hextalls are a famous Manitoba hockey family.

Charles Shilliday

yourself in the valley is to **paddle the Pembina River** during a month-long window of navigability following the spring snowmelt. Put in northeast of Snowflake at the bridge over the river at Road 5 North and paddle 35 km to the takeout at PR 201, just northwest of Pembina Valley Provincial Park. This is a long daytrip, so head out early.

West and North of Winnipeg

The dullest possible drive in Manitoba is the seventy-five-km stretch between Winnipeg and Portage la Prairie along the featureless Trans-Canada Highway. But don't let that discourage you from tooling around the northwestern quadrant of Winnipeg's hinterland, home to the meandering Assiniboine River, world-class birding at Delta and Oak Hammock marshes, and Stonewall, the fastest-growing community in Manitoba.

If you're heading to Portage, consider taking the scenic route. Not only does two-lane Highway 26 have a lot more character than the Trans-Canada, it's less exposed from prevailing winds, which means it may actually be safer when the snow blows horizontally in the winter.

Portage la Prairie

Most motorists heading west from Winnipeg completely bypass **Portage la Prairie** (pop. 12,976), the fourth-largest city in the province. Blame another crime on the Trans-Canada Highway.

This potato-processing centre is almost as old as Winnipeg, as explorer La Vérendrye paddled up the Assiniboine River in 1738 and established **Fort la Reine** on a site northeast of the city, using it as a base of operations for fifteen years. The fort was subsequently moved a couple of times and now exists as a pioneer museum and village on Highway 1A at the junction with Highway 26. It's open May 15 to Sept. 15 from 9 a.m. to 6 p.m. Admission is $5. There's also a tourism info bureau at the site.

If history doesn't turn your crank, visit **Island Park**, an oval of land almost entirely surrounded by Crescent Lake, an oxbow left behind by an earlier course of the Assiniboine River. The park has an aquatic centre with waterslides ($4.75 for adults), a windmill, a U-pick strawberry field, an arboretum, and a large enclosure of fallow deer, an ornamental species from Europe. There are also occasional performances at the **William Glesby Centre** (11 2nd N.E.), which also houses the Craig Media Gallery, a small art gallery named after the broadcasting company that once used Portage as a base for what's now City-TV in Winnipeg.

For munchies, start with **Très Unique** (103 3rd N.E.), a gift shop, art gallery, and restaurant inside an 1889 land titles building. This newish place serves unpretentious country offerings like grilled ham, cheddar and apple sandwiches, rhubarb pie, and iced tea, all made from scratch using local and organic ingredients, whenever possible.

More proletarian fare can be found at rib shack **Bill's Sticky Fingers** (210 Saskatchewan East) and the ultra-reasonable **Wright Spot** (904 Saskatchewan East), an old-school diner where it's okay to read the paper while you eat.

Just outside Portage, the **Portage Sandhills Wildlife Management Area**, about 10 kilometres south of the city on the east side of PR 240, offers cross-country ski and walking trails over grass and tree-covered dunes. Unlike in most Manitoba WMAs, here, motorized vehicles aren't allowed,

About 30 minutes southwest of Portage, there are twenty km of more regularly maintained skinny-ski routes at the fantastic **Bittersweet Cross Country Ski Trails**, which descend the north side of the Assiniboine River Valley. From Portage, head west on the Trans-Canada Highway to Bagot and then south on PR 242. The trail starts on the west side of the road, right before the Assiniboine River.

Delta Marsh

Charles Shilliday

Delta Marsh, one of the province's top birding destinations.

The biggest tourist attraction in the vicinity of Portage la Prairie is one of the world's largest wetlands – **Delta Marsh**, which covers 220 square km of shallow freshwater habitat at the south end of Lake Manitoba. Almost 300 bird species – roughly three out of every four in Manitoba – have been spotted at the fifty-km-wide marsh, making Delta one of Canada's top birding destinations. The marsh also attracts canoeists, hunters, and thanks to the windy, open water on Lake Manitoba, windsurfers.

There are three built-up areas offering easy access to the marsh, each sporting a campground, boat launches, at least one beach, and places to observe (and shoot) birds. Lynch's Point sits at the southwest corner of Lake Manitoba at the edge of the **Lynch Point** Game Bird Refuge. It's forty-five km northwest of Portage la Prairie – take the Trans-Canada west to Highway 16, drive northwest to PR 242, then head north to the end of the road.

Delta Beach, in the centre of the marsh, is the most popular destination. Both the University of Manitoba's **Delta Marsh Bird Observatory** and the pro-hunting **Delta Waterfowl Research Centre** are located in this area. At the observatory, ornithologists and volunteers capture, measure, and release birds during the May-to-June spring migration and the July-to-September fall season. Visit www.dmbo.org for information about volunteer opportunities. Behind the Research Centre, meanwhile, the one-km **Delta Marsh Interpretive Trail** leads to a five-metre observation tower. To reach

Charles Shilliday

the beach from Portage la Prairie, take PR 240 north for 24 km.

Not to be confused with the Observatory or the Research Centre, the University of Manitoba's **Delta Marsh Field Station** sits on a 930-hectare ecological preserve northwest of the Delta Game Bird Refuge. This bird-watching area is not accessible from Delta Beach – from Portage, take PR 240 north to PR 227, drive west across the Portage Diversion canal, and make the first right. Drive north to Lake Manitoba. This is a scientific research station, not a tourist area, so don't expect any amenities.

Finally, on the northeast corner of the marsh, you'll find the town of St. Ambroise and **St. Ambroise Beach Provincial Park**, which has a campground, beach, and a boardwalk trail through a corner of Sioux Pass Marsh. To the west of the small park, the **Clandeboye Bay Special Conservation Area** protects habitat for the endangered piping plover, while to the east, sprawling **Lake Saint Francis Wildlife Management Area** is set aside for hunters.

To reach St. Ambroise from Winnipeg, take either the Trans-Canada or Highway 26 west to PR 430 and then drive north to Lake Manitoba.

St. François Xavier and Headingley

The closest "country" destination available to Winnipeggers is **St. François Xavier**, a village on the Assiniboine River barely 15 km west of the Manitoba capital. The attractions consist of a log-construction restaurant called the **Medicine Rock Café** and one of the more poignant village statues in the province: **The White Horse** at the junction of Highway 26 and the Trans-Canada commemorates the *Romeo and Juliet*-like legend of a Cree brave and Assiniboine bride who were slaughtered by jealous rivals.

Southeast of St. FX, **Beaudry Provincial Heritage Park** sports sixteen km of cross-country ski trails branching off a trailhead just north of PR 241. Farther to the east, the Winnipeg suburb of **Headingley** – once part of the city, but strangely allowed to secede – has a fantastic greasy spoon called **Nick's Inn**. This is the place to load up on burgers and fries if you're heading west on the Trans-Can.

Twin Beaches, north of Delta Marsh.

MUST SEE:
Delta Marsh and Oak Hammock Marsh
World-class bird watching north of Portage la Prairie and Winnipeg, respectively.

Old-growth tree at Beaudry Provincial Heritage Park, just west of Winnipeg.

Charles Shilliday

119

Stonewall and Vicinity

Stonewall Quarry Park in winter.

The fastest-growing town in Manitoba is **Stonewall** (pop. 4,012), a Winnipeg bedroom community at the junction of Highway 67 and PR 236. The main attractions in this commuter town are tea room **McLeod House** (292 Main) and **Stonewall Quarry Park**, a former limestone quarry with a campground, artificial lake, and interpretive centre explaining the geo-cultural history of the area, the latter open daily from 11 a.m. to 5 p.m. in the summer. **Quarry Days**, the town's annual fair, is held in the park during the third weekend in August. You can also grab a rare cup of civilized java at **Timothy Beans Cappuccino Bar** (Centre and Main), which occasionally books live music.

Due east of Stonewall on Highway 67, strawberry-growing Boonstra Farms operates **Murray's Corn Maze**, a labyrinth open in September and October on weekends and Friday evenings. The $7 admission covers the maze, a petting zoo, hayrides, and a round of minigolf.

Two km south, **Stony Mountain** is best known for its federal penitentiary. During the Great Flood of 1826, the high ground northeast of the town provided refuge for Red River Valley settlers on the west bank of the river. Today, the slope of the same hill is known as **Stony Mountain Ski Area**, which caters mostly to snowboarders. Lift tickets are $18 for adults. To reach the hill from Winnipeg, take Highway 7 north for 10 km, turn right into town, and follow the signs to the hill. For more info, visit www.skistony.com or call 344-5977.

If you're a fan of old trains, the **Prairie Dog Central Railway** carries passengers in vintage rail cars on a 2.5-hour return trip from Inkster Junction Station on the outskirts of Winnipeg to farmers' markets in the small towns of **Warren** and **Grosse Isle**, both located west of Stonewall on Highway 6. From May to September, the trains run twice a day on weekends, leaving the station at 10 a.m. and 3 p.m., and at 11 a.m. only on holiday Mondays and Canada Day. There are also special theme trips before Halloween and Christmas – visit www.pdcrailway.com or call 832-5259 for more info. The fare is $18 for adults, reservable in advance at Ticketmaster, 780-3333 or www.ticketmaster.com. Inkster Junction Station is located in the Rural Municipality of Rosser, about two km northeast of the junction of Inkster Boulevard and Sturgeon Road.

Warren is also home to the **Niska Game Farm**, a petting zoo open summer Sundays from 2 p.m. to 4 p.m. ($2 admission), and the **V. Gross Doll Display**, a museum with 3,000 dolls, open Sunday through Friday from May to October, from 10 a.m. to 5 p.m. ($4 admission). Both are located near the town's golf course.

Grosse Isle, meanwhile, marks the south end of the **Prime Meridian Trail**, a 116-km hiking, cycling, and horseback-riding trail that extends north along an abandoned rail line to Fisher Branch in the Interlake. There are few services along the trail; see the *Beaches and Interlake* chapter for more detail about some of the towns along the way.

Oak Hammock Marsh

If you care about birds, you must make the short trip to **Oak Hammock Marsh Wildlife Management Area**, which protects 36 square km of wetlands for 296 avian species. A 30-km network of dike trails covers the whole marsh, but it's best to start at the Oak Hammock Marsh Interpretive Centre at the north end of PR 220.

While the walking trails are free, it's worth spending $5 to enter the Interpretive Centre, which has info on many of the animals and plants in the area, as well as displays about wetlands conservation. The centre is open 10 a.m. to 8 p.m. from May to October, and 10 a.m. to 4:30 p.m. from November to April. The best times to visit are dawn and dusk during spring migration in May or the fall migration in late August and early September. There are also summer canoe rentals and winter snowshoe trails.

You can get an up-close view of Oak Hammock Marsh in a war canoe.

Charles Shilliday

Jason Sorby

THE CANADIAN SHIELD

7

Rivers, lakes, and wild spaces are the main attractions in Manitoba's sparsely populated southeast, a Group of Seven landscape protected by three big provincial parks – Whiteshell, Nopiming, and Atikaki – as well as a patchwork of provincial forests.

A post-glacial playground of exposed granite and coniferous trees, the Canadian Shield is the largest of Canada's physical regions, covering almost half the country, including most of eastern and northern Manitoba. This chapter just deals with the southeast portion of the Manitoban Shield, as well as the sandy deciduous forests that mark the transition and between the Shield and the open Prairie.

Cree and other Algonkian peoples hunted and fished here during pre-colonial times, living off sturgeon, deer, grouse, and other critters. The area opened up to Europeans after La Vérendrye paddled down the Winnipeg River in 1733, leading the way for French-Canadian fur traders, trappers, and, in all likelihood, pea-soup merchants.

After the completion of the Canadian Pacific Railway in 1877, timber from Shield forests supplied Winnipeg's construction industry as immigrants from all over Europe began flooding into western Canada. Logging, gold mining, and finally hydroelectric power dominated the economy until Whiteshell Provincial Park was established in 1961, followed by Nopiming in '76 and Atikaki in '85.

Today, tourism and recreation are the main industries in the southeastern Shield, although logging continues in transitional forests and Crown land to the immediate west.

Summertime Shield attractions include paddling, fishing, hiking, and mellowing out at numerous lake-side cottage areas and campgrounds. Winter is all about snowmobiling and cross-country skiing.

Wildlife in the area includes deer, wolves, moose, river otters, black bears, bald eagles, great blue herons, and, up in the Nopiming, a small population of threatened woodland caribou.

The Shield is also home to most of Manitoba's year-round cabins and lodges, so this is the best place to go for a quick winter getaway from Winnipeg if you can't afford a flight to the Dominican Republic. Just don't expect to suntan in December.

Opposite:
Granite cliffs and coniferous forests dominate the Canadian Shield.

Whiteshell Provincial Park

Southern Manitoba's largest provincial park at 2,726 square km, Whiteshell takes its name from small, white seashells used in ceremonies by the Ojibway, who moved into these forests to hunt and gather around AD 1800. The park's logo – the rock outline of a turtle – is inspired by petroforms assembled by Algonkian-speaking peoples who lived here much, much earlier. Some archeological sites within the park date back to 6,000 BC and remain sacred to First Nations.

Winnipeg Free Press

MUST SEE: Whiteshell Provincial Park
Manitoba's most-popular provincial park, with dozens of resorts and hundreds of lakes, including meteor-created West Hawk, the deepest in the province.

Created out of a former forest preserve, Whiteshell is bounded by the Winnipeg River to the north, the Ontario border to the east, and the beginning of the transition between the Shield and prairie to the south and west.

Every visitor entering Manitoba at the Ontario border passes through the Whiteshell's southeast corner, zooming past meteor-created West Hawk Lake – Manitoba's deepest at 111 metres – and heavily developed Falcon Lake. But Manitobans know the park as an all-season playground, swarming in during the summer but maintaining a year-round presence.

The park can be divided into four regions. The densely populated southeast is dominated by cottage developments at Falcon, West Hawk, and Caddy lakes. The northwest has more cottage areas, campgrounds, and lodges, all snaking along a string of lakes between Highway 44 and the Winnipeg River. The northeast is undeveloped except for lodges, canoe routes, and a Manitoba Hydro generating station at Point du Bois. But no industry, motorized vehicles, or permanent dwellings of any kind are permitted in the eastern Wilderness Section, home to a sizable wolf population and the 63-kilometre Mantario Trail, the longest dedicated hiking trail in the province.

The park entrance fee is the standard $5 per vehicle, collected at gates at Rennie, West Hawk Lake, and Seven Sisters from May to September. Gate staff will waive the fee if you're driving straight through the park along Highway 44. Don't abuse the privilege – Manitoba Conservation is so badly underfunded, they need each dollar they can get.

Falcon Lake

Only 75 minutes from Winnipeg by car on Highway 1, **Falcon Lake**'s proximity to the Prairie metropolis makes it one of the most popular lakes in Manitoba, for better and for worse. Three-quarters of the cigar-shaped lake is lined by cottage developments, which means rarely a summer day goes by without the roar of personal watercraft and powerboats reverberating across the water.

Despite the racket, Falcon Lake remains one of the province's prettier resort areas. The **Falcon Lake townsite**, located at the west end of the lake, is home to a beach, marina, tennis court, campground, hotels, restaurants, 18-hole golf course (home to a four-km ski loop during the winter), and, best of all, one of the largest and most-challenging miniature golf courses in the province. Never underestimate the recuperative powers of a round of minigolf. There's also a horseback-riding stable and a 2.2-km (return) self-guiding trail just northeast of town.

The road along the south side of lake ends at the year-round **Falcon Trails Resort** (349-8273, falcontrails.mb.ca), which encompasses a lodge, cabins, the eleven-run **Falcon Ridge ski-and-snowboard hill**, and a modest but well-maintained trail system groomed for hiking and mountain biking in the summer and cross-country skiing in the winter. The longest ski route, the 7.5-km **High Lake Trail**, takes you past the resort's two solar-powered eco-cabins ($160 to $250 per night), on to the High Lake ice, and then back to the resort. Just watch out for snowmobiles.

On the north side of Falcon Lake, the thirteen-km **South Whiteshell Trail** hooks up with West Hawk Lake, swooping beneath the Trans-Canada Highway. You can bike in the summer or cross-country ski in the winter, when the trail connects to three ski loops south of West Hawk Lake. There's also a four-km winter ski trail that crosses the east end of Falcon Lake, connecting the West Hawk ski loops with the Falcon Ridge and the High Lake trails.

West Hawk Lake

Only one click away from the Ontario border at the east end of Highway 44, **West Hawk Lake** is smaller than Falcon but almost as busy, thanks to cottages that ring its southern and western shores. The unusually deep lake, formed when a meteorite smashed into the Shield about 150,000 years ago, attracts scuba divers to a permanent **dive site** near the West Hawk townsite, and to a marina at the south end of the lake.

A vintage aerial view of meteorite-created West Hawk Lake, Manitoba's deepest at 111 metres.

Sights below the surface include a submerged windmill, the wreck of a sailboat, and freshwater fish. The water gets frigid below 10 or 15 metres, so divers should suit up. For more information about this site – and Manitoba diving in general – contact the Manitoba Underwater Council at 254-0362 or www.manunderwater.com.

If diving into the deep, cold blackness doesn't sound like fun, you can learn about the lake's origins at **West Hawk Museum**, open from the May long weekend to Labour Day (9 a.m. to 5 p.m.) at the **West Hawk Campground**. The town, meanwhile, offers the usual

Manitoba Department of Natural Resources

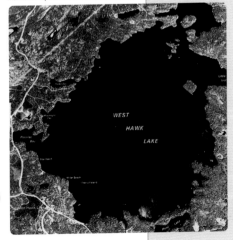

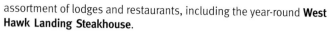

Mantario Trail
Manitoba's longest dedicated backpacking trail, a sixty-three-km trek over granite ridges and alongside lakes in Whiteshell Provincial Park's wilderness zone.

The six-km (return) hike from Hwy 44 to Bear Lake may also be undertaken in the winter.

assortment of lodges and restaurants, including the year-round **West Hawk Landing Steakhouse**.

If you're looking to stretch your legs, the longest day hike in the Whiteshell begins just east of the townsite. The 12.6-km **Hunt Lake Trail** is a pulse-stimulating there-and-back scramble over granite ridges on the east side of West Hawk Lake. There's a warm-up shelter at the turnaround point in case the wind is howling.

West Hawk Lake to Rennie

One of the nicer short drives in Manitoba is a winding stretch of Highway 44 from West Hawk Lake to the Whiteshell's eastern gate at Rennie.

Heading west, the first paved road on your right is PR 312, one of the access points to **Caddy Lake**, a popular staging ground for **canoe trips down the Whiteshell River**. Paddling north from Caddy, you can circumnavigate the Whiteshell's Wilderness Section or head all the way up to the Winnipeg River. One of the highlights of the Caddy Lake paddle is accessible to daytrippers, as Caddy is connected to northern neighbour South Cross Lake not by a portage but by a tunnel blasted below the Canadian Pacific Railway line. The **Caddy Lake tunnel** is only four paddling kilometres northwest of the lake's boat launches.

Continuing east on PR 312, you'll find a parking lot that serves as the southern staging ground for the **Mantario Trail**. This is the place to clip your toenails and jettison extra weight in preparation for the 63-km slog to Big Whiteshell Lake. If that sounds too daunting, you can always whip around the easy 2.8-km **White Pine Trail**, which starts at the same parking lot.

Charles Shilliday

The 312 continues east into Ontario, where it dead-ends at the small community of **Ingolf**, home to network of mountain-biking trails accessible from the CPR tracks. The trailhead isn't obvious, so don't be afraid to ask for directions.

Back on Highway 44, there are four diversions between Caddy Lake and Rennie. The **McGillivray Falls self-guiding trail** offers walks of 2.4 or 4.6 kilometres along a set of rapids. The Lily Pond, a picnic spot, attracts climbers to a set of steep cliffs. The moderate **Bear Lake Trail** offers a slightly more strenuous six-km scramble, while the twenty-five-km **Centennial Trail** can take you all the way from Caddy Lake to the Bear Lake trailhead along a portion of the Trans-Canada Trail. For a more manageable day hike, shorten the route to eleven km by starting at the McGillivray Falls trailhead and heading west.

The main attractions in **Rennie** are a Manitoba Conservation District Office where backcountry paddlers and hikers can leave their itineraries, and the **Alfred Hole Goose Sanctuary**, a pond harbouring thousands of Canada honkers. The best times to visit Alf Hole are the spring, when impossibly cute goslings are yellow and fuzzy, or right before the fall migration, when adult geese congregate in disturbing numbers.

The **Alfred Hole interpretive centre**, open from June to Thanksgiving (10 a.m. to 5 p.m. weekdays; 10:30 to 6 p.m. weekends and holidays), will give you the lowdown on the geese and other wildlife you'll find in the Whiteshell. A 2.5-km walking trail follows the pond, while in the winter, a seven-km ski loop extends east to Jean Lake and then back to the interpretive centre.

The Mantario Trail

Jason Sorby

Straddling lakes and climbing ridges in the eastern fringe of Whiteshell Provincial Park, the **Mantario Trail** is the prettiest, most-pristine, and most-strenuous hiking route in Manitoba. Disturbingly fit trail runners complete the 63-km slog from Caddy Lake to Big Whiteshell Lake in less than two days. But they're insane. Backpackers typically take three to five, depending on their fitness level and on how much time they want to chill out and enjoy the scenery and solitude.

Compared to high-elevation Rocky Mountain hikes or the tidal challenges of the Pacific Coast Trail, Mantario is a literal walk in the park. But every year, hundreds of people who've never hiked a day in their life head out on this trail and are defeated within 36 hours, carelessly discarding cooking utensils, clothing, and food along the way, and sometimes bush-crashing into cottage areas at isolated Florence and Nora lakes in a desperate – and usually futile – attempt to get a lift back to civilization.

Hard to reach but worth it: Granite cliffs and bogs along the 63-kilometre Mantario Trail, the province's longest and wildest back-packing route.

If you've never strapped on a backpack, this is no place to start. But hikers with wilderness-camping experience should have no problem. Navigation is fairly easy, as most of the trail is well marked and well used. But you need a compass and map for a handful of tricky areas, particularly near Peggy and Olive lakes. Pick up a $10 laminated trail guide at Manitoba Conservation's Map Sales office in Winnipeg (1007 Century, 945-6666, or canadamapsales.com), even if you've been here before, as the southern portion of the trail was re-routed to the east of Caribou Lake in the late '90s.

Most hikers find it easier to hike the route from south to north, as the stretch around the north trailhead at Big Whiteshell is flat and easy. Leave a vehicle at each trailhead and register your route and licence-plate numbers with Manitoba Conservation staff in Rennie. There is no fee for using the trail.

The best time to go is September and early October, when days are cool, bugs are non-existent, the autumn foliage is beautiful, and low-lying areas are dry. But you should still take a pair of gaiters and hiking poles to remain dry and upright while negotiating at least three beaver-dam crossings along the way.

There are nine dedicated campsites along the route, plus one dead-end site on the west side of Caribou Lake, perfect for a there-and-back overnight. Each site has a firepit, tenting space, bear boxes, and outdoor biffies. Keep the Wilderness Section wild and you will be rewarded: The last time I hiked the Mantario, I was serenaded by a pack of wolves at Olive Lake.

The only service along the trail can be found at Mantario Lake, where the Manitoba Naturalists Society runs wilderness-education programs and guided canoe trips out of rustic Mantario Cabin. Week-long canoe trips take place in July and August at a cost of $410 per adult. But you can't just show up – register in advance at www.manitobanature.ca.

North Whiteshell

Leaving Highway 44 at Rennie, PR 307 snakes north past five lake-front cottage communities until it parallels the Winnipeg River and heads west to the park's northwestern gate at Seven Sisters Falls. You can spend a fantastic day checking out trails and scenery along this route, or spend the night at one of six campgrounds or eleven lodges/rental cabins. Just don't drive through if you're in a hurry, especially during the summer, as the 307 is notoriously busy and slow.

Heading north from Rennie, the first community is **Brereton Lake**, which has a campground, two beaches, and the **Amisk hiking trail**, a 4.8-km loop that leads to Inverness Falls, home to the year-round **Inverness Falls Resort** (www.invernessfalls.mb.ca) and an eight-km cross-country ski-trail system.

A side road at **Red Rock Lake** takes you to the 4.6-km (return) **Cabin Lake Trail**, while five paths across the highway from **Jessica Lake** are groomed for cross-country skiing in the winter and walking in the summer. The loops range from almost two to eight km.

White Lake offers a beach, campground, and fishing spot at **Rainbow Falls**. Less than a kilometre farther on, PR 309 heads east to **Big Whiteshell Lake**, home to more cottages and cabins, a marina, a beach campground, and the north end of the Mantario Trail.

Continuing north on 307, there's yet another campground and beach at **Betula Lake**, plus **the only dedicated mountain-bike trail in the Whiteshell**, a 4.2-km loop that shares space with the short **Forester's Footsteps hiking trail**.

The next trailhead along the highway is the start of the most-travelled trail in the Whiteshell, the 8.2-km walk to **Pine Point Rapids**, two small sets of falls on the Whiteshell River. This is a very popular picnic spot, so consider a midweek visit or go early in the

Jason Sorby

morning to avoid crowds. In winter, you can ski a 6.5-km stretch of this trail.

Next up along the highway are the **Bannock Rock petroforms**, the most-accessible archeological site in the Whiteshell and a sacred place for Ojibway and other First Nations. The petroforms are 2,500-year-old artworks created by indigenous people of undetermined identity, who placed rocks on the ground to form the outlines of turtles, snakes, and people. The petroforms likely served both navigational and spiritual purposes. But they're very sacred today, so moving the rocks or tampering with any offerings left at the site is strictly forbidden – never mind absolutely moronic.

PR 307 meets the Winnipeg River at **Nutimik Lake** just below **Sturgeon Falls**, an excellent playboating spot for whitewater paddlers. In the eighteenth and nineteenth centuries, sturgeon were so plentiful that anglers had only to place sharpened sticks in the rapids and wait for a large fish to impale itself. Nutimik Lake also offers a modest **natural history museum**, with exhibits about sturgeon, wild rice, and the petroforms (May long weekend to Labour Day, 9 a.m. to 5 p.m., closed at lunch). There's also the five-km (return) **Picket Creek cross-country ski trail**.

There are five more cottage communities along the highway in the Whiteshell's northwestern arm, at Nutimik Lake, Barrier Bay, Dorothy Lake, Otter Falls, and Eleanor Lake, all of which are portions of the Winnipeg River. Campgrounds can be found at Nutimik, Barrier, and Otter, while there also are four lodges in the area, including excellent riverfront cabins with decks and lofts at Dorothy Lake's **Pinewood Lodge** (348-7549, www.mypinewood.com), which recently opened a sixteen-suite addition with hotel-style rooms, a pool, and an exercise room. This is the most modern place to stay in the north Whiteshell. Rates run from $79 to $149 for guest rooms and $249 to $599 for two nights at the cabins.

In the winter, there's a three-km snowshoe trail south of Pinewood Lodge and two cross-country ski loops (three and seven km) at Otter Falls.

At any time of year, your best bet for a meal in the north Whiteshell is just outside the park in the hydro town of **Seven Sisters. Jennifer's** offers Central European dishes such as schnitzel, shots of Czech liqueur, and some authentic decor from rural Slovakia – implements hanging over the dining room include a *fujara*, a wind instrument that looks like a flute crossed with a didgeridoo, and a long axe belonging to Juraj Jánocik, Slovakia's answer to Paul Bunyan.

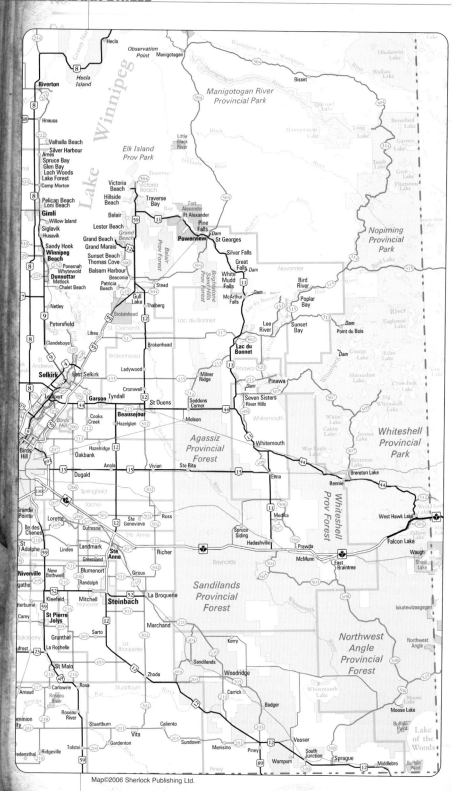

Canadian Shield Daytrips

1. North Whiteshell Circle

All daytrips
start and end
at Winnipeg.

Time to go: May to October
Prerequisite: Nothing but basic
curiosity.
Highlights: A short morning walk at
a wildlife sanctuary, an eight-km (return) hike to a scenic picnic
spot, and a visit to eastern Manitoba's most important Aboriginal
spiritual site.
The goods: From Winnipeg, head east on Highway 15 until it ends
at the town of Elma. Turn north at Highway 11, then east at Highway
44 to the town of Rennie, the western entrance to Whiteshell
Provincial Park.

Just at the entrance, pull in at the Alfred Hole Goose Sanctuary on
the right. Learn about eastern Manitoba wildlife at the visitor centre
and loosen up your legs along the short (2.5-km) walk along the
pond. Marvel and/or be disgusted by the agglomeration of Canada
geese. In May, the fuzzy yellow goslings are frickin' adorable.
Just past the Alf Hole sanctuary, turn left at PR 307 and drive north
along the winding road. About two km past Betula Lake, you'll see
the Pine Point Rapids trailhead on the right. Park your car, grab your
daypack, and scramble over Canadian Shield ridges to two sets of
rapids at the Whiteshell River. Hang out and eat lunch – you have a
better chance of having this spot to yourself if you go in midweek.
Walk back to your vehicle and drive another one km north to the
Bannock Rock Petroforms, a collection of rock sculptures assembled
as long as 8,000 years ago by some of Manitoba's first inhabitants.
Look, but do not touch.

Continue north and then west on 307, following the Winnipeg
River out of the park. If you're peckish, stop for schnitzel at Jennifer's
Dining Room in Seven Sisters Falls (348-7135). If not, continue west
to Highway 11, south to the junction with Highway 44, and west to
Beausejour, where it's time for a bison burger and shoestring fries
at Vickies Snack Bar (719 Park Avenue, 268-1922). Continue west to
Highway 59 and then southeast to Winnipeg.
Driving time: Roughly 3:30 for the whole loop.
Total time commitment: A complete day.
Fees: $5 per vehicle to enter the Whiteshell, or a Manitoba
Parks Pass.

2. Bike the Sandilands

Time to go: May to Thanksgiving.
Prerequisite: Moderate fitness level and some biking experience.
This isn't gruelling, but it's not for novices.
Highlights: Forty km of off-road bike trails through a sandy forest or
a sixty-five-km road-cycling route along gently rolling hills.
The goods: From Winnipeg, take the Trans-Canada Highway east to

Highway 12 and head south to Ste. Anne. Exit the highway and follow PR 210 through the town and then southeast past Giroux, La Broquerie, and Marchand to Marchand Wayside Park, just past PR 404.

The extensive off-road trails start at the south of the highway, immediately opposite the wayside park. You can download a trail map from the Manitoba Cross Country Ski Association website (see *Stuff to See and Do*).

For the bicycle road trip, park your car at the wayside park and drive southeast along the rolling pavement to the town of Woodridge. Fuel up with ice cream and head west on gravel PR 203 to a three-way junction with Highway 12 and PR 404. Take the 404 north to the town of Sandilands and follow the highway or the wide, gravel Old Bedford Road the final 13 kilometres back up to the wayside park.

For munchies on the drive home, detour west to Steinbach for Mennonite grub at MJ's Kafe (408 Main Street, 326-2224).

Driving time: 1:30 to the trailhead and back.

Total time commitment: Half a day.

Fee: Make a donation at the trailhead lockbox.

3. Ski Falcon and West Hawk

Time to go: Christmas to early March.

Prerequisite: Basic cross-country skis and experience.

Highlights: About thirty-five km of cross-country ski trails connecting three year-round resorts, plus a modest downhill-ski and snowboard hill at Falcon Ridge.

The goods: From Winnipeg, head east to Falcon Lake in at least two vehicles. Park the first at the Falcon Lake Resort Hotel (349-8400 or www.falcon-resort.mb.ca) and cram into the second for the short drive along the south side of the lake to the Falcon Ridge Ski Area. To warm up, spin around the 7.5-kilometre High Lake loop. Stop at the lodge for hot chocolate and bear north on the Falcon Lake Trail, heading up to West Hawk Lake via the east side of the McHugh Lake loop. Detour to a West Hawk lakefront resort for another beverage, or head southwest to the Falcon Lake townsite along the thirteen-km South Whiteshell Trail. Spin around the four-km golf-course loop. Stop for yet more libations, or shuttle yourself to the other vehicle.

On the way back to Winnipeg, stop at the McMunn Hotel on the Trans-Canada Highway for an over-sized, butter-slathered cinnamon bun.

Driving time: 2:30 to the trailhead and back.

Total time commitment: Most of the winter daylight hours.

Fees: A Manitoba Parks Pass.

Map©2006 Sherlock Publishing Ltd.

Oversized Statues

When it comes to building monuments, small Prairie towns like to think big. Many of the communities in this book have erected large, colourful, and sometimes ridiculous statues of flora, fauna, and mythological figures in the hope that tourists will stop to take a snapshot. Oddly enough, the gambit usually works. Here's a list of selected towns and their oversized objets d'art.

Altona: Van Gogh's Sunflowers; old tricycle
Arden: Crocuses
Ashern: Sharptail grouse
Austin: Tractor
Boissevain: Turtle
Dauphin: Beaver
Deloraine: Cookie jar
Dominion City: Sturgeon
Dunrea: Goose
Elm Creek: Fire hydrant
Emerson: Mountie
Erickson: Viking ship
Flin Flon: Flintabatty Flonitan
Gilbert Plains: Golfball
Gimli: The Viking
Gladstone: The Happy Rock
Glenboro: Camel
Holland: Windmill
Inwood: Garter Snakes
Komarno: Mosquito
La Broquerie: Cow
La Rivière: Wild turkey
Lundar: Canada goose
McCreary: Alpine Archie
Meleb: Mushrooms
Minnedosa: Canvasback duck
Neepawa: Birdhouse
Oak Lake: Ox
Onanole: Elk
Petersfield: Mallard

Pinawa: Sundial
Poplarfield: King Buck
Portage la Prairie: cola can; grey owl
Roblin: Diamond
Roland: Pumpkin
Roseisle: Roses
Russell: Bull
St. Claude: Tobacco pipe
St. François Xavier: White Horse
St. Malo: Deer
Ste. Rose: White bull
Ste. Rose du Lac: Manipogo (lake monster)
Selkirk: Catfish
Sifton: Spinning wheel
Steinbach: Red Rolls-Royce
The Pas: Trapper
Thompson: King Miner
Transcona, Winnipeg: "Neighbourhood Greeter"
Virden: Oil derrick
Winnipeg: Bison
Winnipeg Beach: Totem

Bigger is better: Boissevain's Tommy the Turtle and Minnedosa's Canvasback Duck.

Wilf Taylor

MUST SEE:
*Nopiming
Provincial Park*
*A boreal forest
playground with
abandoned mining
towns, rustic
resorts, and access
to the Manigotagan
River, one of
the province's
most accessible
canoe routes.*

Just west of Seven Sisters Falls, the Whitemouth River tumbles into the Winnipeg at the appropriately named **Whitemouth Falls**, which you can see from **Whitemouth River Wayside Park**.

North Whiteshell Gateway Towns

The billion-year-old Canadian Shield bedrock is among the most stable land on the planet. In this central part of the continent, earthquakes occur as often as tsunamis. Knowing this, Atomic Energy of Canada Limited constructed a nuclear laboratory on the north side of the Winnipeg River in 1960 and built the nearby town of **Pinawa** (pop. 1,470, 15 km east of Highway 11 on PR 211) to house scientists and technicians. At its peak in 1991, the lab employed 1,100 people, but a series of government cuts reduced the staff to a skeleton crew by 1999.

The nuclear plug was finally pulled in 2003, but the overeducated town of Pinawa survived, re-inventing itself as a retirement community and commuter residence for Winnipeg professionals. To visitors, the main attractions are a 10-metre-wide **sundial** built as a millennium project, a beach, a golf course, and an extensive series of trails, including the **Ironwood Interpretive Trail** along the Winnipeg River, the excellent **Whiteshell Cross-country Ski Trails** east of the town (six loops totalling thirty-seven km), and the **Pinawa Channel Heritage Walk**. This last walk follows the north side of the Pinawa Channel from the Winnipeg River to a suspension bridge built in 1998.

Across the bridge, a section of the Trans-Canada Trail continues north toward **Pinawa Dam Provincial Park** (by road, ten km north of Pinawa on PR 520), which preserves what's left of Manitoba's first hydroelectric project, a generating station that operated from 1906 to 1951. Today, water tumbles through the concrete ruins, which were partially destroyed during army training exercises. The park also has canoe launches and an interpretive trail.

Northwest of Pinawa, the town of **Lac du Bonnet** (pop. 1,089) lines the shore of the Winnipeg River at the confluence of Highway 11 and Provincial Roads 317, 313, and 502. The logging town and cottage community has a beach, a marina, and a free museum called **Lac Du Bonnet House** (408 Lake, open mid-June to October), but most visitors merely travel through on their way to the northern Whiteshell, Nopiming, Atikaki, or Ontario's Woodland Caribou Provincial Park. Heading into the bush from Winnipeg, this is the last place on any size to load up on groceries, fuel, booze, and park passes.

MUST SEE:
Pinawa
*Founded by nuclear
physicists, this
hyper-educated
former nuclear
energy town has
remade itself as
a laid-back
Shield gateway
community with
kilometres of
trails and a great
golf course.*

To the east of Lac du Bonnet on PR 313, **Point du Bois** is an odd duck of a town that sits entirely within Whiteshell Provincial Park but has an economy based around a hydroelectric generating station. It's also the northernmost gateway to the park: Car campers as well as canoeists paddling around the northern Whiteshell can make use of three campgrounds, two in town and one to the south at **Eight Foot Falls**.

Nopiming Provincial Park

Nopiming is like Whiteshell's younger, wilder brother. Roads are gravel instead of paved, there are fewer cottages and lodges, and even canoeists and hikers are not allowed to camp inside a caribou-calving zone in the centre of the park in the summer months.

Nopiming came into being like most Manitoba parks. First, we logged the heck out of it. Then, we protected it as a provincial forest so we could log some more. Logging even continued after Nopiming was granted provincial-park status in 1976, when the north-south PR 314 was connected with the gold-mining town of Bissett via the east-west PR 304.

To reach the park from Lac du Bonnet, head east on PR 313 and turn north at the junction with PR 315. From there, it's a thirty-km drive to the park. Shortly before the entrance, you'll pass a turnoff to **Bernic Lake**, where mining company Tanco works the world's richest deposit of rare, volatile cesium as well as the almost-melt-proof metal tantalum. Both elements are used in electronic components. I only mention this because cesium, if you ever have the occasion to light it on fire, is really freaking scary.

It's easy to miss the entrance to Nopiming: there's no gate, and visitors are expected to obtain a park pass in Lac du Bonnet. Most visitors keep going east on PR 315 to the **Bird Lake area** in Nopiming's southeastern corner, home to most of the park's cottage developments, as well as campgrounds at both the **Bird Lake townsite** and **Tulabi Falls**.

Bird Lake is also the staging ground for **canoe trips up the Bird River** (also known as the Oiseau, to Francofolks) into Elbow Lake, McGregor Lake, Snowshoe Lake, and eventually Crown land in Ontario. This short route sees a lot of paddlers during summer weekends, so go during the week or shoulder seasons if you want a quiet campsite.

Taking a breather along a hike in Nopiming Provincial Park, where solitude is easier to find than in the more popular Whiteshell.

Bartley Kives

The main artery in Nopiming is PR 314, which heads north from the park entrance. After 30 kilometres of winding nothingness, you'll pass the abandoned **Irgon Mine** and then come to access points to three canoe routes. The **Rabbit River route** is an overnight trip upriver to Cole Lake and back. Head downriver at the same point to embark on a five-day, 100-km paddle down the **Black River**, out of the park, and to the edge of Lake Winnipeg. A short distance to the north lies the start of the **Seagrim Lake trail**, another short, popular paddling route.

A couple of kilometres up the highway, pull into the **Black Lake campground**, the start of a nine-km (return) lakeshore path marked with rock cairns. The campground also houses **an outdoor exhibit about Nopiming's small herd of woodland caribou**, the southernmost caribou herd in Manitoba. The critters are so skittish while calving that the area around Flintstone Lake and Lost Claim Lake is closed to overnight visitors all summer.

You can get a glimpse of Flintstone Lake, albeit from a long distance, from the top of the **Walking on Ancient Mountains trail**, a short self-guiding trail that climbs up a granite ridge. The trail is piddly in length – only 1.8 km, return – but offers a nice panoramic view of the area, including Tooth Lake stretching out to the west.

Continuing north on PR 314, you'll cross the **Manigotagan River**, the most accessible A-list whitewater river in the southeastern Shield. You can spend four to six days paddling 135 kilometres down the scenic Manigotagan to Lake Winnipeg, passing dozens of rapids, waterfalls and probably river otters along the way. In 2004, the lower fifty-five km of the river was protected from logging, mining, and hydro development by the creation of Manigotagan Provincial Park, a narrow corridor that follows the river up to the town of Manigotagan. If you're interested in paddling the river, there's good advice in John Buchanan's *Canoeing Manitoba Rivers* or Hap Wilson's *Wilderness Rivers of Manitoba* (see *Selected Sources*). It's usually navigable between Victoria Day and Thanksgiving.

There are two cottage areas in Nopiming's northern section: Beresford Lake, which also sports a campground, canoe launch, and the remains of an old trapper's cabin; and Long Lake, home to the only lodge in this part of the park. Before the Beresford Lake turnoff, the short **Fire of '83 trail** takes you through an area of recovering forest. But the most interesting aspect of this part of the park is the **remains of gold and silver mines** that operated in the area between 1927 and 1951. You can see the capped remains of four mine sites near Beresford Lake and Long Lake, the latter accessible via a short but slightly gnarly four-wheel-drive track that starts at the end of PR 314. You know you've come to the right place when you see a big pile of old core samples.

In the extreme north of the park, at the beginning of PR 304, you'll drive through a clearing that looks like a giant mudflat. It's actually the remains of a mining town called **Wadhope**, which was completely dismantled after the nearby Kitchener mine was closed during the Depression. A small plaque stands at the site, which you could call a ghost town, if there were any town left here at all. The

Winnipeg Free Press

The San Antonio Gold Mine at Bissett, where 1.2 million ounces of gold were extracted in the 20th century.

clearing has an eerie quality, especially since vegetation has yet to reclaim the site, even after 60 years. Who would have guessed mine tailings could be bad for the environment?

Provincial Road 304

PR 304 extends in an arc from Nopiming's north entrance to the Lake Winnipeg town of Manigotagan, then down to the twin communities of Pine Falls and Powerview on the Winnipeg River. The east-west drive between Nopiming and Powerview is dusty and lonely, and seems longer than its eighty-eight km. People mostly come up here to hunt, fish, or paddle – or to charter a floatplane to do more of the same. I can't recommend the drive, otherwise.

Just northwest of Nopiming, you'll find a turnoff to Wallace Lake and the **Wallace Lake Provincial Recreation Park**, a popular campground and boat launch. The lake is a magnet for fishing, but also marks the start of the most infamous set of portages in Manitoba – the **Siderock and Obukowin portages**, six boggy kilometres of misery that allow paddlers access into roadless Atikaki Provincial Wilderness Park without having to pony up big bucks for a floatplane lift. Canoeists can also head west from Wallace Lake to begin a ninety-km, two-to-four-day paddle down the narrow but mostly pristine **Wanipigow River**, which enters Lake Winnipeg at Hollow Water First Nation.

Continuing west on the 304, the town of **Bissett** (pop. 167) is most famous for the San Antonio gold mine, where 1.2 million ounces of gold and 190,000 ounces of silver were extracted during sporadic periods of activity between 1932 and 1985. Manitoba's modest gold rush started here in 1911, when an Ojibway trapper named Duncan Twohearts gathered up some yellow rocks on Rice Lake and showed them to a trader in Manigotagan.

MUST SEE:
Kasakeemeemis-ekak Islands
A spectacular archipelago on the east side of Lake Winnipeg, with amazing numbers of eagles, double-crested cormorants, and pelicans.

MUST SEE:
Atikaki Provincial Wilderness Park
A roadless wilderness sanctuary with some of the best whitewater paddling in Canada on the historic Bloodvein and the raging Pigeon River.

As the mine stands idle, Bissett is now used as a gateway to Atikaki Provincial Wilderness Park. Silver Falls – based Blue Water Aviation carries hunters, anglers, and paddlers and their canoes from a floatplane base on Rice Lake.

There are three campgrounds between Bissett and Manigotagan: **Caribou Landing**, on Quesnel Lake in the western arm of Nopiming Provincial Park, may be used to shave thirty km off the 100-km Manigotagan River canoe trip; **Wanipigow Lake** is popular for fishing; and **English Brook** is usually empty, even during the summer.

Two kilometres west of English Brook, a winter road heads north from 304 to the Bloodvein River, crossing the **Rice River** thirty km up. Canoeists and kayakers park here, paddle about five km down to Lake Winnipeg, and explore a gorgeous archipelago called the **Kasakeemeemisekak Islands**, where amazing numbers of white pelicans, cormorants, and bald eagles gather during the summer. The islands make for a fantastic daytrip, as long as you're prepared to deal with rough water on Lake Winnipeg and the navigational challenges of finding your way in this maze. Bring a GPS, just in case.

You can also reach the Kasakeemeemisekak Islands and spend several days exploring the Lake Winnipeg narrows region from **Hollow Water First Nation**, an Ojibway community located eight km north of the 304.

South of the Hollow Water turnoff, PR 304 becomes a paved road, and the settlement of Manigotagan appears. The main attraction is the impressive falls at the Manigotagan River, overlooked by a campground to the south.

The seventy-one-km drive between Manigotagan and the Winnipeg River is fast and mostly featureless, with the exception of a **two-km hiking loop** just north of Powerview.

Atikaki Provincial Wilderness Park

In 1985, Manitoba protected 4,000 square km of Canadian Shield forests and wetlands on the east side of Lake Winnipeg with the creation of **Atikaki Provincial Wilderness Park**, home of five of the province's most celebrated rivers and a woodland caribou population of about 350.

Since there are no roads in the park, the only way to enter is by floatplane, canoeing up from Garner Lake in Nopiming Provincial Park, or taking the arduous Obukowin Lake portage. The expense and effort required to reach Atikaki has helped keep the park pristine, as the only visitors are hunters and anglers flying to one of five wilderness lodges, and paddlers heading down the **Gammon**, **Bloodvein**, **Sasaginnigak**, **Leyond**, and **Pigeon** rivers.

The most popular attraction is the **Bloodvein**, a fur-trade waterway that flows 340 kilometres from Red Lake, Ont., to Lake Winnipeg. One of seventeen Canadian waterways designated as a heritage river, the Bloodvein possesses spectacular beauty, historical significance, and dozens of challenging rapids. But much of its whitewater can be bypassed via portages, making this river accessible to any paddler with prior wilderness experience.

Canoe-in paddlers usually approach the Bloodvein from the Gammon River, accessible via the Obukowin portage. The classic fly-in route begins at the Ontario border at pictograph-laden **Artery Lake** and continues 225 kilometres to Lake Winnipeg. The latter trip takes ten days to two weeks, but you don't need to fly out, as a free weekday ferry operates between Bloodvein First Nation and the west side of the Lake Winnipeg Narrows.

Atikaki's other big attraction is the less-visited **Pigeon River**, reputed to be one of Canada's best whitewater rivers. This northern-most Atikaki waterway looks similar in size to the Bloodvein, but has almost twice the flow, which makes it too hairy for anyone but experienced paddlers.

Both the Bloodvein and Pigeon are navigable from Victoria Day to Thanksgiving. John Buchanan and Hap Wilson's canoe guide-books (see *Selected Sources*) have the intelligence you'll need.

Floatplane companies that serve Atikaki include **Bluewater Aviation** (www.bluewater aviation.com) for flights out of Bissett, and **Northway Aviation** (www.biscuitharbour.com) out of Pine Dock on Lake Winnipeg. You can also get outfitted or arrange fully guided Bloodvein, Pigeon, and Manigotagan river trips through **Northern Soul Wilderness Adventures** (www.northernsoul.ca) or **Wilderness Spirit** (www.wilder-nessspirit.com), two respected Winnipeg ecotourism outfits.

The Shield-Prairie Transition

Between the rocky Canadian Shield and the open Prairie farmland, you'll find mixed forests with sandy soils created by the retreat of glacial Lake Agassiz. Most of this area – a rough triangle extending south from Pine Falls to the US border and across to Lake of the Woods – is covered by provincial forests, the largest being Agassiz, Whiteshell, Sandilands, and Northwest Angle.

Logging is the main activity here, followed by tourism and the old-school outdoor recreations of fishing, hunting, snowmobiling, and ATVing. Since most of these practices are restricted if not com-pletely banned in provincial parks, the forests of the southeast are sort of like redneck playgrounds.

Don't get offended: I use the term in the most affectionate way possible, because there's no longer a big cultural gap between urban ecotourist types and rural outdoorsmen. Hunters are among the world's most-committed conservationists, catch-and-release sport fishing is both sustainable and growing in popularity, and modern snowmobiles are quieter and produce fewer pollutants than their archaic counterparts. But I have nothing good to say about the ATV crowd, who do more to disfigure the landscape than any other group of backcountry users.

In any case, take care when hiking, mountain biking, or skiing in the southeast, as you may be sharing a trail with motorized vehicles. And, if you head into the bush during hunting season, wear bright colours such as blaze orange to avoid being mistaken for something with fur, claws, or antlers. You'd look stupid up above somebody's mantle.

Pine Falls to the Trans-Canada Highway

Highway 11 is the main north-south artery in southeastern Manitoba. Beginning at the edge of the Eastern Beaches region (see the *Beaches and Interlake* chapter), it follows the Winnipeg River southeast until Seven Sisters Falls, when it parallels the Whitemouth River to the Trans-Canada Highway.

About 3,000 people live in a cluster of communities, each with its own character, at the top of the highway near the confluence with PR 304. Driving southeast, you'll pass through the mostly Ojibway **Fort Alexander First Nation**; the paper-mill town of **Pine Falls**; hydroelectric centre **Powerview**, where you can walk across the boiling froth of the Winnipeg River at PR 304; and the partly Francophone **St-Georges**, home to a free museum, **La Societé historique de St-Georges** (19 Baie Caron), open June to September.

Go back 100 years and most of the Winnipeg River was a raging ribbon of whitewater. Today, six dams between the Ontario border and Lake Winnipeg have mellowed it out and swollen its width to create Lac du Bonnet and other pseudo-lakes within the Whiteshell.

The drive from St-Georges to the town of Lac du Bonnet is more pastoral than wild, as Highway 11 heads south through a narrow band of cleared farmland east of the **Brightstone Sand Hills Provincial Forest**. The scenery grows tamer as you head south, as the road follows a ribbon of open prairie between Agassiz and Whiteshell Provincial Forest, past the towns of **Whitemouth** and **Elma** to **Hadashville** at the Trans-Canada Highway.

For a very short detour, take PR 406 between Whitemouth and Elma to stick close to a string of rapids along the Whitemouth River. Kayakers and playboaters paddle into **Nakka Falls**, **Oak Falls**, and **Cook Falls** to keep their whitewater skills sharp. Campgrounds at the latter two falls are open from May to October – you can also go tubing if kayaking doesn't appeal to you.

In winter, the town of Whitemouth grooms six km of cross-country ski trails, while the **Whitemouth River ski-trail system** south of Hadashville offers loops of 2.5, 5.5, and seven km. To find the trailhead, drive south on Highway 11, cross Highway 1, and follow the access road as it curves to the right. Hadashville also has a **forest centre** with interpretive displays.

Charles Shilliday

Sandilands Provincial Forest

Driving east on the Trans-Canada from the Red River Valley, the flatness gives way to a wide, green ridge created by sediments left behind when the final glaciers retreated from southern Manitoba. This is **Sandilands Provincial Forest**, the highest area in south eastern Manitoba, home to forests intercut with logging roads and fireguards.

The maze of dirt tracks is a playground for quad yahoos as well as hunters in pursuit of moose and deer. To stay out of their way, mountain bikers and cross-country skiers focus their attention on forty km of trails near the confluence of provincial roads 210 and 404, officially known as the **Sandilands Cross-Country Ski Trails**. The volunteer-maintained system is accessible from a trailhead across PR 210 from Marchand Wayside Park, just east of the 404.

Popular with motorcyclists, PR 210 is a gently winding road that curves southeast through the southern Sandilands, where a slew of small communities are cut into breaks in the forest. If you choose to carve out a backcountry campsite in the Sandilands, stick to the north of the forest and avoid areas near the towns of Woodridge, Carrick, Badger, and St. Labre. But do pay a visit to the town of **McMunn** at the northeast corner of the forest. Right on the Trans-Canada Highway, the unassuming-looking **McMunn Hotel** toasts enormous cinnamon buns and slathers them in butter – the perfect, high-carb pick-me-up after a day of skiing, either in the Sandilands or the Whiteshell. In the summer, you can peruse hand-made crafts at **Birch River Arts and Crafts**, an artists' co-op on the south side of the highway.

A rainbow brightens up an open stretch of Sandilands Provincial Forest.

Aurora borealis, a.k.a. the northern lights.

Northwest Angle Provincial Forest

Manitoba's extreme southeast corner is mostly comprised of bogs, fens, and marshes passable only in the winter on snowmobile. Most of the area belongs to **Northwest Angle Provincial Forest**, which takes it name from a chunk of Minnesota that wound up affixed to Manitoba when the final borders between Canada and the US were settled (See *Northwest Angle,* below).

The only road cutting through the forest is PR 308, which is entirely gravel and extends from the delightfully named community of East Braintree to tiny **Moose Lake Provincial Park and Campground**. The road to Angle Inlet, Minn., is just northeast of the park.

The two main attractions in this area are **Whitemouth Lake**, an extremely popular fishing spot accessible from a gravel road that connects Woodridge to PR 308, and **Buffalo Bay**, a tiny corner of Lake of the Woods that belongs to Manitoba.

The southernmost reaches of both the Sandilands and Northwest Angle Provincial Forest are traversed by Manitoba Highway 12, which passes by the towns of Piney, South Junction, and Sprague on the way to Warroad, Minn., the southernmost port on Lake Of The Woods.

Just before the border, at the turnoff to cottage area Buffalo Point, the modest **Buffalo Point Cultural Centre** offers Aboriginal crafts and cultural displays.

Northwest Angle

If you look at a map of North America, you'll notice the Canada-U.S. border follows a nice, even path along the 49th Parallel until you get to Lake of the Woods, where a little thumb of Minnesota known as the **Northwest Angle** sticks up into the Great White North.

When the UK and US were settling their North American borders at the end of the American Revolution, they agreed to separate Ontario from Minnesota along the historic voyageur canoe route between Lake Superior and Lake of the Woods. All the lakes and rivers along the way – including Rainy Lake and Rainy River – were divided down the middle. For some reason, Lake of the Woods was supposed to bisected its northwestern point, which was later determined to be a small bay called Angle Inlet.

This became a problem when the rest of the Canada-US border was set at the 49th Parallel, creating a 43-kilometre gap. So in 1841, border negotiators decided to draw a line south from Angle Inlet, connect the dots on paper and call it a day.

This decision meant a chunk of Minnesota wound up an orphan, attached by land only to Manitoba and separated from the rest of the US by the choppy waters of Big Traverse Bay. Today, the bulk of this mapmaking oddity belongs to Minnesota's Red Lake Ojibway Nation, while the shoreline is protected by the Northwest Angle State Forest. The sole town, **Angle Inlet**, sits on the north side of the peninsula.

Residents of this small fishing community periodically threaten to secede from Minnesota whenever Ontario makes it tougher for US residents to fish in Canadian waters. But the protests are never serious – even orphaned Americans take their nationality seriously.

The chief attraction in the Angle is history, and bloody history at that. On **Magnusons Island** in Angle Inlet, explorer La Vérendrye established **Fort St. Charles** soon after he reached Lake of the Woods in 1732. Four years later, the star-crossed adventurer sent his son Jean Baptiste, local priest Jean Pierre Aulneau and 19 other men east to pick up supplies from what's now Thunder Bay. Along the way, the canoe party was ambushed by a Sioux war party, who beheaded all 21 men and left their corpses on **Massacre Island**, which sits inside Canadian waters in Little Traverse Bay.

From Angle Inlet, you can take a motorboat ride to Magnusons Island and tour Fort St. Charles, which was rediscovered in 1890 by St. Boniface Jesuits and rebuilt in the 20th Century by Minnesota Catholics. Kayakers may also retrace the route of the doomed canoe party from Magnusons to Massacre Island, a 15-km trek across choppy, open water.

Some Americans, however, claim a smaller island inside US waters, Ile du Massacre, is the real site of the massacre. Yet again, borders are an issue in Lake of the Woods.

To reach the Northwest Angle from Winnipeg, take the Trans Canada Highway east to the town of East Braintree, PR 308 south to PR 525, and head east to an unmanned US border post, where you're supposed to show your passport to a US customs guard stationed elsewhere. From here, it's a short drive northwest to Angle Inlet. Allow two hours for the entire jaunt.

Heading north from the US border, Angle Inlet can be reached by taking Highway 12 northwest to Sprague and then PR 308 northeast to PR 525.

BEACHES AND
THE INTERLAKE

8

Crusty Manitobans can often be heard griping about two things: the weather, which is always too cold, humid, dry, muggy, or buggy; and "those bastards in Ottawa," regardless of whoever happens to be in power. But nothing really stirs emotions like the province's most dominant feature, Lake Winnipeg. The world's eleventh-largest freshwater lake is the destination of choice for vacationing Winnipeggers, a meal ticket for hundreds of fishers – and an environmental disaster waiting to happen.

Despite its massive size – roughly 24,000 square km, which is bigger than all of Israel or El Salvador – Lake Winnipeg is very shallow, with an average depth of only twelve metres. That gives it a very small volume – 284 cubic km – relative to its immense drainage basin, a 950,000-square-km chunk of North America that includes half of Manitoba, Saskatchewan, and Alberta, sizable pieces of Ontario, North Dakota, and Minnesota, and a couple of corners of Montana and South Dakota.

As a result, Lake Winnipeg is the lucky recipient of pollution created by farms, factories, mines, logging operations, cities, towns, and cottage communities from Edmonton to Fargo to Atikokan, all places residents rarely think about where their wastewater winds up. Raw sewage, fertilizers, industrial effluent, and sediments all threaten the lake, whose ecology has already been messed up by the destruction of lakeshore habitat and the introduction of foreign fish, invertebrates, and micro-organisms since Europeans showed up en masse in the 1800s.

In recent years, fertilizers and possibly sewage have led to summertime toxic algae blooms in the lake's larger northern basin, while freshwater snails, mussels, and other rungs on the food chain are disappearing. If the situation worsens, as some biologists and water-quality experts predict, the lake could lose its lucrative commercial pickerel fishery and become unattractive to vacationers. Almost every Manitoban shoulders some responsibility for the future of the lake, and most want the provincial government to do whatever's necessary to prevent or at least mitigate the looming disaster.

Opposite: Gulls at Winnipeg Beach, one of the largest of dozens of cottage communities ringing the southern basin of Lake Winnipeg.

In the meantime, it's still perfectly safe to visit Lake Winnipeg, whose densely populated southern basin is the main focus of this chapter. I've only dished out the bad news to instill a sense of urgency in travellers: Enjoy this big, shallow baking pan right now, while you still have the opportunity.

Winnipeg Free Press

Lake Winnipeg's southern basin is lined by dozens of sandy beaches, two excellent provincial parks (Grand Beach and Hecla/Grindstone), and the fishing community/resort of Gimli. Meanwhile, the low-lying marshes, forests, and meadows to the west – dubbed the Interlake, due to its location between Lake Winnipeg and Lake Manitoba – sport attractions like the garter-snake pits of Narcisse, the 116-km Prime Meridian Trail, and the limestone cliffs of Steep Rock.

Hitting the waves at Grand Beach Provincial Park.

In the lakeshore communities, the bulk of the population is seasonal. Among the year-round population, dominant ethnic groups include Icelandic, Cree, Ojibway, and Métis, along with the usual Manitoban mix of British, German, and Ukrainian.

The best time to visit both the beaches and the Interlake is obviously the summer, but ice fishing, snowmobiling, and cross-country skiing draw year-round visitors. I've personally snowshoed straight across the frozen southern basin of Lake Winnipeg in the middle of March, so a little cold weather is no reason to avoid cottage country.

MUST SEE:
Grand Beach
Manitoba's most popular beach, packed with tens of thousands of sun-worshippers on hot summer days.

Eastern Beaches

Two provincial parks, a dozen beaches, and about twenty cottage communities line the east side of Lake Winnipeg's southern basin, a fifty-km shoreline characterized by unusually fine sand, impressive glacial erratics (large boulders left behind by retreating glaciers), and a mix of deciduous and coniferous trees. A transition zone between prairie and the Canadian Shield, this ecologically diverse area feels a lot wilder than the west side of the lake – and not just because of the hard-partying hardbodies who flock to Grand Beach.

To reach most of the beaches, you have to dawdle through quiet cottage areas. But there are no barriers to three of the best, each with its own distinct character: Grand is the biggest and busiest, Patricia is the best choice for families, and Beaconia is the most secluded and least developed.

For the purposes of orientation, I've listed the beaches from north to south.

Victoria Beach

If any place in Manitoba couldn't care less about tourism, it's **Victoria Beach**, an unusual community that bars motorized traffic from its streets and gears most services to resident cottagers. Except on special occasions, cottagers are required to leave their vehicles at a parking lot at the entrance to the community and walk in. This

Charles Shilliday

once-exclusive – as in, no Jews or visible minorities, if you go back half a century – cottage area works extremely hard at being relaxed. Victoria Beach feels more like a New England island resort than a Manitoba beach town, especially when you factor in the presence of a sailing club and numerous social events throughout the summer.

Still, Victoria Beach is hardly xenophobic – visitors are more than welcome to stroll its narrow streets and swim at its sandy beach. If you make the trek, stop in at **Einfeld's Victoria Beach Bakery** (112 Birch), a seventy-year-old establishment famous for its moon cookies.

Patricia Beach.

Victoria Beach is located at the end of Highway 59, about 110 km northeast of Winnipeg.

Elk Island Provincial Park

One of the weirder (and wetter) day hikes in Manitoba is the trek to **Elk Island Provincial Park**, a 900-hectare protected wilderness located off the north shore of the Victoria Beach peninsula. To reach the island, you have to wade across a narrow strait that's usually about a metre deep, carefully following a submerged sandbar. Venture too far to the left or right and you'll end up swimming – or worse.

There's nothing on the other side of the strait but forest, sand, and swamp; hence the attraction. You can circumnavigate Elk Island (about eight km) or merely hang out and the south end and enjoy the solitude. Overnight camping, however, is not permitted.

To reach the island, drive north on Highway 59 but go straight past the turnoff to Victoria Beach at PR 504. At the end of the road, turn left and drive until you can't go any farther. Park, walk as far north as you can, and begin wading cautiously across the strait, being mindful of currents and waves. You might want to take a lifejacket and, in cooler weather, a dry bag full of warm clothes.

Grand Beach Provincial Park

On hot July and August weekends, the remarkably fine silica sands of **Grand Beach Provincial Park** attract tens of thousands of Winnipeggers, creating a scene that looks a lot more like southern California or Florida than the Canadian Prairies. Originally served by rail, this seasonal sunspot causes traffic headaches on Highway 59.

The three-km-long beach is the best open-air meat market in Manitoba, as the young, the genetically gifted, and the surgically augmented crowd along the **West Beach**, home to a boardwalk with beachwear vendors, a hotel/restaurant, a tennis court, and a cramped cottage area. On busier days, families usually stick to the middle of the beach or the **East Beach**, which sports a campground, an amphitheatre, and access to most of the trails in the park.

Aside from the beach and lake, natural attractions include active sand dunes that reach a height of twelve metres, a large lagoon and marsh full of fish and waterfowl, a small protected nesting ground for the endangered piping plover, and eight trails totalling thirty-two km.

Three of these trails are short walks suitable for the young kids or people pressed for time. The one-km **Spirit Rock trail** rounds a bluff near the West Beach; the equally brief **Wild Wings trail** circles part of a marsh along the causeway that connects the East and West Beaches; while the two-km **Ancient Beach trail** offers a glimpse of the mixed forest that characterizes the mostly undeveloped east side of the park.

A separate East Beach trailhead is the staging ground for five longer trails that make for dull hiking but decent mountain biking and excellent cross-country skiing. The longest route is the thirteen-km **Beaver Pond trail**, which is officially closed during the summer but is passable to anyone willing to make stream crossings.

Grand Beach is about eighty km northeast of Winnipeg. Take Highway 59 north and then Highway 12 west to reach both the East Beach and West Beach gates. A Manitoba Park Pass is required for vehicle entry from the start of the Victoria Day long weekend to Labour Day.

Around Grand Beach

Immediately outside the West Beach gate, the town of **Grand Marais** – literally, "big marsh" – is a quaint but faded beach town offering cheap cabin rentals and greasy comfort food. The most popular destinations for munchies are **Lanky's** (85 Grand Beach), a shack that specializes in hot dogs and deep-fried perogies, and licensed pizza joint **Potenza** (42 Parkview), which makes better 'za than most joints in Winnipeg. As well, a handful of commercial fishers live here and occasionally sell smoked whitefish and goldeye.

The marsh that gives Grand Marais its name extends southeast from the town and is best explored by canoe. From mid-June to mid-August, you're all but guaranteed to see great blue herons, red-winged blackbirds, cormorants, and white pelicans, the latter two nesting on narrow **Stevens Island**, which is usually covered with Hitchcockian quantities of gulls. Unfortunately, idiots on personal watercraft routinely buzz the nesting grounds, while the marsh itself is slowly being destroyed by the one-two punch of introduced, non-native carp and artificially maintained water levels.

You can also bike or walk into the interior of the marsh along a section of the Trans-Canada Trail that follows a railbed used during Grand Beach's early-twentieth-century heyday. Starting at an entrance hidden behind the Sand Bar Motor Inn, the path leads across the marsh, then through seven cottage communities, until it veers toward Highway 59 at Beaconia, eight km to the south.

Immediately outside the Grand Beach's east gate, you'll find **Thunder Mountain Waterslides** (open mid-June through August) and a more unusual attraction: a Manitoba Hydro substation capped by an enormous osprey nest. This is an easy place to spot North America's most spectacular fishing bird: four of the big raptors usually perch in the nest all summer.

Three km to the southeast, the far side of sandy Balsam Hill has been carved into a 10,000-seat concert amphitheatre and campground called the **Grand Beach Entertainment Centre** (Highway 59 at Road 102 North), which usually hosts at least one classic-rock festival per summer. And two km up Highway 50, northeast of the park, an off-road driving route called the **North Star Trail** curls around the glacial moraines of Belair Provincial Forest to PR 304, offering eastward views across the Catfish Creek Valley to the Brightstone Sand Hills near Pine Falls. An old fire tower is officially off-limits but frequently climbed – I legally can't recommend it, but people have been to the top and lived to tell the tale.

Beaconia and Patricia Beach

If you love beaches but can't stomach crowds, head to idyllic **Beaconia Beach**, about 1.8 km of pristine sand and absolutely nothing else. There are no services here, and in some places, no bathing suits – the southern section the beach is clothing-optional, albeit by custom and not official sanction.

Generally speaking, the north end of the beach is for people in bathing suits, straight nudists frequent the middle section, and the bottom of the sandbar is a gay nude beach. You can wear clothing wherever you like, but don't go naked on the north section, as some of the locals aren't cool with exposed flesh.

To reach Beaconia Beach, drive north on Highway 59, turn left at PR 500, and enter the hamlet of Beaconia. When the main road veers to the right, go straight and follow a gravel causeway to the sandbar that comprises the beach. Since this is a wilderness area, pack out all your trash.

A similarly mellow vibe can be found at **Patricia Beach Provincial Park**, about 1.5 km long but usually busier and a little more family-friendly. You'll find actual washrooms and a snack bar here, but little of the hustle and bustle of Grand Beach. The secluded eastern corner (that is, the righthand side of the sandspit) is another unofficial nude beach. To reach the park, take Highway 59 north, turn left at PR 319, and follow the winding road to the beach.

Brokenhead First Nation

Perched on the northeast corner of Netley Marsh, the Ojibway community of **Brokenhead First Nation** serves as the gateway to the Eastern Beaches. Only recently has Brokenhead begun to take advantage of all the traffic that passes through: In 2005, the reserve opened **South Beach Casino**, a year-round gaming facility with a Miami Beach motif.

More traditionally, **Brokenhead Ojibway Village** (766-2494) offers Aboriginal cultural immersion and overnight stays in teepees. The First Nation is located on Highway 59, about seventy km northeast of Winnipeg.

Immediately to the south of the reserve, the **Mars Hill Wildlife Management Area** encloses a tangle of sandy trails used by horseback riders and ATVs during the summer and cross-country skiers and dogsledders in winter. This is also a popular forage spot for

MUST SEE:
Beaconia and Patricia Beach
Quiet white-sand beaches where the vibe ranges from mellow to idyllic.

mushroom, herb, and berry pickers. Take a map and compass, because most trails aren't marked, or follow a section of the Trans-Canada Trail through the area. The hills are accessible from PR 317, east of the community of Libau.

Netley Marsh

In stark contrast to the dense cottage developments on the east and west sides of Lake Winnipeg, the very bottom of the inland ocean remains wild. A 240-square-km wetland called **Netley Marsh**, one of the largest waterfowl nesting areas in North America, is uninhabited aside from a handful of communities on its fringes.

Although larger than Delta Marsh, Netley sees relatively few visitors. Boaters pass through the three mouths of the Red River on their way to Lake Winnipeg, while anglers, the occasional canoeist, and a handful of intrepid birders negotiate the labyrinth of canals and shallow lakes in the rest of the marsh. Needless to say, it's incredibly easy to get lost here – take a GPS unit as well as a topographical map and nautical chart if you decide to go exploring. Also be aware of the tide-like effect of winds: gusts from the north engorge the shallow marsh with water from Lake Winnipeg, while south winds empty it out, turning navigable channels into impassable muck.

The only road-accessible destination inside the marsh is **Breezy Point**, a cottage area, campground, and small marina at the end of PR 320, a northern extension of Selkirk and Winnipeg's Main Street. An observation tower at the end of the road offers views of the massive marsh.

Southwest of the marsh on Highway 9, a string of marinas in the settlement of **Petersfield** offers water access to the marsh via Netley Creek, the most northern tributary of the Red before the river splits into three branches.

Western Beaches and New Iceland

MUST SEE:
Winnipeg Beach
An increasingly artsy beachfront community within 45 minutes of Winnipeg.

While the Eastern Beaches are all about nature, the west side of Lake Winnipeg's southern basin offers culture. In 1875, immigrants from Iceland established a colony near the present-day town of Gimli, where the Scandinavian influence remains.

Fishing and farming dominated this shoreline before crowds from boomtown-era Winnipeg discovered the beaches about 100 years ago, brought *en masse* by a branch of the Canadian Pacific Railway. In recent years, retirees and a handful of artists have started to move in and transform the character of Dunnotar, Winnipeg Beach, and Gimli from purely rural communities into urban-friendly extensions of the Manitoba capital. But due to the seasonal nature of the cottage business, the area has largely resisted colonization by fast-food franchises and other tendrils of corporate culture. The main arteries are Highway 9 and PR 222 along the shore of Lake Winnipeg, and the faster but less scenic Highway 8, which continues north to the marine playground of Hecla/Grindstone Provincial Park.

Winnipeg Beach and the Village of Dunnotar

Only sixty km north of Winnipeg, the lakefront hamlets of Matlock, Whytewold, and Ponemah, collectively known as the **Village of Dunnotar,** own the closest set of beaches to the Manitoba capital. These communities only sport a handful of small beaches and a decent summer-only country restaurant in **Janet's Place** (30 Gimli Rd. in Matlock, 389-5303), but they're cute enough to warrant the brief detour off Highway 9 – PR 232 follows the shore through the entire village.

Winnipeg Free Press

Extras from the Global TV drama *Falcon Beach* enjoy some downtime at Winnipeg Beach.

Immediately to the north, **Winnipeg Beach** is no rival to Grand Beach when it comes to sand or hotties, but the lakefront services are vastly superior and are open for more of the year. The main attraction is the beach itself, part of it protected by tiny **Winnipeg Beach Provincial Park,** but the town offers superior country food along the lakefront boardwalk at the nouveau-Italian **Casa Bianca** (22 Murray, 389-5007, May to September) and middlebrow diner **The Boardwalk** (30 Main, year-round), plus espresso and loose-leaf tea at **The Breakwater** (Main and Robinson, year-round), much to the dismay of townies who prefer an old-fashioned cup of joe.

Also on the boardwalk, leaf through dog-eared titles at **Barb's Used Books** or stop into one of the most creative art retailers in small-town Manitoba, the **Fish Fly Gallery** (18 Main), where proprietors Heidi Hunter and Cheryl Tordon sell works by forty-odd Manitoba artists, including nine from the Winnipeg Beach area. They pay all their artists up front, which means the pieces on display are excellent, compared to consignment galleries where the proprietor doesn't really care whether the pieces sell. Tordon herself makes intriguing willow-branch furniture.

Winnipeg Beach to Gimli

In total, there are at least thirty potters, painters, sculptors, luthiers, and other artists working full-time along a strip of Lake Winnipeg shoreline from Matlock to Gimli. Many sell their work out of their studios. You'll find a complete listing and virtual tour online at the Winnipeg Beach Art and Culture Co-op's website, www.mts.net/ ~hroggere/.

Along the same Matlock-to-Gimli strip, dozens of Lake Winnipeg outfits sell fresh and frozen pickerel, pickerel cheeks, and fantastic smoked goldeye from garages or storefronts advertised along the road. Don't be squeamish about the cheeks – they're boneless nuggets of meat, perfect for pan-frying. If you'd rather have someone cook your fish for you, drive four km north on Highway 9 to Sandy Hook for a pickerel dinner at the totally old-school **Jane & Walter's** (May to September), a delightfully untrendy family restaurant.

Another five km north, **Willow Creek Heritage Park** marks the landing site of the Interlake's original Icelandic and Ukrainian settlers. The creek itself is navigable to paddlers. You can head upstream during the spring and early summer, when water levels are high, or downstream all summer through the community of Siglavik to Lake Winnipeg.

Gimli

The capital of all things Icelandic in Manitoba, **Gimli** combines the hardscrabble hardiness of a maritime fishing village with the Neverland vibe of a summer resort. It's also the largest community in the Interlake, with about 5,000 people living in and around the lakefront town – and more retirees coming from Winnipeg every year.

Charles Shilliday

At the east end of Centre Street, **Gimli Harbour** is worth a brief visit, but don't expect to see actual fishers hauling in their catch. You can rent kayaks and windsurfers here, or hang out at Gimli Beach. But you absolutely must take a walk along First Avenue and have a meal of pan-fried pickerel – among half a dozen downtown restaurants, **The Beach Boy** (70 1st) appears to be the most popular. There are also a dozen places in and around the town where you can buy fresh pickerel (in season) and smoked fish, including goldeye. Just keep your eyes peeled along Highways 8 and 9.

Gimli Harbour – quaint, but don't expect to meet Captain Highliner.

Over the August long weekend, downtown Gimli hosts **Islendingadagurinn** ("Icelandic Days"), a cultural festival that celebrates the 130-year Norse presence in the Interlake. It's basically your typical town fair, with Viking hats, free performances by decent indie-rock bands, and the excellent **Gimli Film Festival**, which features both indoor screenings and outdoor night-time movies on a 10-metre screen right in the lake, facing the beachfront.

From 1875 to 1887, Gimli was the unofficial capital of the New Iceland reserve, a semi-autonomous entity reporting to the federal government. You can learn about the twelve-year colony at the **New Iceland Heritage Museum**, whose exhibits are divided between the **Waterfront Centre** (94 1st, year-round), the **Lake Winnipeg Visitor Centre** (just west of Gimli Harbour, May to September), and **Gimli Public School** (62 2nd, May to September). The Waterfront Centre houses multimedia displays and the visitor centre has a freshwater fish aquarium, while the school maintains a heritage classroom. Admission to the museum is $6.

For shoppers, the compulsory Gimli stop is **H.P. Tergesen & Sons** (First and Centre), a retail store established in 1899 but now specializing in beachwear, books and street clothes. But the place for hand-made jewellery, pottery, and other artwork is the **Mermaid's Kiss Gallery** (85 Fourth), located a little off the beaten path but well worth it for fans of original art.

MUST SEE:
Gimli
Once the centre of Icelandic commercial fishing on Lake Winnipeg, now a mixed community with a laid-back resort vibe in the summer.

Gimli to Hecla

Eight km north of Gimli on PR 222, **Camp Morton Provincial Recreation Park**, a former Roman Catholic summer camp, has seven km of footpaths along the shore of Lake Winnipeg. The highlight is the formal gardens in the northern section of the small park. In winter, the Gimli Cross-Country Club maintains thirteen km of ski trails along both sides of the road.

There are province-run campgrounds at both Camp Morton and tiny **Hnausa Provincial Park**, located twenty-one km farther north on PR 222. Another eleven km up, the fishing village of **Riverton** (pop. 594) is worth a detour for a summer swim at underused **Sandy Bar Beach**, or for fried pickerel at **Doreen's** (32 Main, 378-5185), a homey lunch spot.

MUST SEE:
Hecla/Grindstone Provincial Park
An undervisited marine park near the Lake Winnipeg Narrows.

Hecla/Grindstone Provincial Park

Eleven km north of Riverton, Highway 8 veers east toward Lake Winnipeg and **Hecla/Grindstone Provincial Park**, an 1,084-square-km block of open water, islands, and peninsulas that comprises Manitoba's only real marine park. This is one of the best places in Manitoba for sea-kayak touring and sailing, and also offers a glimpse into the past at the fishing village of **Hecla**, one of the original New Iceland settlements.

The park can be divided into three components: **Grindstone Peninsula**, road-accessible **Hecla Island**, and a **wilderness area** encompassing Black Island, Deer Island, and dozens of smaller islets.

The mainland peninsula has a pair of cottage communities and public beaches at Blacks Point and Little Grindstone. Most visitors

Rocky Beach around Hecla.

Grassy Narrows Marsh on Hecla Island.

Charles Shilliday

Charles Shilliday

The lighthouse at Gull Harbour, in Hecla/Grindstone Provincial Park.

head to Hecla Island, crossing over the Grassy Narrows Causeway to **Grassy Narrows Marsh**, a waterfowl nesting area ringed by twenty-five km of hiking and bike trails along a system of dikes just outside the park gate. The two longest trails are the 10.5-km **Fox Loop** and the 7.5-km **Turtle Loop**, located on either side of Highway 8.

A little less than two km ahead, a wildlife-viewing tower offers a chance to spot moose in the distance. It's fourteen more km to **Hecla Village**, which resembles a Newfoundland fishing outport.

At the end of Highway 8, the resort of **Gull Harbour** has a campground, restaurant/hotel, and marina that serves as the launching point for sailing and sea-kayaking excursions. There are also two trails: the ten-km (return) **West Quarry Trail** and the shorter walk to the **Gull Harbour lighthouse**, which serves as Hecla's trademark.

Sea kayakers with experience on open water can spend three to five days circumnavigating the park's wilderness area, whose highlights include amazing numbers of pelicans and cormorants, a heron rookery at Cairine Island, limestone cliffs at the northern tip of Hecla Island, a secluded beach at the east end of Deer Island, and, best of all, the **Kasakeemeemisekak Islands**, a stunning archipelago on the east side of Lake Winnipeg. There are also several beaches along **Black Island**, the largest used for spiritual ceremonies by nearby Hollow Water First Nation. Obtain permission from the band before camping at this particular beach – it's the only one with a lawn.

The most awe-inspiring part of this wilderness trip is the way the landscape changes from the limestone-dominated Manitoba Lowlands at Gull Harbour to Prairie-Shield transition landscape on Black Island to rugged Canadian Shield granite in the Kasakeemeemisekak Islands, all in the span of twenty-five km.

There are dozens of natural harbours in this area for sailboats, but the waves are often too freaky for canoeists. Alternate water access is available on the east side of the lake at Manigotagan, Hollow Water First Nation, or the Rice River. See the *Canadian Shield* chapter for more info.

Lake Winnipeg Narrows

Branching off Highway 8 just before the turnoff to Hecla/Grindstone, gravel PR 234 snakes along the west side of Lake Winnipeg until it reaches a point where the lake's shallow southern basin meets the larger, wilder north. This is the **Lake Winnipeg Narrows**, a two-km gap prone to crazy currents, especially when winds force water from one basin to another through the narrow bottleneck.

PR 234 snakes for forty km before you reach **Beaver Creek Provincial Park**, the most northerly campground on Lake Winnipeg, which faces the top of Grindstone Peninsula across Washow Bay. Next up is the floatplane terminal of **Biscuit Harbour**, where canoeists heading to Atikaki Provincial Wilderness Park catch a one-way ride. Following soon after is the start of a winter ice road across the narrows to Bloodvein First Nation.

After ninety-three km, PR 234 ends in a ferry terminal where you can catch a ride to Bloodvein, Princess Harbour, or the quaint fishing community of **Matheson Island** (pop. 111), where the newish **Matheson Island Lodge** (www.eaglewatching.com) specializes in September and October bald-eagle-watching tours.

Central Interlake

Drive north through the middle of the Interlake, and you'll see why they call this area the Manitoba Lowlands. The forests and swamps are as flat as the Red River Valley, with only the occasional limestone crevice offering some relief. The chief attractions here are the 116-km Prime Meridian Trail, the world's largest agglomeration of snakes at Narcisse, and the rarely visited wildlands north of Peguis First Nation.

The main arteries are north-south Highways 7 and 17, and the east-west Highway 68.

Gunton to Arborg

Heading north from Winnipeg's hinterland on Highway 7, tiny **Gunton** used to be a daytrip destination for rock climbers, who practised in two old quarries south of the town. Most of the anchors have been removed from well-established climbing routes, so this is no place for novices to learn the art. Choose a Winnipeg indoor facility instead.

Continuing north, **Teulon** (pop. 1,058) offers the requisite **pioneer museum** (June to September, 2 p.m. to 4 p.m., $3), while **Komarno** is worth an ironic visit if you want to see a town named (in Ukrainian) after Manitoba's most reviled creature, the mosquito. A giant mosquito swings with the wind but, unfortunately, does not suck blood from other oversized statues, which means Oak Lake's giant ox and Onanole's elk are safe, for the time being.

Thirty-eight uneventful km later, **Meleb** sports the only culinary monument in Manitoba, a statue of three edible wild mushrooms prized by Polish and Ukrainian babas: the boletus, the morel, and the

Derelict structures, such as this church, are common sights in the central Interlake.

Charles Shilliday

honey mushroom. Highway 7 ends at **Arborg** (pop. 959), one of the few Interlake towns where Icelandic is still spoken as a first language. If a local tells you his name is Thor, he isn't messing with you.

Winnipeg Free Press

Every spring, about 70,000 garter snakes emerge from limestone caves in the Narcisse Wildlife Management Area – the largest collection of reptiles anywhere on earth.

MUST SEE:
Narcisse
Snake Pits
A spring-and-fall gathering place for 70,000 red-sided garter snakes, the largest agglomeration of reptiles on the planet.

Narcisse Snake Dens and Bender Hamlet

On warm, sunny days in late April and early May, more than 70,000 red-sided garter snakes wriggle out of underground pits in a corner of the **Narcisse Wildlife Management Area**. The four dens rank as the largest concentration of reptiles in the world, and are easily among of the planet's weirdest wildlife-watching destinations: Few ecotourism hotspots allow visitors actually to handle the creatures they observe.

Normally antisocial, the snakes have somehow learned to huddle together all winter in porous limestone caves in the middle of the Interlake. They emerge in the spring in massive mating balls, where – in a scene reminiscent of closing time at any human bar – dozens of males coil around a single female. Manitoba Conservation staff is on hand during the spring to show you how to pick up the non-poisonous serpents without harming them.

The snakes are absent from the dens during all summer, but return in September to gather at the mouths of the pits until frosty weather drives them back underground. Every Manitoban makes a visit to this spot at some point in their lives, and tourists are usually amazed – just make sure the reptiles are present before you make the drive. Call Manitoba Conservation at 945-6784 just to make sure.

To reach the snake dens from Winnipeg, take Highway 7 north to Teulon and take a left on Highway 17, following it north to Inwood, home to a statue of two giant garters. Continue north on Highway 17 for twenty-three km until you pass the town of Narcisse. The entrance to the snake dens is another six km ahead, clearly marked alongside the highway. Amazingly, there is no entrance fee.

Narcisse, contrary to popular belief, does not derive its name from the Greek legend of Narcissus. The village is actually named after Narcisse Leven, a resident of the ghost town of **Bender Hamlet**, the first Jewish farm colony in Manitoba.

In 1903, a group of Jewish immigrants led by Ukrainian emigre Jacob Bender settled in the central Interlake east of the present-day site of Narcisse and began farming and raising cattle. Despite the fact that Jews were lousy farmers – persecuted in Europe, most were not allowed to own land and never developed the skills required to live off it – the community lasted more than two decades. There was a synagogue, a school and at the town's peak, about 150 people.

Despite their modest success, the Jews of Bender Hamlet soon migrated into larger cities and towns, following the rest of the rural Jews on the Canadian Prairies. By 1927, Bender Hamlet was abandoned and its synagogue and other buildings later fell into disrepair.

All that remains today is a plaque, a cemetery and some foundations. From the village of Narcisse at Highway 17, take a gravel road due east across PR 231 for about 3.5 kilometres, where it will then swing south to the ghost town. A little farther south, the road will reconnect with PR 231.

Prime Meridian Trail

Manitoba's Prime Meridian has nothing to do with Greenwich, England: it refers to a colonial-era survey line that marks the centre of Manitoba and, via happenstance, an old railway bed that stretches up the middle of the Interlake.

After the rail tracks were removed, volunteer trail-builders established a 116-km-long hiking and fat-tire biking route called the **Prime Meridian Trail,** which runs from Grosse Isle, northwest of Winnipeg, up to the northern Interlake town of **Fisher Branch**. While the trail is extremely flat as well as disturbingly straight, it's mostly free from motorized vehicle traffic. It also crosses a diverse landscape that takes through-hikers from grain fields around Argyle to the marshes of Inwood Wildlife Management Area, and eventually into boreal forest.

Since the trail is relatively new, camping facilities along the route are sketchy, as some farmers allow camping on their lands and others don't. Trail-use fees are $5 for three days, payable in a drop-box at the trailhead in Grosse Isle.

North-Central Interlake

Driving north on Highway 17 past Highway 68, the swampy agricultural land that dominates the lower Interlake gives way to boreal forest and the occasional glacial ridge. Nine km north of Fisher Branch, a gravel road on the right marked "Interlake Forest Centre" leads to a pair of short trails: the one-km **Spruce Grove loop**, home to unusual orchids in late spring, and a wider three-km (return) walk along a rough road that leads east to an old marble quarry. Both trails are extremely buggy in mid-summer, so consider a June or September visit, if you're in the area.

Continuing north, Highway 17 becomes PR 224 at **Peguis First Nation** (see East Selkirk in *Central Plains & Valleys*, for the history) and follows the Fisher River to Lake Winnipeg at Fisher Bay. The bay's entire shoreline may one day encompass a new provincial wilderness park; Manitoba has granted interim protection to the east side of the bay and large Moose Island, while Fisher River First Nation – wisely recognizing the ecotourism potential – supports the inclusion of the west side, too.

Between Peguis and Fisher River, a side road heads north to Kinonjeoshtegon First Nation, passing between narrow Lake St. Andrew – home to bat hibernacula – and Lake St. George, site of the rarely visited **Lake St. George Provincial Park**. The Kinonjeoshtegon Nation hopes to make these lakes part of an even larger provincial wilderness park stretching west to the Mantagao River and north to existing Lake Winnipeg park reserves at Sturgeon and Kinwow bays.

A visitor centre and a modest trail-building effort would make this area very attractive to visitors from Winnipeg, only a 2.5-hour drive to the south. For now, however, there is no tourism infrastructure.

Lake Manitoba

At 4,624 square km, Lake Manitoba is the third-largest lake in the province and is second only to Lake Winnipeg in importance as a commercial fishery. The east shore of the lake is a cross-section of Interlake culture – there are cottage areas, Métis fishing towns, Icelandic farming communities, Cree nations, and a pair of modest provincial parks.

You can explore Lake Manitoba's 250-km east shoreline from Highway 6, which loosely parallels the lake as it heads northwest from Winnipeg.

Twin Lakes, St. Laurent, and Lundar

Heading northwest from Winnipeg through the towns of Grosse Isle, Warren, and Woodlands (see *Central Plains and Valleys*), Manitoba Highway 6 hits Lake Manitoba right above Lake Francis, an eastern extension of the Delta Marsh system. To take the scenic route here, exit Highway 6 at the town of Woodlands and drive north on PR 518 through the West Shoal Lake Provincial Wildlife Management Area, then due west on PR 415.

Winnipeg Free Press

Otherwise, keep going northwest on Highway 6 until you reach the turnoff to the cottage community of **Twin Lakes Beach**, which occupies a sandspit between Lake Francis and Lake Manitoba. This is one of the closest natural beaches to Winnipeg – only Matlock takes less time to reach, if getting the heck out of Winnipeg is a matter of urgency.

Just north of the Twin Lakes turnoff, the fishing town of **St. Laurent** is one of the few places on the Prairies where you can still hear Michif, the Métis language. While few Winnipeggers ever visit, the town's unique culture is on display at the National Museum of the American Indian, part of the Smithsonian Institute in Washington, DC, where Métis hunting and fishing implements – including the Bombardier, a motorized ice-fishing sled – are on display. The town celebrates its culture during **Métis Days**, held during the August long weekend.

Thirteen km northwest of St. Laurent, **Marshy Point Provincial Game Refuge** preserves a chunk of Lake Manitoba shoreline between the Métis settlement of Oak Point and **Lundar Beach Provincial Recreation Park**, the latter accessible via PR 419 from the Icelandic town of **Lundar**. The refuge sees about 10,000 geese per year, while its shoreline reputedly makes for decent sea kayaking.

The provincial park, meanwhile, has a beach, a campground, and a three-km hiking trail. Lundar itself has a **pioneer museum** in a former railway station, and on Friday afternoons from July to mid-September, a **farmer's market** near an oversized statue of a Canada goose.

Winnipeg Free Press

Above and opposite: Fishers from the mostly Metis community of St. Laurent use motorsleds called bombardiers to haul their catch off the surface of Lake Manitoba.

Lake Manitoba Narrows

While Lake Winnipeg's blustery narrows are only traversable by ferry boat and winter ice road, you can drive right across the narrow strait dividing Lake Manitoba's northern and southern basin. Highway 68 crosses **the Narrows** sixty km west of Highway 6, after exiting about ten km north of the community of Eriksdale.

The Narrows is a fishing hotspot, usually packed with vacationing families on summer long weekends. But the **Narrows Campground and Lake Manitoba Narrows Lodge** (www.narrowslodge.com or 768-2749, $75-$298 for rooms) are considerably less busy midweek.

Aside from fishing, the sole attraction is **Manitou Island**, a small chunk of land just north of the Narrows Bridge that may have provided the province with its name. To some First Nations, pounding waves on the north side of the island evoked the sound of Gitchi Manitou, the "Great Spirit" of pantheistic Aboriginal cosmology, thereby giving the lake – and the entire province, by extension – its monicker.

About forty km north of Eriksdale, **Ashern** is a haven to motorists, as the Petro-Canada outlet is the last 24-hour gas station on Highway 6 before the road gets extremely lonely on its way north. The small community also sports a – yep, you guessed it – pioneer museum in the former CNR station, and holds a rodeo every September long weekend.

Twelve km to the north, PR 237 heads west from the town of Moosehorn to **Watchorn Provincial Park**, a seasonal campground at Watchorn Bay, on Lake Manitoba.

Steep Rock

Bartley Kives

Limestone is the official rock of the Interlake, and there's no better place to see it than the town of **Steep Rock**, a small Lake Manitoba hamlet blessed with stunning cliffs that wind along the shore for kilometres. About 10,000 years of wave action and winter ice have carved the cliffs into ledges, seats, and other eroded shapes that make this shoreline an interesting place to stop on the long drive north to Thompson or elsewhere in Manitoba. As a daytrip destination, it's a little out of the way – Steep Rock is 210 km from Winnipeg's perimeter.

To reach the cliffs from Highway 6, drive five km north past Grahamdale and turn left at PR 239. Follow the road into town and then down to a government dock, where you can leave your car for walks along the shoreline.

The cliffs at Steep Rock are comprised of the dominant substance in the Manitoba Lowlands – limestone, which easily erodes into cliffs, caves and other unusual geological formations.

One warning, though: There's nothing much to do besides check out the cliffs. There are campgrounds just northeast of the town, as well as at Fairford, twenty-three km up Highway 6, at the entrance to Little Saskatchewan First Nation.

If you plan to continue north toward The Pas or Thompson, take notice of your fuel gauge. St. Martin Junction has the last gas station for 178 km, as the next section of Highway 6 is the loneliest stretch of asphalt in the entire province.

Beaches and Interlake Daytrips

1. Reach the Beach

Time to go: Mid-June to late August.
Prerequisite: The ability to chill, a long-lost art in North America.
Highlights: Sun, sand, solitude – and some diversions along the way and back.
The goods: As early as you can stand it, head north from Lagimodière Boulevard on Highway 59 in an effort to beat the beach-going traffic. When that clearly becomes futile, quickly exit Highway 59 at PR 213 – also known as Garven Road – and drive east to PR 212. Take a left, and drive a few minutes north to the Immaculate Conception Ukrainian Greek Catholic Church and the colourful Grotto of Our Lady of Lourdes. Marvel at the effort put into the grotto, then continue north to Highway 44, and east to Garson for brunch at Harvest Moon Café.

All daytrips start and end at Winnipeg.

After lunch, continue east on Highway 44 to Highway 12. Make a left and take the long, scenic route north to the beaches, crossing the idyllic Brokenhead River farmland.

When you hit Highway 59 again, you have a choice – straight to ultra-mellow Beaconia Beach, right to the boisterous, beautiful people at Grand Beach, or left to the middle-ground compromise at Patricia Beach? Whichever way you turn, it's only minutes to the sand, and you have the option of changing your mind. Spend the entire day doing nothing but sleeping, reading, removing grains of sand from your sandwiches, and maybe swimming, assuming anyone actually does that at the beach any more.

On the way home, take Highway 59 south to the 44 then west across the Red River into Lockport (see *Central Plains and Valleys*).
Driving time: 2:30.
Total time commitment: Most of a day.
Fees: None at Beaconia. A Manitoba Parks Pass is required for Patricia and Grand Beach Provincial Parks.

2. Take the Lake

Time to go: Late April to mid-September.
Prerequisite: An appreciation of folk art and smoked fish – and no irrational fear of snakes.
Highlights: Shopping for art, scarfing down smoked goldeye, going for strolls along the Lake Winnipeg shoreline, and – if it's late April/early May or mid-September – a visit to the incredible agglomeration of red-sided garter snakes at the Narcisse Wildlife Management Area.

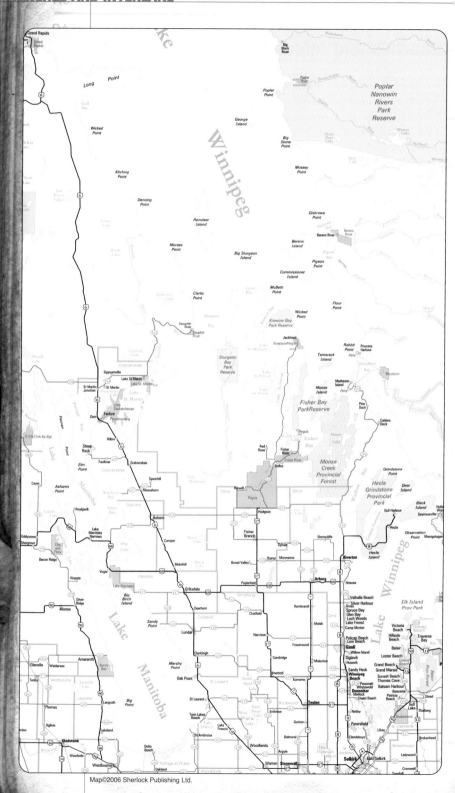

Map©2006 Sherlock Publishing Ltd.

The goods: From McPhillips Street, drive north on Highway 8 for about nine km, then quickly exit on PR 230 to avoid the boredom of four-lane blacktop. Continue north to Highway 9 and keep driving north about forty km to PR 232, exiting at the turnoff to Matlock. Turn right and slowly amble along the beachfront road through Matlock, Whytewold, Ponemah, and, finally Winnipeg Beach, stopping anywhere along the way that advertises local art or smoked fish.

Map©2006 Sherlock Publishing Ltd.

At Winnipeg Beach, find the lakefront, park your vehicle, and check out the boardwalk shops, paying special attention to Fishly Gallery if you're a fan of sculptures. Grab a cup of loose-leaf tea to go at The Breakwater, check out the beachfront, then continue driving north on Highway 9, still keeping your eyes peeled for private art studios or smoked fish retailers, assuming you haven't found the goldeye you desire yet.

When you reach Gimli, head for the harbour, park the car, and hope the lunch rush isn't too busy at the Beach Boy. Order the pickerel – otherwise, there's no point being in Gimli. After the last morsel of flesh is in your belly, check out Mermaid's Kiss Gallery for more regional art, shop for beachwear at Tergesen's, and maybe learn a little about the town's Scandinavian heritage at the New Iceland Heritage Museum's Waterfront Centre or Harbourfront units. Once you've had your fill of Gimli, continue north along the Lake Winnipeg shoreline on PR 222 for about nine km to Camp Morton. Go for a lakeside stroll to check out the gardens – and burn off that breaded fish.

Back in your vehicle, head south barely a km to PR 324 and drive west to Highway 8. If it's mid-May to early September, turn south as quickly as possible and call it a day. But if it's late April, early May or the middle of September – and reasonably sunny outside – only drive south for eight km to PR 231, because this is the prime viewing time to see Narcisse's garter snakes. On PR 231, head west to Fraserwood at Highway 7, drive north three km, and then west again on the gravel portion of PR 231 to Highway 17. Turn north and drive about six more km to the entrance to the Narcisse Snake Pits. Walk the entire circuit, stopping at each of four snake pits to witness the largest collection of reptiles on the planet. Return home to Winnipeg via Highway 17, Highway 7, and – if you're jonesing for caffeine – a slight detour on PR 236 to Stonewall for some java at Timothy Beans.

From here, take Highway 67 and then Highway 7 to reach the city.

Driving time: 1:45 for the shorter option; 2:30 when you include Narcisse.

Total time commitment: A full day.

Fees: None.

C anadians have a distorted view of southwestern Manitoba, thanks to the unfortunate
placement of the Trans-Canada Highway. For
the most part, Highway 1 crosses some of the most
yawn-inducing terrain in the province, which makes
for great long-distance trucking but lousy sightseeing.

The gently rolling prairie south of the Trans-Canada is way more
interesting, thanks to the winding Souris River Valley, the western
reaches of the Pembina Valley, forests in Spruce Woods and Turtle
Mountain provincial parks, a patch of sand dunes, and a couple of
biggish bodies of water, including birdwatching spots Oak Lake,
Pelican Lake, and Whitewater Lake.

North of the Trans-Canada, the Yellowhead Highway marks the
transition between Prairie farmland and the more rugged parkland
on the approach to Riding Mountain National Park.

And smack in the middle of the region is the second-largest
community in Manitoba – Brandon, an underappreciated city where
even the residents don't seem to recognize what they have.

Getting out to this region from Winnipeg usually demands an
overnight, but you can hit certain destinations as a daytrip if you're
really motivated.

Opposite: The
suspension
bridge at Souris, a
quaint town of
1,700, southwest
of Brandon.

Spruce Woods Provincial Park

A remnant from an earlier, wetter time when forests covered southwestern Manitoba, **Spruce Woods Provincial Park** is a 250-square-
km island of greenery in the middle of Prairie farmland. This popular
park is famous for the **Spirit Sands**, a small patch of active sand
dunes that stand out spectacularly against the surrounding parkland. But it also encompasses a particularly scenic stretch of the
Assiniboine River Valley, and one of the best long biking and
cross-country skiing routes in the province, the **Epinette Creek/
Newfoundland Trail system**.

Located east of Highway 5 between the Trans-Canada and
Highway 2, Spruce Woods is a patch of forest and grassland with
sandy soil that used to mark the bottom – and later, edge – of
glacial Lake Agassiz. The preponderance of sand prevented the
area from being developed in the late 1800s, when the rest of

southwestern Manitoba was getting ploughed to shreds. Spruce Woods formally became a park in 1964.

Today, the vast majority of visitors head straight to the southwest corner of the park and the nine-km **Spirit Sands trail system**, which offers easy access to not just the fantastic dunes, but also an unusual colour-shifting sinkhole called the **Devil's Punchbowl** and a nice bend of the Assiniboine River Valley. The trailhead is located on the west side of Highway 5, just north of the river. Given the fragility of the landscape, bikes, ATVs, and off-trail hiking are not allowed, but that doesn't stop idiots from occasionally scarring the dune faces.

Charles Shilliday

Night sky over the prairies.

On the south side of the River, the only developed portion of the park houses a campground and swimming hole at an oxbow called **Kiche Manitou Lake**, a replica **Pine Fort** with a restaurant and a **Visitor Centre** (open May to September) with a bookshop and museum. There are also two short walking trails: the 1.4-km **Isputinaw Trail** is just east of the campground; meanwhile, the 1.2-km **Springridge Trail**, four km to the northeast at Steels Ferry Overlook, offers views of the Assiniboine River Valley.

Kiche Manitou Campground also marks the start of a ten-km section of the Trans-Canada Trail that heads to an equestrian campground and a network of dirt tracks used by horseback riders and hikers in the southeast corner of the park. The highlight of this area is an unusual, bald-faced ridge called **the Hogsback**, about five km east.

North of the Assiniboine, a 1.5-km interpretive trail called **Marshs Lake** explains the formation of oxbow lakes, the crescent-shaped sloughs created when meandering prairie rivers forge a more direct course. It's located about one km north of the Spirit Sands trailhead.

Another six km north, just outside the park boundary, you'll find the entrance to the **Epinette Creek/Newfoundland trail system**, one of the few Manitoba provincial park loops to offer hike-in, bike-in, and ski-in camping. This is a fantastic trail. There are five campsites and four warm-up shelters along the 42-km route, which traverses sandy hills, grasslands, forests, and two ravines. The first ten km of the trail are okay for hiking, but the entire route is more fun for mountain bikes – you can whip through here in four to six gruelling hours. Just be prepared to push your bike up the occasional patch of deep sand. **Jackfish Cabin**, at the far end of the loop, may be reserved as a winter shelter for cross-country skiers – call 834-8800 after Oct. 1.

During the winter, the close end of the Epinette trail system makes for good day-skiing and there are twenty-five more km of cross-country loops nearby. The **Seton Cross Country Ski Trails** depart from a trailhead on the west side of Highway 5, one km south of the Epinette turnoff, while the **Yellow Quill Trails** are on the east

Ruth Bonneville/Winnipeg Free Press

side, another two clicks down the road. The northeast and southern sections of the park are devoted to snowmobiles.

In addition to hiking, biking, skiing, sledding, and horseback riding, you can also see Spruce Woods from the water. The lazy **Assiniboine River** is navigable for canoes and kayaks from the spring snowmelt until the end of the summer. Paddlers usually put in east of the park at PR 340 or at Stockton Ferry and spend two to four days on the river, taking out at Highway 34 east of the park. There are two established canoe campsites inside the park itself, one northeast of Kiche Manitou, the other near the Hogsback. The only annoyance is drinking water, as pesticides and other farm chemicals make Assiniboine water disgusting, even when filtered.

Visitors to Spruce Woods are subject to the usual fees: $5 per vehicle for a three-day pass, or $20 for a seasonal pass covering all Manitoba provincial parks.

Some people liken the Spirit Sands of Spruce Woods to a desert, but the region is actually far too moist.

Around Spruce Woods

Immediately to the west of the provincial park, **Spruce Woods Provincial Forest** has more interesting hills that few people ever get to see: The Canadian Forces out of Shilo use this area as a training ground and artillery range. If you think you hear shells going off while you're in the nearby park, you're not imagining it.

Charles Shilliday

The largest town outside the park is **Carberry** (pop. 1,513), Manitoba's self-proclaimed potato capital, located ten km north of the boundary on Highway 5 near the Trans-Canada Highway. Get a post-trail burger at **Ray's Diner** (43 Main, 834-2174), or check out two relatively interesting small museums. **Carberry Plains Museum** (520 Fourth, mid-June through August, 1 p.m. to 6 p.m.) has exhibits honouring pioneer wildlife painter Norman Criddle (see *Criddle/Vane Homestead*) and former resident Tommy Douglas, the architect of Canada's publicly funded healthcare system. The even tinier **Seton Centre** (116 Main, June through August, afternoons only) is dedicated to the life of British-born wildlife illustrator, naturalist, and Aboriginal rights activist Ernest Thompson Seton, who spent his early twenties in the Carberry area. The Spirit Sands inspired his life's work.

Beware of giant grasshoppers around the Criddle/Vane Homestead Provincial Heritage Park.

Southwest of the park, the last remaining river ferry in Manitoba carries vehicles across the Assiniboine northeast of the hamlet of **Stockton**, itself twelve km west and four km north of the Spruce Woods gateway town of **Glenboro**. There's a statue of a camel at Glenboro, in honour of the Spirit Sands.

Charles Shilliday

Northeast of the park at **Austin** (Trans-Canada and Highway 34), the **Manitoba Agricultural Museum** is a thirty-two-hectare shrine to farm implements, vintage tractors, and the like. Located three km south of the Trans-Canada, it's open daily from May through September from 9 a.m. to 5 p.m. Admission is $5. The museum grounds also sport a campground and are used to host the **Austin Threshermans Reunion**, a large fair held the last week of July.

Horse team at the Threshermen's Reunion at Austin, a big community along the Trans-Canada Highway.

Southeast of the park, **Holland** (Highways 2 and 34) is home to the modest **Tiger Hills Art Gallery** and the **Abbey of Our Lady of the Prairies**, a community of monks that moved here from St. Norbert in 1978 to get away from Winnipeg's urban sprawl. Their current residence is a modernist concrete structure with a small gift shop up front. Hours vary, but these are monks after all – if they wanted a constant stream of visitors, they'd have stayed in Winnipeg.

Brandon

Manitoba's second-largest city, **Brandon** (pop. 39,716), is a lot like Winnipeg in that the locals seem to be unusually hard on their hometown. Built up on the Assiniboine River Valley where Highway 10 and the Trans-Canada meet, the small city with the big inferiority complex is particularly gorgeous in September, when the leaves on more than 20,000 elms begin to turn. Brandon also makes an excellent base of operations for a weekend exploration of southwestern Manitoba.

MUST SEE: Brandon
Manitoba's second-largest city is a great base to explore nearby attractions like a World War II air force training museum, a snake-alligator-menagerie, and the Brandon Hills, home to the best mountain-biking in western Manitoba.

Brandon's similarities to Winnipeg are numerous, starting with the city's beginnings as a railway boomtown in the 1880s, a long period of stagnation in the twentieth century, and a relatively recent period of renewed growth. Brandon also has its own urban-doughnut problem, as the handsome, 100-year-old buildings of its turn-of-the-twentieth-century downtown seem deserted at night, when Brandonites flock to the franchises and malls on the suburban fringe of 18th Street, the city's main north-south artery, and Victoria Avenue, the primary east-west route.

Brandon's most attractive feature is the river valley, which runs east-west through the northern part of town. The **Assiniboine Riverbank Trail System**, a seventeen-km network of mostly paved footpaths, lines both sides of the river and connects to both downtown and small **Eleanor Kidd Gardens** (18th Street at the river). A good place to begin a walk is the **Riverbank Discovery Centre** (545 Conservation Drive), where you can pick up a trail map and tourism info for the whole region.

It's also worth a stroll through the city's picturesque inner core, a ten-block-wide rectangle bounded by 18th Street, Pacific Avenue, First Street, and Victoria Avenue. While the old residential streets are quaint, the most cosmopolitan stretch of downtown Brandon is **Rosser Avenue**, where you'll find some global craft retailers, the Town Centre mall, and the adjacent **Art Gallery of Southwestern Manitoba** (710 Rosser), which specializes in contemporary Prairie art. It's open Monday through Saturday from 10 a.m. to 6 p.m. Admission is free.

Rosser Avenue also boasts one of the best pubs in Manitoba, the **Double Decker** (943 Rosser), which has a good selection of

Suzanne Braun

brews on tap and a large bar menu that extends beyond spicy wings into bison-burger and steak-and-kidney-pie territory. Two doors down, steakhouse **Olivier's** (935 Rosser, 727-3333) has a knack for Greek-style spareribs and lamb chops, while the Caribbean-influenced **Rhapsody Grill** (926 Rosser, 727-7781) reputedly has the most ambitious kitchen in the city. For dessert, **Scarlatti's** (908 Rosser, 757-2820) serves latte and Belgian chocolates late into the evening – a rarity for downtown Brandon – and occasionally hosts

performances by students at Brandon University's respected School of Music. Other downtown eateries beloved by the locals include **Romana Pizza** (39 Ninth Street, 727-8486) and **Alessio's Pasta** (121 10th Street, 728-4804), the latter famous for enormous portions.

The decommissioned Brandon Mental Health Centre, which looms over Brandon like a Gothic asylum out of a Batman comic.

Just west of downtown, the **B. J. Hales Museum of Natural History** (270 18th, 727-7307) houses about 500 animal, plant, and geological specimens in the lower level of Brandon University's Richardson Library complex. It's free, but open only on weekdays from 1:30 p.m. to 4:30 p.m. There's also the usual pioneer museum: **Daly House** (122 18th Street, 727-1722), the former residence of Brandon's first mayor, open seven days a week from July to September and Tuesday through Saturday the rest of the year. Hey, some people like this pioneer stuff.

South of downtown, the **Keystone Centre** dominates five long blocks of 18th Street with exhibition grounds, curling rinks, and the 5,000-seat Keystone Arena, home of the Western Hockey League's **Brandon Wheat Kings**, the province's biggest spectator-sports draw outside of Winnipeg. Tickets to see the junior-aged Wheaties, who play from October to March, range from $6 to $14 at 726-3555 or www.ticketmaster.ca.

In late March and into early April, the Keystone Centre hosts the week-long **Royal Manitoba Winter Fair**, Manitoba's largest agricultural and equestrian show. On the other end of cultural spectrum, the **Brandon Folk Music and Art Festival** sets up on the centre's grounds over the third weekend in July. The centre also sports a Canad Inns hotel and the attached **Roadhouse**, one of the two most popular nightspots in the city.

The other leading watering hole is **Houston's**, the barn-shaped country bar at the Royal Oak Inn (3130 Victoria), on the west side of Brandon. Also worth checking out in this western corner of the city is **Forbidden Flavours** (Victoria and 34th), a locally owned coffeehouse and ice-cream franchise.

Suzanne Braun

Unfortunately, the most fascinating attraction in Brandon is all but ignored by the local tourism authorities and all-but-impossible to visit. The decommissioned **Brandon Mental Health Centre**, originally known as the Asylum for the Insane, looms over the northeast portion of city like a Gothic institution out of a Batman comic, surrounded by chains and No Trespassing signs. This is the place where an infamous psychiatrist named Ewan Cameron, later reviled for experimentally administering LSD to patients in Montreal, began to develop controversial ideas about "re-creating" entire personalities from scratch. Today, the four main buildings, built between 1912 and 1932, can be viewed from a distance, along First Street between the Low Road to Shilo and Ross Avenue.

Thanks to its location at the confluence of two major highways, Brandon has more than twenty hotels and motels, most located inside the city on 18th Street or just north along the Trans-Canada Highway. There are also three campgrounds and four bed-and-breakfast options, the most convenient being **Casa Maley** (1605 Victoria, 728-0812), an early-twentieth-century heritage home located within walking distance of downtown Brandon.

Around Brandon

The biggest bonus of visiting Brandon is the close proximity of great cycling in the Brandon Hills and a number of idiosyncratic attractions around the city. The following destinations are within fifty km of Brandon, which translates into no more than a half-hour drive.

North of Brandon

Two minutes north of Brandon, World War II buffs will dig the **Commonwealth Air Training Plan Museum**, a monument to the days when air force pilots and support crews from around the English-speaking world trained in the Brandon area before heading off to Europe to battle the Nazis. The museum boasts vintage aircraft and a pair of lovingly curated galleries, but the chapel up front really

Old and new come together in a Dakota Sioux community.

drives home how different the wartime era was from today: On display are samples of terse telegrams informing parents and spouses of the loss of their loved ones. It's chilling stuff.

Charles Shilliday

The museum is housed inside Hangar 1 at Brandon Municipal Airport, accessible from Highway 10 just north of town. It's open daily from 10 a.m. to 4 p.m. Admission is $5. In the early 1990s, the airport and some of the planes from the museum served as the backdrop for *For the Moment*, Australian movie star Russell Crowe's first North American feature.

Charles Shilliday

Thirty minutes northwest of Brandon, **Rivers Provincial Park** sits on Lake Wahtopanah, a dam-created reservoir on the Little Saskatchewan River. The small park has a campground and a beach, though you might want to think twice about a dip if you're susceptible to swimmer's itch. You can walk from the beach to the nearby town of Rivers (pop. 1,119) along three-km **Aspen Walking Trail**, which passes by a series of railway-excavated gravel pits.

In late April and early May, when water levels are high, Rivers Provincial Park also makes a good starting point for a thirty-seven-km **paddle down the Little Saskatchewan River**, which drops 100 metres and passes through many sets of Class I rapids before it meets the Assiniboine River northwest of Brandon. Again, Buchanan's canoeing guide (see *Selected Sources*) has the goods on this trip.

Shilo and Wawanesa

East of Brandon on PR 457, also known as the Low Road to Shilo, **Westman Reptile Gardens** houses a surprisingly large collection of snakes, iguanas, lizards, crocodiles, turtles, and other cold-blooded creatures inside a nondescript bunker of a building. Proprietor Dave Shelvey took care of unwanted reptiles for years before opening this menagerie in 2005. His collection is as impressive as it is hard to find – heading east on PR 457 from Brandon, drive south on Brown Road then east on Thompson Road. Keep your eyes peeled for a sign on the right. If you hit Wagglesprings Road, you've gone too far east. Hours are 10 a.m. to 8 p.m., Monday through Saturday, and noon to 5 p.m. Sundays. Admission is $5.

One km to the east, PR 457 meets PR 340 and slides into the town of **Shilo** and **Canadian Forces Base Shilo**, once a home away from home for the German military, now a barracks-cum-blasting ground for the Canadian Forces. While most of the base is off-limits to civilians, armchair warriors can get up close to big guns at the newly renovated **Royal Canadian Artillery Museum** (PR 340 at the base), the largest collection of its kind in Canada, open weekdays all year from 9 a.m. to 5 p.m. and also summer weekends from 1-5 p.m. Admission is by donation.

Ten km south of Shilo, **Criddle/Vane Homestead Provincial Heritage Park** is a monument to one of Manitoba's most colourful pioneer clans – and when I say colourful, I actually mean downright weird. In 1882, British businessman Percy Criddle immigrated to Manitoba with his wife Alice (Mrs. Criddle), his German mistress, Elise (Mrs. Vane), and a total of nine offspring. The family patriarch was a less-than-fantastic farmer, but the women and children made the best of a probably awkward situation, somehow thriving on the land and excelling at sports and sciences. The Criddles even built their own golf course and tennis court. One of the sons, Norman Criddle, eventually became a celebrated entomologist. The

Winter on the Little Saskatchewan River northwest of Brandon.

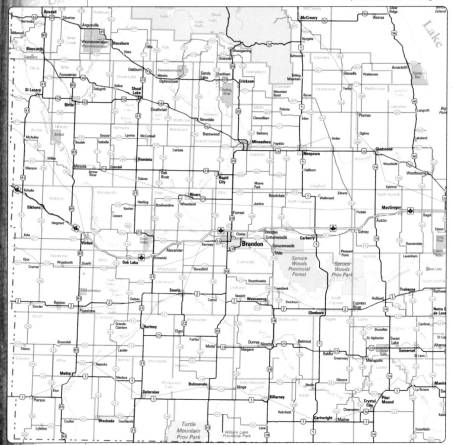

Map©2006 Sherlock Publishing Ltd.

All daytrips start and end at Winnipeg.

Southwestern Daytrips

1. Yellowhead and Shoulders

Time to go: May to August – you'll need a lot of daylight to pack this all in.

Prerequisites: A lot of stamina and time-management skills.

Highlights: Small-town Manitoba civility, a blip of a trip through Brandon, captive bison and anacondas, and an evening visit to Manitoba's most famous day hike.

The goods: From Portage Avenue, go west on the Trans-Canada. Head quickly west to Portage la Prairie to dispense with the boring portion of the drive. Enter the town, load up on old-school bacon 'n' eggs at the Wright Spot, if you haven't eaten breakfast, and continue through town and along the Trans-Can to Sidney. Congratulations: the dull getting-there portion of the drive is over.

At Sidney, turn right on PR 352 and follow the gravel road northwest along the Arden Ridge, part of a glacial end-moraine, past the hamlets of Firdale and Edrans to Highway 16, the Yellowhead Highway. Turn left and drive about ten minutes into Neepawa, stopping in at Prairie Seasons Bakery for organic munchies to picnic on at Rotary Park, just south of town, where the geese will eye up your snack. Check out Manawaka Gallery and Margaret Laurence House, if that sort of thing turns your crank.

From Neepawa, continue west fifteen more minutes to Minnedosa. Drive down into town and then get on PR 262 to visit the walking trails and bison compound right below the dam on the Little Saskatchewan. Return to Highway 16 and drive west two km to Highway 10, where you'll turn south and make the slow, twenty-minute descent to Brandon. Enter the city along 1st Street, checking out the Gothic structures of the unused Brandon Mental Health Centre on your left before you descend "The Hill." At the bottom, turn right and make your way to the Riverbank Discovery Centre, where you'll park your vehicle and walk east along the Assiniboine River, up over the footbridge, and into Brandon's downtown. Check out the Art Gallery of Southwestern Manitoba on Rosser Avenue, then pop into Scarlatti's for a latte, or the Double Decker pub for something a little more substantial. If you're starving, Alessio's is a better choice. Continue west along Rosser until you reach 18th Street, then walk north back across the river, shortcutting at Eleanor Kidd Gardens, if you see a river taxi.

Get back in your vehicle and then take PR 457, also known as the Low Road to Shilo, east for about ten minutes to Brown Road, then south to Thompson Road and west to the cleverly hidden Westman Reptile Gardens, Manitoba's largest collection of cold-blooded creatures outside the provincial legislature. When you've had your fill, continue west to PR 340, then drive south a couple of minutes to Canadian Forces Base Shilo, where the recently renovated Royal Canadian Artillery Museum has all kinds of big guns.

After the military museum, head south on PR 340 for about ten km until you see the exit to St. Albans and Criddle/Vane Homestead Provincial Heritage Park, the former home of one the province's strangest pioneer families. Check out the interpretive info and, if there's still plenty of daylight, follow one of the two short trails.

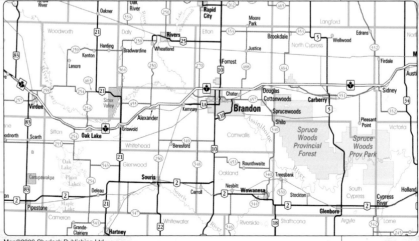

Map©2006 Sherlock Publishing Ltd.

Continue south on PR 340 to Wawanesa, where you can learn about suffragette Nellie McClung at Sipiweske Museum and pop into Kurt's Schnitzel House for flat-pounded chicken or pork. But if there's only a little bit of daylight left, hurry east along Highway 2 to Highway 5 and then north into Spruce Woods Provincial Park for a pre-dusk walk to the Spirit Sands, where the dunes look spectacular in the late-day light.

Return to your vehicle before dark, drive north to Carberry, and head east on the short but pretty PR 351. This will take you back to Sidney and the hour-long return drive east along the Trans-Canada. Feel free to omit any of these pit stops for the sake of getting home at a reasonable time.

Driving time: About 5:30 for the whole loop.

Total time commitment: A very long day.

Fees: $5 for Westman Reptile Gardens, an optional donation for the Artillery Museum, and a Manitoba Park Pass for Criddle/Vane Homestead and Spirit Sands.

2. Pembina Valley West and Turtle Mountain

Time to go: May to August.

Prerequisites: More stamina, and a keen eye for hawks and water-fowl. Bring binoculars!

Highlights: The best tiny museum in Manitoba, a pair of short hikes, an idealistic monument to Canada-US unity, and no less than four crossings of the Pembina Valley.

The goods: From McGillivray Boulevard, head west on Highway 2 for a flat, eventless hour until you climb the Manitoba Escarpment and reach Holland. Pay a brief visit to the monks at the Abbey of Our Lady of the Prairies – they have a gift shop – and drive south on Highway 34, crossing the Pembina Valley just south of Swan Lake First Nation and continuing to Highway 3.

Drive southwest to Pilot Mound and quickly exit at PR 253. The actual mound that inspired the town, a former Sioux-Métis battle-ground, is located north of the road, which continues west through the Pembina Valley, along the shore of Rock Lake, and back into the valley again before ending at Highway 18.

Drive south on Highway 18 to Killarney, popping in at the Danish Mermaid if you have a sugar craving. Continue south to PR 341 and then head west on the gravel road, keeping the binoculars handy to spot birds along myriad prairie potholes.

After about a quarter-hour, turn south to William Lake Provincial Park and hike the six-km Turtle's Back loop to get a look at Turtle Mountain. Return to your vehicle, double back to PR 341, drive a couple of minutes west to Highway 10, then head south about twelve more minutes to the International Peace Gardens. Make sure there's nothing illicit in the car – e.g. marijuana, unregistered guns, your subscription to *Al Qaeda Weekly* – and cross the Canadian border to enter the gardens, where the chief attraction is the central walkway with the gardens, Peace Tower, and September 11 monument.

Return to your car, stop at Canadian customs, and then head back up Highway 10 to Highway 3. If you love birds, make a short detour

Map©2006 Sherlock Publishing Ltd.

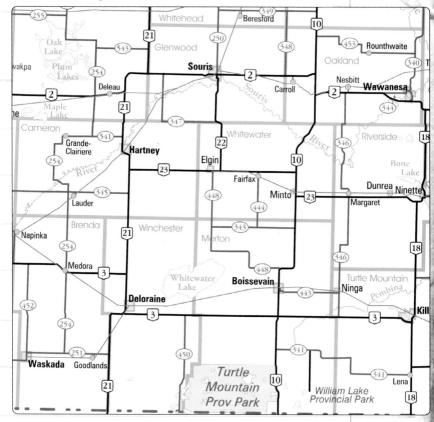

west to Whitewater Lake to check out the marsh, which is actually better to visit at dusk or dawn. If you're not a waterfowl fan, continue north to Boissevain and peruse the Moncur Gallery's collection of pre-European Aboriginal artifacts.

Continue north on Highway 10 to Highway 23, drive east about five minutes to Margaret, and drive north on PR 346 until you cross the Souris River. Pull into a trailhead on the right side of the highway and walk down into the valley to check out the Souris Riverbend. When you return to your vehicle, double back to Highway 23 and drive east through the Pembina Valley once more at Ninette, stopping to check out pelicans and – if you're lucky – sandhill cranes.

Continue east on Highway 23 all the way to the 3, where you have a choice of returning to Winnipeg three ways – north to Carman then northeast on Highway 3; east to Morris and then north on Pembina Highway; or, if there's still daylight, go east only until PR 422, then head north Rosenort, east to McTavish, and north on PR 330 to Winnipeg via Osborne, Domain, and La Salle.

Driving time: About 6:30 for the whole loop.

Total time commitment: One very, very long day.

Fees: $10 for the International Peace Gardens, $2 per person for the Moncur Gallery, and a Manitoba Parks Pass for William Lake Provincial Park.

Criddle/Vane descendents maintained a presence at the hamlet of Aweme until 1960. In 2004, their land became a provincial park with a pair of interpretive trails, located east of PR 340.

About 12 km farther south, the village of **Wawanesa** (PR 340 at Highway 2) is familiar to most Manitobans in name only, thanks to Wawanesa Life Insurance, a multinational corporation founded here in 1896. With a population of 516, the town hasn't grown along with its financial offspring, but the 1903 Wawanesa Mutual building now houses **Sipiweske Museum** (102 Fourth), whose subjects include the Criddle/Vane Family and early feminist Nellie McClung, who lived

Charles Shilliday

in the area before moving to Winnipeg and winning women the right to vote in Manitoba. The museum is open daily in July and August from 1 p.m. to 9 p.m., with an hour off for dinner. Admission is a loonie. A couple of doors down, **Kurt's Schnitzel House** (123 4th Street, open Wednesday to Sunday) is the best place to snag a meal – the German military may have left nearby Shilo in 2001, but the Teutonic food remains.

Sipiweske Museum in Wawanesa.

Brandon Hills

Due south of Brandon, some of the best mountain biking in Manitoba – and good cross-country skiing, too – can be found in **Brandon Hills Provincial Wildlife Management Area**, a glacial ridge that looms over the surrounding prairie. There are forty-five km of mostly unmarked trails, ranging in difficulty from easy loops on well-maintained single track to technical sections with plenty of challenging switchbacks and annoying deadfall.

The best place to hike in the hills, meanwhile, is near the southeast corner of the ridge, where the exposed hilltop offers long views of southwestern Manitoba. To reach the main ski-and-bike trailhead, drive south from Brandon on Highway 10 to the intersection of PR 349 but turn left on the gravel road opposite. Drive about three km east, turn right, and drive about 1.5 km up the ridge. Another left turn will lead to the Brandon Hills trailhead parking lot.

Souris

Southwest of Brandon, **Souris** (pop. 1,683) is one of the prettier towns in western Manitoba. The main attractions are the 182-metre **Swinging Bridge**, Canada's longest suspension bridge, and **Victoria Park**, a large green space with free-roaming peacocks, six km of walking trails, a campground, and access to hour-long cruises down the Souris River on a modified barge.

MUST SEE: Souris
A quaint small town on a bend in the Souris River, with Canada's longest suspension bridge swinging across the river valley – and an oddball rock-collectors' pit.

Between the park and the west side of the bridge, **Hillcrest Museum** ups the usual pioneer-museum ante with an entomological oddity: a collection of 5,000 (quite dead) butterflies from all over the world. The museum is open Canada Day to Labour Day from 10 a.m. to 6 p.m. Admission is $2. The nearby **Plum Heritage Church Museum** (140 1st, also Canada Day to Labour Day) offers just what you'd expect in a town with peacocks – a **Victorian tearoom**.

Charles Shilliday

The oddest attraction in town is the **Souris Agate Pits** (Highway 2 at PR 250), an open pit with precious stones scattered amidst the sand and grit. Rock collectors show up in the summer with buckets and start feeling their way through the gravel. You too can be a rock-hound, after paying a pit permit – $10 per vehicle – at The Rock Shop (8 1st), which also sells precious gems and fossils.

To reach Souris from Brandon, drive south on Highway 10 and then west on Highway 2.

Fog rises over Souris in morning.

Pembina Valley West

Charles Shilliday

Carved out of southern Manitoba by a torrent of glacial meltwater, the Pembina River Valley snakes across southern Manitoba along a course roughly parallel to the US border. The eastern portion of this valley, described in the *Central Plains and Valleys* chapter, is the most-affluent rural region in the province. The western Pembina Valley has a completely different character – it's seen a lot less growth in recent years, but remains a beautiful stretch of the Prairies, especially in the middle of the summer.

West of Highway 34, the valley widens out into three trough-like lakes: Swan, Rock, and Pelican, the latter being a busy cottage area. Farther west, the Pembina is merely a stream that tumbles down from the Boissevain area.

Away from the river, the farmland is dotted with thousands of tiny lakes and sloughs that attract impressive numbers of birds. As a result, a pair of binoculars is compulsory for any spring, summer or fall road trip through this region.

Heading east or west, you have three routes to choose from: Highway 23 skirts the north side of the valley, Provincial Road 253 heads straight through it, and Highway 3 curves below the river, hugging the US border.

Not just in Alberta! Oil pumps, like this small contraption near Boissevain, are a common site in southwestern Manitoba.

The Pilot Mound Region

Tucked into a bend in Highway 3, **Pilot Mound** (pop. 676) takes its name from a thirty-six-metre-high glacial formation with a fascinating history. In late prehistoric times, Aboriginal peoples – Sioux ancestors, in all likelihood – used the hill for ceremonies and built

MUST SEE:
Boissevain
A small town with three museums, including the excellent Moncur Gallery of pre-European Aboriginal artifacts.

an artificial mound on its summit. But the hill became a Sioux grave-yard in the 1850s, after hundreds were killed in a battle with Métis bison hunters on a plain just north of the mound.

In the decades to come, white settlers used the mound as a navigational aid and built a town on the site in 1881. Sir John A. Macdonald, Canada's first Prime Minister, held a political rally here in 1885. But when the Canadian Pacific Railway bypassed the town, the hill was abandoned for a new site two km to the south. The original mound is a very short drive from the current village, but treat it with respect – Sioux from North Dakota occasionally hold cere-monies on the summit. More mounds built in pre-colonial times line the north shore of Rock Lake, a prime birding area about fifteen km west of Pilot Mound on PR 253.

Eight km southwest of Pilot Mound, the village of **Crystal City** (pop. 414) is worth a stop for the **Crystal City Community Printing Museum** (212 Broadway South), a quirky living monument to 100-year-old typesetting and publishing gear. Some of the vintage equip-ment is fully operational, as the museum staff still handles print jobs. You can visit on any weekday, between 9 a.m. and 5:30 p.m. Express some genuine interest and the staff may print something up for you.

Another six km west of Crystal City on Highway 3A, the even tinier hamlet of **Clearwater** is on the map thanks to the **Harvest Moon Festival**, a folk and roots music festival featuring performers from Winnipeg during the second-last weekend in September. Ostensibly created to promote organic farming in the region, this cross-cultural event has carved out a niche as the last Manitoba folk festival of the season. For the current festival lineup and ticket info, visit www.clearwatermb.ca.

Continuing west, the village of **Cartwright** (pop. 304, Highway 3 at Highway 5) offers another glimpse at pre-European history. Three km to the north, a set of cliffs known the Clay Banks were used 2,500 years ago as buffalo jumps by early Aboriginal peoples.

In mid-July, one of the communities in this area hosts the Gathering of Nations Festival, a multicultural celebration of south-central Manitoba's Aboriginal, British, French, and Dutch heritage. The festival moves from town to town every year – look for a poster at a local gas station in early July.

Pelican Lake and Vicinity

The largest navigable body of water in southwestern Manitoba, **Pelican Lake** sits above the spot where the Pembina River spills into the long, post-glacial trench that once held the lower portion of the Assiniboine River. The lake is twenty-three km long but only 2.5 km wide, with cottage communities and rental cabins ringing the shoreline.

Pelican Lake peaked about ninety years ago as a resort area, but a yacht club remains at the largest community, **Ninette** (Highways 23 and 18, at the northwest corner of the lake). Aside from boating and fishing, birding is the chief activity, especially dur-ing the fall migration season.

About fifteen km west of Ninette, north of the town of Margaret (Highway 23 and PR 346), there's more attractive valley scenery in the **Souris Riverbend Provincial Wildlife Management Area**, a protected patch of river-bottom forests and grasslands. This is the place where the Souris River abruptly turns northeast to flow into the Assiniboine. Equestrians and hikers use about ten km of trails, some of which cross private land. From Margaret, drive about eleven km north on PR 346, cross the Souris River, and look out for a trailhead on the east side of the road.

An aerial view of Souris River Valley.

South of Pelican Lake, **Killarney** (pop. 2,221, Highways 3 and 18) is a quiet town that's lucky enough to have its own beach and marina at small Killarney Lake. Despite the Irish name, the main tourist attraction is the **Danish Mermaid** (433 Broadway, 532-8109), a kitschy shop that specializes in handmade chocolates but also sells candy, ice cream, and assorted knicknacks.

Turtle Mountain Area

When the glaciers started retreating from southwestern Manitoba, the first dry land to see the light of day was Turtle Mountain, a plateau that straddles the Canada-US border about 100 km south of Brandon.

The first people moved in some time between 10,000 and 12,000 years ago, making the area the oldest inhabited corner of the province. Hunter-gatherer cultures persisted until European colonists arrived in the nineteenth century, but Turtle Mountain remains a relatively wild place, home to Turtle Mountain Provincial Park, an excellent birding area at Whitewater Lake, and the interesting little town of Boissevain.

Boissevain

American tourists heading up from North Dakota, and Brandonites heading south, have helped make **Boissevain** (pop. 1,495) a worthwhile stop on Highway 10, six km north of Highway 3. The town actively promotes its **Outdoor Art Gallery**, a series of murals painted on the sides of eighteen buildings, but the most unique attraction is the tiny **Moncur Gallery** (436 South Railway, below the public library), an extremely impressive museum devoted to 12,000 years of Aboriginal presence in southwestern Manitoba.

If you have any interest in pre-European history, this will be the best $2 you'll ever spend. The gallery features more than a thousand ancient and more recent artifacts found in fields and forests around Boissevain and Turtle Mountain, the first part of the province to emerge from glacial ice. Amazingly, a single collector – William Moncur – found most of the arrowheads, awls, and hammers. His donations form the basis of the collection.

To fully appreciate this place, pick up the self-guided tourbook, which explains the exhibits and helps illuminate Manitoba's early human history. The museum is open Tuesday through Saturday from 10 a.m. to 5 p.m. If the librarian tells you it's closed, ask nicely and you may be let in anyway.

Boissevain also has two other museums: **Beckoning Hills** (425 Mill South) is your standard pioneer museum, open June to September from 1 p.m. to 5 p.m., with admission by donation. The much freakier **Irvin Goodon International Wildlife Museum** (298 Mountain) is really a monument to taxidermy, featuring stuffed wolves, bison, bears, moose, eagles, and dozens of other critters. Basically, this place is a zoo where all the animals are dead. The museum is open 10 a.m. to 6 p.m. Monday though Saturday and noon to 6 p.m. on Sundays. Admission is $7. An attached gift shop specializes in fur clothing and rustic handicrafts.

Outside the wildlife museum, it's impossible to miss **Tommy the Turtle**, a seven-metre-high statue of a painted turtle at the corner of Mill and Mountain. In mid-August, townsfolk really do race turtles as part of the **Boissevain Turtle Island Festival**, whose name refers both to nearby Turtle Mountain and to the Aboriginal name for North America.

In 2005, Boissevain began the process of further honouring southwestern Manitoba's Aboriginal roots by beginning the consruction of Medicine Wheel Park, an astronomical calendar comprised of stones.

Turtle Mountain Provincial Park

There's no shortage of irony in the fact that Manitoba's oldest inhabited spot is now a protected wild area. **Turtle Mountain Provincial Park**, established in 1961, encompasses 184 square km of forests, marshes, and shallow lakes on rolling terrain along the US border, providing a playground for off-road cyclists, hikers, horseback riders, cross-country skiers, snowmobilers, and the occasional canoeist.

There are 175 km of trails in the park, most of them concentrated in a built-up eastern section along Highway 10. **Adam Lake**, the most popular spot in the park, has a beach, campground, interpretive centre (open mid-May to Labour Day), 1.6-km walking trail to a wildlife-viewing tower, and access to a sixty-five-km trail system for day-hikers, trail runners, cyclists, horses, and cross-country skiers. While there are no backcountry campsites along these routes, the fifteen-km **James Lake Trail** leads to a backcountry cabin that must be reserved in advance at Manitoba Conservation's Boissevain office (534-7204).

You can reach the wilder western side of the park from **Max Lake**, accessible from Highway 10 via McKinney Road, about 1.5 km north of the park. This lake has a beach, campsites, and a canoe

MUST SEE:
Turtle Mountain Provincial Park
The oldest inhabited corner of Manitoba is now a preserve for lakes and forests, right next to the US border.

Winnipeg Free Press

launch for flatwater paddling trips down to seven other lakes connected by well-used portages. It also marks the start of the forty-three-km **Sharpe Lake Trail**, a former fireguard that circumnavigates the west side of the park, coming within metres of the US border. It's used both as a ski/bike route, and to provide motor-vehicle access to two short hiking trails: the one-km **Disappearing Lakes** self-guiding trail, and a two-km hike to a back-country campsite at **Oskar Lake**.

Other long routes include the thirty-km **Bella Lake Trail**, which requires cyclists to ford a chest-deep lake, and the thirty-two-km **Gordon Lake Trail**, which straddles the north side of the park. After a big rainfall, the Sharpe, Bella, and Gordon trails all get obnoxiously muddy – gummed-up gears will be an issue unless you have calves of steel.

Visitors to Turtle Mountain are required to pay the usual fees: $5 per vehicle for a three-day pass, or $20 for a seasonal Manitoba Parks Pass.

International Peace Gardens

Tucked into the southeast corner of Turtle Mountain Provincial Park and extending south into the US, the **International Peace Gardens** celebrate Canada's (sometimes) buddy-buddy relationship with its southern neighbour. Founded in 1932 as a Depression-era make-work project, the park is designed to allow both Canadians and Americans to visit without crossing an international border or passing through customs. The entrance sits precisely on the boundary, between the Canadian and American border stations on Highway 10, which means you do have to pass through customs when you leave the gardens.

The park is divided into a Canadian side, with a 2.4-km hiking trail; an American side, with a campground, sports camp, and **Game Warden Museum** (early June to mid-August, weekdays from 10 a.m. to 6 p.m.); and a central corridor housing three sets of gardens and a pair of poignant monuments that make the trip here worthwhile.

Just west of the park entrance, you'll find the **All-American Gardens**, the **Formal Gardens**, and the **Peace Gardens Interpretive Centre**. The interpretive centre offers garden tours at 10:30 a.m. and 1 p.m. throughout the summer. Continuing west on foot, you'll pass through the **Sunken Gardens** then walk up a gentle slope to the **Bell Tower**, which chimes every 15 minutes, and a **9/11 Monument** comprised of steel girders salvaged from the wreckage of the World Trade Center in New York.

At the end of the corridor, the concrete columns of the **Peace Tower** eerily resemble the destroyed Twin Towers, which is especially creepy considering they were built in the early '80s. When you get

MUST SEE: International Peace Gardens *A park dedicated to the long history of friendship between Canada and the United States, with gardens, the monolithic Peace Tower, and a monument to the victims of the September 11, 2001, terrorist acts.*

up close, you'll notice there are actually four pillars here, each extending 37.5 metres off the ground. This concrete message of unity is illuminated at night, all year long.

The International Peace Gardens are open 24 hours a day, 365 days a year. Admission is $10 per vehicle or $5 per pedestrian, with Canadian and US funds at par.

William Lake Provincial Park

A small satellite of Turtle Mountain Provincial Park, **William Lake Provincial Park** sits about five km east of its larger neighbour. This small crescent of a park has a beach, a campground, and one decent day hike: the six-km **Turtle's Back loop**, which follows the shore of William Lake before climbing to one of the highest viewpoints in Turtle Mountain. To reach the park from Highway 10, take gravel PR 341 east for about seven km and then head south.

Whitewater Lake

While it's easy to make fun of birdwatching, **Whitewater Lake Provincial Wildlife Management Area** actually makes this arcane-sounding activity exciting.

A wetlands restoration project on the east side of this shallow lake attracts incredible numbers of birds, including the usual Manitoba suspects – Canada geese, pelicans, cormorants, and smaller waterfowl – but also egrets, uncommon shorebirds, tundra swans, sandhill cranes, and snow geese, especially during the fall migration period. During the middle of the summer, a system of dikes around the artificial marsh makes for an amazing walk at dusk and dawn, when clouds of swallows are so dense they look like airborne schools of fish.

Whitewater Lake is fed by streams flowing down from Turtle Mountain and has no drainage at all, which means water levels fluctuate greatly from year to year. To reach the viewing area and dike trails from Boissevain, head west on Highway 3 for 11 km, turn north at a gravel road marked with a Wildlife Watching sign and follow more signs eight km to the trailhead.

Along the way from Highway 3 to the marsh, you'll pass by oil wells and a captive bison herd that give the place a decidedly western feel. If you're lucky, you'll see cattle egrets perched on bison.

Metigoshe and Deloraine

Just west of Turtle Mountain Provincial Park, **Lake Metigoshe** straddles the Canada-US border, with one small bay belonging to Manitoba. There's a beach and cabin rentals at the town of Metigoshe, plus a short interpretive trail, a boardwalk, and a viewing tower at nearby **Lake Metigoshe Natural Area**. The lake is at the southern end of PR 450, which heads south from Highway 3 a few km west of the Whitewater Lake turnoff.

Fourteen km west, **Deloraine** (pop. 1,026) is a former coal-mining town best known as the home of Peter Nygard, a Winnipeg

Charles Shilliday

clothing magnate. The main attraction here is **Flags of the World**, a collection of national emblems from 193 countries, located in the centre of town at Nygard Park. Give 'em a break – it's better than another stupid statue.

Green and yellow canola stands out against a bright blue Manitoba sky.

The Far West

Manitoba's extreme southwestern corner is unlike anywhere else in the province, thanks to distinctly Saskatchewan-like features such as oil wells and dryish grasslands. Towns like Melita and Virden are almost as close to Regina as they are to Winnipeg. But that's just geography – culturally, these places feel worlds away from the Manitoba capital.

The far west is defined by the US border to the south; the Trans-Canada Highway, to the north; the Saskatchewan border to the west; and PR 21 to the east. The north-south arteries in this region are Highways 83 and 21.

Melita and Vicinity

The town of **Melita** (pop. 1,111) straddles a flood-prone stretch of the Souris River where Highway 3 meets Highway 83. The main thing to see in town is the **Antler River Historical Society Museum** (71 Ash, 522-3103), a collection of pioneer and First Nations artifacts with a tearoom, open June to August.

Yes, there are cacti in Manitoba! A pin-cushion cactus in Lauder Sand Hills.

There are a handful of natural attractions in the scrubland around the town, the driest region of Manitoba. Four km north of the American border, southeast of the village of Waskada, **Lowe Natural Heritage Area** protects a ten-hectare tract of unbroken grassland. From

Charles Shilliday

Waskada (PR 251 at 452), follow the signs six km south and three km east.

At the confluence of the Antler and Souris rivers, you'll find **Sourisford Park**, believed to be the oldest park in western Canada. It sits on Road 158 West, east of Highway 83 and north of the small community of Coulter. And about 30 minutes northeast of Melita, **Lauder Sand Hills Provincial Wildlife Management Area** protects an area of sandy hills best visited in late June and early July, when prickly-pear and pincushion cacti are blooming. (Yes, there are small cacti all over southern Manitoba.) A maze of trails is accessible from PR 254 west of the town of Hartney (Highway 21 at the Souris River).

On some maps and local tourism pamphlets, you might notice a reference to **Linear Mounds National Historic Site** somewhere in the Melita area. This is not a place you can visit – it's an Aboriginal burial ground dating back to times before European contact, when the Siouan-speaking Assiniboine were the dominant First Nation in southwestern Manitoba. (Their descendents have since moved southwest into Montana.) The site is part of a network of burial mounds extending across Montana, Saskatchewan, Manitoba, and North Dakota. For now, Parks Canada is keeping the Melita-area burial mounds closed to the public, both to protect the sanctity of the site on behalf of First Nations and to prevent relic-hunters from sacking graves for pottery shards.

If you're interested in pre-European burial mounds, there's a fully developed historic site that's far more spectacular and just as close to Winnipeg: **Manitou Mounds**, a Laurel Culture site maintained by Parks Canada and several Ontario Ojibway nations, sits on the north bank of the Rainy River, south of Ontario Highway 11.

Trans-Canada West

The westernmost major waterfowl area in southwestern Manitoba is **Oak Lake**, a shallow marsh subdivided by a two-km-long dike. You can look for birds along the dike or launch canoes at either **Oak Lake Beach** or **Oak Lake Provincial Recreation Park**, both accessible from PR 254, which heads south from the Trans-Canada west of the town of Oak Lake.

To the west, **Virden** (pop. 3,109) is one of the worst speed traps along the entire 7,821-km length of La Transcanadienne. Slow down and assume that Mounties are watching you. When you come to a halt, check out the chateau-style **former CP Rail Station** (425 6th), which now houses the local art gallery and gift shop, open weekdays from 10 a.m. to 3 p.m. Another unusual structure is **The Aud** (228 Wellington West), a 450-seat opera house built in 1912 and still in use today. You likely won't be able to take a peek inside, however – it's usually only open for performances.

As the last sizable town on the Trans-Canada before Saskatchewan, Virden is a wise place to grab a bite if you're continuing west. Non-franchise options include homespun diner **D & L King Street Café** (269 King East, 748-3528) and **The Elegant Moose** (King and Highway One, 748-3005). Continuing west, the village of **Elkhorn** (pop. 470) is worth a pit stop for the **Manitoba Antique Auto**

Museum, a collection of 75 vintage cars built between 1902 and 1933. Located right on the Trans-Canada, it's open daily from May to September.

The Yellowhead

A ribbon of road extending northwest from Portage la Prairie, the Yellowhead – also known as Highway 16 – marks the transition between the southwestern Manitoba Prairie and the wilder Parkland. The highway leads through the pretty towns of Neepawa and Minnedosa, where the Whitemud and Little Saskatchewan rivers flow down from Riding Mountain, before continuing across a relatively empty stretch of farmland on its way to the Assiniboine River and the Saskatchewan border.

A harvest moon over the Yellowhead Highway.

This will probably be the highway you'll take to reach Riding Mountain and the rest of the Parkland, so it's worth familiarizing yourself with the towns along the way.

Gladstone and Big Grass Marsh

Heading west on the Yellowhead, the first community of any size is **Gladstone** (pop. 848), infamous for the Happy Rock, a supremely silly statue that looms over Highway 16 near the junction of Highway 34. Pull in anyway, as the town is the gateway to **Big Grass Marsh**, the first conservation project ever undertaken by Ducks Unlimited in North America. This marsh encompassed 400 square km before misguided drainage projects about 100 years ago dried up the wetlands and created a dustbowl. Happily, Ducks Unlimited succeeded in restoring part of the swamp to its original soggy state, beginning in 1938.

Today, **Big Grass Marsh Provincial Game Bird Refuge** protects fifty square km for the likes of Franklin's gulls, snow geese, and sandhill cranes. To reach the south end of the refuge, drive north from Gladstone on Pembroke Road and head east on Road 86 North. To see more of the marsh, continue north on Pembroke Road to PR 265 and head east.

Continuing west on the Yellowhead, the community of **Arden** (PR 352, six km north of Highway 16) offers a chance to stretch your legs along a five-km walking trail at the Whitemud River, where you'll also find a swinging bridge and an oversized statue of a crocus. The surrounding area is covered with crocuses, which bloom spectacularly right after the spring snowmelt.

About 1.5 km west of PR 352, **Prairie Orchard Tea House** offers lunch and organic produce from mid-May to mid-September. It's open 11 a.m. to 4 p.m., Thursday through Monday.

Charles Shilliday

Long, narrow Lake Minnedosa, created by the damming of the Little Saskatchewan River, complements the idyllic setting of one of western Manitoba's most picturesque towns. Late CanWest Global founder Izzy Asper got his start here, sweeping his father's movie theatres.

Neepawa

One of the most idyllic-looking towns in Manitoba, **Neepawa** (pop. 3,235) is best known as the home of the late novelist Margaret Laurence, whose fictional hamlet of Manawaka was based on this picturesque community. The very definition of quaint, the town bills itself as the lily capital of the world. The annual fair is called the **Lily Festival**, usually held in the third week of July, when every available patch of soil in town is covered with the colourful and hardy prairie flowers. Needless to say, there are few biker bars here.

If you want to buy lilies, no less than 1,500 varieties are on sale at **The Lily Nook**, four km south of Neepawa on Highway 5. Other Neepawa attractions include **Rotary Park** (Park Lake Drive, at the south end of 1st Avenue), a quirky lakeside picnic area with an emu, turtles, and geese inside an enclosure; and **Margaret Laurence House** (1st and Brydon), the author's former home, open May to Thanksgiving.

Inspired by Laurence's prose, the **Manawaka Gallery** (388 Mountain) displays local art Tuesdays through Fridays, while **Beautiful Plains Museum** (west end of Hamilton Street) offers the usual assortment of pioneer artifacts in an old CN station, Victoria Day to Labour Day. On the west end of town, **Two Barns Antiques** (159 Main) boasts the largest collection of salt-and-pepper shakers you're likely to encounter at any curio shop. The place doubles as a free museum, much to the chagrin of the somewhat crusty proprietor, who seems to enjoy chastising "tire-kickers."

The most civilized place to grab a bite here is **Prairie Seasons Bakery** (370 Mountain), an organic bakery, while **Agassiz Drive-In** (30 Main, summer only) is a non-franchise ice-cream option.

Neepawa also marks the start of one of Manitoba's most road-free portions of the **Trans-Canada Trail**. A 49-km stretch of TCT's Rossburn Subdivision follows an abandoned railbed between Howden, a hamlet five km north of Neepawa on Highway 5, and the town of Erickson, just south of Riding Mountain National Park. Trail conditions vary from fair to awful, but the attraction here is solace – head out and you'll probably have the route to yourself.

Minnedosa

Another attractive Yellowhead town, **Minnedosa** (pop. 2,426) sits on the Little Saskatchewan River at the junction of Highway 16 and Highway 10. Media mogul Izzy Asper, the late founder of the CanWest Global Corporation, was born in this quiet valley town, and began his career here sweeping up the family-run movie theatre.

Today, the main attraction is **Lake Minnedosa**, an artificial lake and beach created by a dam on the Little Saskatchewan. In the late 1990s, a lakefront amphitheatre played host to massive mid-summer classic rock festivals, but financial troubles have led to smaller shows with fewer marquee headliners.

Right below the dam, a short network of walking trails criss-crosses a low-lying area with a marsh boardwalk, a swinging bridge, and a bison compound. The walk isn't challenging, but it's usually soggy enough to warrant hiking boots.

The beach, dam, and trails are all accessible from PR 262, just northeast of Main Street. After your walk, pop into **Brede's** (121 Main South, 867-2162) for a heaping helping of German grub.

Yellowhead West

West of Minnedosa, the next 100 km of the Yellowhead can be fairly dull, except in July, when bright-yellow canola and deep-green wheat fields stand out against the blue sky. Diversions along the way include the **Police Museum** (July and August only), a replica of a nineteenth-century Northwest Mounted Police barracks at the town of Shoal Lake (Highways 16 and 21); hiking or cross-country skiing along picturesque **Birdtail Creek Valley** at Birtle (10 clicks south of the Yellowhead at Highways 42 and 83); or minigolf and a chlorinated dip at **Binscarth Park and Pool** (late June through August), immediately off the highway two km south of the town of Binscarth (Highway 16, just north of the junction with Highway 41).

One of the last remaining examples of the wooden grain elevator, once the symbol of the Canadian Prairies.

Charles Shilliday

A big, triangle-shaped chunk of western Manitoba, the Parkland takes its name from two of the largest natural areas in the province, Riding Mountain National Park and Duck Mountain Provincial Park.

Neither of these places are actual mountains, but plateaus that rise about 400 metres off the Manitoba Lowlands. During the fur trade, travellers would ditch their canoes and switch to horses to make their way up the Manitoba Escarpment and across the densely forested high ground. During the pioneer era, most of the land in the region was cleared for agricultural use, which turned Riding Mountain and Duck Mountain into the ecological equivalent of islands.

Within the parks, especially Riding Mountain, there are impressive numbers of moose, elk, black bears, beavers, coyotes, and other mammals, including small populations of wolves and cougars. Outside the parks, you're more likely to see white-tailed deer, relative newcomers to Manitoba that seem to thrive wherever humans go.

The largest community in the Parkland is Dauphin, a mainly Ukrainian city in a valley between the prairie "mountains." The other dominant features are the west sides of lakes Manitoba and Winnipegosis, a dramatically deep stretch of the Assiniboine River Valley, and the tallest hills in Manitoba – Baldy Mountain in Duck Mountain Provincial Park, and Hart Mountain in the Porcupine Hills.

Riding Mountain National Park

The only road-accessible national park in Manitoba, **Riding Mountain** is one of the few places in the province you absolutely must visit. I am adamant about this. The 3,000-square-km park offers amazing wildlife-watching opportunities, the largest network of cross-country ski trails in Manitoba, multi-day off-road bike trips, and hiking that actually involves some elevation. Add in deep, cold Clear Lake and the resort town of Wasagaming, and you have a park for every kind of tourist, from merino-clad weekend warriors to young families to senior citizens in RVs.

Riding Mountain lost much of its forests and grasslands to logging and fires when settlers arrived in large numbers about a century

Opposite: Snowshoeing in deep, mid-February powder near the Bead Lakes in Riding Mountain National Park.

MUST SEE: Riding Mountain National Park Manitoba's only road-accessible national park, with amazing wildlife-watching opportunities and hundreds of kilometres of hiking, cross-country skiing, and mountain-biking trails.

ago. By the time the park was established in 1933, much of the wildlife had already been wiped out by a combination of hunting, trapping, and habitat destruction.

Female moose grazing right along Highway 10 in early July. Drivers are urged to lay off the gas anywhere inside the park to avoid hurting themselves and wildlife.

Most of the mammals have since recovered, as Riding Mountain now boasts 10,000 beavers, thousands of elk, moose and deer, hundreds of black bears and coyotes, about seventy-five wolves, a captive herd of thirty-five bison, a small number of lynx, and a handful of cougars. Motorists driving through the park on Highway 10 or 19 should drive slowly and cautiously to avoid wildlife collisions, as moose, deer, and bears are often spotted along roadsides. But you might have more trouble spotting critters from the trail, as high brush during the summer will obscure your view. Wildlife watchers may want to travel by bike or horseback to get a better perspective, or visit during the leafless fall or winter.

There are more than 425 km of hiking, biking, backpacking, and bridle paths within the park, with about 270 km open for cross-country skiing, skate-skiing, or snowshoeing during the winter. Since many of the routes follow old logging roads, very few are physically demanding or technical. The biggest danger you'll encounter in the Riding Mountain backcountry is the potential loss of your food to black bears – or run-ins with aggressive elk or moose during the spring rutting season. Needless to say, keep your distance from animals and lock your food up in bear boxes or vehicles.

As a national park, Riding Mountain charges a set of fees that are different from those in all other Manitoba parks. Daily entrance fees are $6 per adult or $15 for a group of up to seven people.

Black bears are common in Riding Mountain.

Car-camping sites range from $14 for unserviced campgrounds to $33 for full hookups at the extremely popular Wasagaming Campground. Backcountry camping is $9 per person, per night, while fishing permits are $8 per day or $25 for the season. You can reserve campsites at Wasagaming at 1-888-737-3783 and backcountry campsites at 848-7275.

Generally speaking, Riding Mountain can be divided into four main areas. The vast majority of visitors heads to heavily developed Wasagaming and Clear Lake, home to all the hotels and restaurants in the park.

Highway 10 slices through the middle of the park, connecting Wasagaming and Dauphin. The slightly steep trails of the Manitoba Escarpment, on the east side of the park, attract the largest numbers of mountain cyclists and hikers. The western section of the park, arguably the heart of Riding Mountain, has most of the longer trails and truly wild places.

Wasagaming and Clear Lake

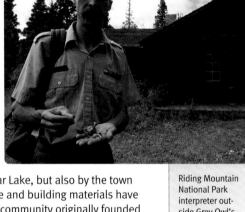

Winnipeg Free Press

Just like Banff, Jasper, and Grand Canyon Village, the mostly seasonal resort of **Wasagaming** looks and feels like a typical national park town. Hundreds of cottages, a dozen hotels and souvenir shops, three golf courses, and the 500-site Wasagaming Campground are crammed into a townsite on the south side of **Clear Lake**, the largest body of water in Riding Mountain.

Wasagaming is the only place most visitors see, which is a shame. They're drawn by the beach and marina at consistently chilly Clear Lake, but also by the town itself, as restrictions on neon signage and building materials have preserved the historic character of a community originally founded in 1908 as Clark's Beach. The name Wasagaming, Cree for "clear water," wasn't adopted until the park's 1933 opening.

Riding Mountain National Park interpreter outside Grey Owl's cabin.

Besides the lake, townsite attractions include the **Riding Mountain Visitor Centre** (Wasagaming Drive at the lakefront), where you'll find interpretive displays, a library, a gift shop, park info, and backcountry permits. It's open from the Victoria Day long weekend to Thanksgiving, from 9:30 a.m. to 8 p.m. in July and August, but only until 5 p.m. in the shoulder season. Nearby **Pinewood Museum** (154 Wasagaming) offers more Riding Mountain history, including exhibits about Grey Owl, the British-born naturalist who lived in the park with two pet beavers in 1931. It's open 2 p.m. to 5 p.m. in July and August only. You'll learn way more about Grey Owl here than you would from the crappy Pierce Brosnan movie.

Non-rodent-related flicks are screened daily at first-run movie house **Park Theatre** (117 Wasagaming), which bills itself as the largest log cinema in North America. The same rustic structure houses **T. R. McKoy's**, a middlebrow pasta and pizza joint that ranks as the best of Wasagaming's dozen restaurants. Other dining options include **Mountain Grill** at the Elkhorn Resort (southeast of the Wasagaming townsite, across Highway 10), and **The Martese**, a cruise ship that encircles Clear Lake four times daily from the Wasagaming marina.

The nineteen-metre, ninety-eight-passenger yacht plied the waters of Lake Okanagan, BC, before Wasagaming entrepreneur Sheldon Willey trucked it to Manitoba in pieces and reassembled it on Clear Lake. From Victoria Day to Labour Day, the ship leaves daily at noon and at 3, 6, and 9 p.m. The dinner-hour cruises are $60 for adults, while the regular fare is $15. In-port breakfast is also offered from 8 a.m. to 11 a.m.

A network of trails allows you see most of Clear Lake on foot or by bike. The twelve-km **Southshore Trail** extends from Wasagaming northwest to Keeseekowenin Ojibway First Nation's reserve on the northwest side of the lake. The 3.5-km **Lakeshore Trail** follows the shoreline through the town, while the 9.5-km **Northshore Trail** encircles the east side of Clear Lake. Other trails in town include the 5.5-km **Wasagaming Bike Trail**, the two-km **Ominisk Marsh Trail**, and the 3.5-km **South Lake loop**, the latter two located just west of the town proper, and open only to hikers.

There are more trails just east of Clear Lake, within a ten-minute drive from Wasagaming. The short **Arrowhead** (3.4 km) and **Brûlé** (1.9 km) trails, the moderate **Kinosao** (7.3 km), and the long day hike to **Grey Owl's Cabin** (17.4 km return) all depart from trailheads on both sides of Highway 19. Both the Kinosao and Grey Owl trails are also open to mountain bikes.

One km farther east of the Grey Owl trailhead, a short access road leads south from Highway 19 to small **Lake Katherine**, where you'll find the 2.4-km **Loon's Island Trail** and also **Shawenequanape Kipi-Che-Win**, a.k.a. Southquill Camp, a replica of a traditional Ojibway village. It offers overnight stays inside teepees, and Ojibway cultural programs.

Another five km east on Highway 19, a side road leads to an unserviced campground at Whirlpool Lake and the eight-km **Cowan Lake Trail**, which passes by a single backcountry campsite before hooking up with the Grey Owl trail.

Unlike its Alberta cousins Banff and Jasper, Wasagaming almost turns into a ghost town every winter, with only **Elkhorn Resort** ($105 to $525, www.elkhornresort.mb.ca) operating year-round. While the regular rooms are dorm-like and the private cabins are overpriced, the resort redeems itself with an open-air Jacuzzi, spa, and, in the summer, riding stables at adjacent **Triangle Ranch**.

Elkhorn also works closely with Earth Rhythms (www.earthrhythms.ca), a unique ecotourism outfit run by former Riding Mountain ranger Celes Davar, an experienced guide who seems to know every beaver and cattail in the park. **Earth Rhythms** offers not just wildlife-watching trips, but also the opportunity to tag along with elk and wolf researchers and tread lightly into areas where there are no trails. Tours, ranging in length from an hour and a half to half a day, average around $95 per person. Earth Rhythms operates all year, with activities dependent on the season. Most winter visitors, however, come to Riding Mountain for the cross-country skiing, basing themselves out of the Elkhorn resort or accommodations in the nearby town of Onanole (see *Approaching Riding Mountain*, below).

There are three short **ski trails** at the Wasagaming townsite alone, plus another route extending behind Elkhorn to Lake Katherine. The nearby Grey Owl and Kinosao trails are groomed for

MUST SEE:
Wasagaming
A rustic national-park town on the southern edge of Riding Mountain, with lodges, touristy retailers, even a cruise ship.

cross-country skiing, while the seven-km summer road to Whirlpool Lake can be used for skate-skiers. In the winter, the Cowan Lake trail is ungroomed but open to backcountry users, while the Brûlé trail is reserved for snowshoeing.

For the precise locations of all Riding Mountain trails and trailheads, pick up a park guide at the south gate or at the lobby of Elkhorn resort.

The Escarpment

Riding Mountain actually looks like a mountain when you're at the eastern fringe of the park, home to some of the steepest inclines on the Manitoba Escarpment. These slopes rise about 400 metres off the low-lying farmland to the east, an elevation gain roughly equivalent to a quarter of the depth of the Grand Canyon.

Bartley Kives

Put in the trail time, and you'll see critters: A bull moose bathes in a bog along the Moon Lake hiking trail.

Highway 19 winds down the escarpment before exiting the park at the **East Gate National Historic Site**, a fort-like wooden structure built in 1933, when the gravel road provided the only vehicle access to Clear Lake. No other road in Manitoba has such steep switch-backs, which makes it a fun, short drive.

Four separate trails allow hikers to climb or descend the escarpment in the east side of the park. The most-popular route is the **Gorge Creek Trail**, a day-hiking trail that follows Highway 19 for 6.4 km, with the eastern trailhead near the East Gate site.

The slightly longer **Packhorse**, **J. E. T.**, and **Bald Hill trails** – also open to mountain bikes and equestrians – connect with the hilltop **North Escarpment trail** and a backcountry campsite at East Deep Lake. Despite the elevation gain, there are only a handful of look-outs along these trails – this area is a little more rewarding for bikers than it is for hikers. To reach the eastern trailhead for these routes from Highway 5, drive north past Highway 19 and turn left at the gravel road opposite PR 462. When you reach the park boundary, turn left and keep your eyes peeled for the parking lot on the right. It comes up quickly and is very easy to miss.

There are two more trails in the northeast corner of the park. The 6.4-km **Oak Ridge Trail** is a day-hiking route, while the two-km **Scott Creek Trail** leads to a hike-in campsite overlooking the north-east corner of the escarpment. To reach these trails, drive north on Highway 5 to the town of McCreary, then west on PR 261 through the McKinnon Creek entrance. Keep going until you see the trailhead on the right.

South of Highway 19, the thirty-seven-km **South Escarpment Trail**, seven-km **Muskrat Lake spur**, and the seven-km **Robinson Lake loop** are all open to hikers, cyclists, and horses. As well, three eastern trails are open to cross country skiers in winter: the North Escarpment (17.6 km, return, from Highway 19), the South Escarpment (18 km, one way), and Oak Ridge (10.4 km).

If you're driving up from Neepawa to this area and don't have a Riding Mountain park pass, purchase your permit at the Tempo station in McCreary to avoid an hour-long detour to Wasagaming.

The Highway 10 Corridor

The only road straight through Riding Mountain, the 10 is the most direct way to get from Brandon to Dauphin – and one of the biggest threats to wildlife in the park. The speed limit along the fifty-km stretch between Clear Lake and the park's north entrance is 80 km an hour, but it's a good idea to drive even slower at night. Moose head onto the highway in March and April to lick road salt, deer and bears frequently cross during the summer and fall, and coyotes jog along the shoulder to avoid deep winter snow. For obvious reasons, this is a great place to observe animals, provided you drive slowly and are aware of other motorists, who may not be so careful. If you see a large critter, do not get out of your car – bears, moose, and elk are a lot faster than you think.

There are six trails along this stretch of road. Ten km north of Clear Lake, the twenty-five-km **Ochre River Trail** heads northwest through the park, descending along the Ochre River most of the way. Along the way, there are two backcountry campsites, one horse camp, and Cairns Cabin, which cross-country skiers may reserve during the winter as an overnight shelter for a twenty-nine-km (return) trip from Highway 10.

Continuing north, the four-km **Bead Lakes loop** makes for an easy summer hike or winter snowshoe excursion, while the one-km **Boreal Trail** is accessible to people in wheelchairs. **Moon Lake** has a campground, a swim dock, and a nine-km hiking/snowshoeing loop. There are more short day hikes at **Kippan's Mill** and **Beach Ridges**, the latter just south of the park entrance, while the **Crawford Creek trail** can be used for a twenty-four-km (return) summer overnight hike or a ten-km there-and-back cross-country-ski jaunt. There are also three shorter ski loops near the Crawford Creek trailhead – Edwards Creek (5.4 km), Beach Ridges (3.5 km), and **Broadleaf** (4.2 km) – as well as the sixteen-km (return) **Hilton Trail** on the west side of the highway, near Edwards Lake.

The Wilder West

Riding Mountain's large and almost-roadless west side is the wildest portion of the park, with few sightseers going farther west than the **captive bison range** at Lake Audy, in the middle of the park. About three dozen of the beasts graze inside the three-square-km enclosure. You can observe the bison from inside your vehicle or from a covered interpretive display. Just don't go walking around – bison can sprint up to fifty km per hour, and tend to be very aggressive. Located west of Clear Lake, the range is accessible from a summer road that branches off Highway 10 just north of the lake, or via PR 354 just south of the park.

Bartley Kives

The only other road-accessible destinations in the west half of the park are campgrounds at **Audy Lake** – outside the bison enclosure, of course – and **Deep Lake**, about three-quarters of the way through the park, going westward.

The rest of the attractions are all hiking and cycling trails. The granddaddy of them all is the sixty-seven-km **Central Trail**, which follows an old logging road from Audy Lake to a western trailhead at Bob Hill Lake. Allow three to five days for hiking, or two to three for mountain biking.

Every other trail in the west side of the park connects to the Central Trail. The ten-km (one-way) **Strathclair Trail**, which heads north from Lake Audy, is popular with wildlife watchers during the fall elk-mating season, when bulls issue dramatic and surprisingly loud bugling noises. The fifteen-km **Grasshopper Valley Trail** loops around the lake and makes for a relatively easy overnight hike, while just to the west, the fourteen-km **Long Lake Trail** can be added on to Strathclair and part of Grasshopper to create a north-south Riding Mountain through-hike.

Ferns, ferns, everywhere: Lush mid-summer foliage in Riding Mountain National Park.

Farther west, there are three more spur trails and two long loops. The thirty-nine-km **Tilson Lake loop**, which partly follows steep Birdtail Creek Valley, is not recommended for cyclists. The **Birdtail Trail** is a better riding choice – it's listed as eleven km, but actually makes for a twenty-five-km return if you start at Bob Hill Lake, the nearest access point.

There are 12 designated backcountry campsites scattered throughout the west side of Riding Mountain, all featuring firepits and bear boxes. It's a good idea to reserve in advance.

If you're interested in riding through this area on horseback, **Trailhead Ranch** (www.trailheadranch.com) offers trail rides, daytrips and overnights at affordable rates. An hour-long ride is $25, full days with a lunch and lessons are $80, and backcountry trips with meals start at $185 a day. Nearby **Riding Mountain Guest Ranch** (www.ridingmountain.ca) specializes in wildlife-watching package tours guided by veteran naturalists Jim and Candy Irwin, starting at around $280 a day. Both ranches are located just south of the park, near the Lake Audy entrance.

Riding Mountain staff groom seven cross-country ski loops in the west side of the park, ranging in length from five to fourteen km. They're located at the east end of the Central Trail, as well as at park entrances at Lake Audy, Baldy Lake, Deep Lake, Moose Lake, and the Sugarloaf warden station.

Riding Mountain Gateway Towns

While rustic Wasagaming is a pretty little tourist town, there are some things you can't do inside a national park. Only three km south, the Riding Mountain gateway town of **Onanole** (Highway 10 at PR 262) is the place to buy booze and watch fireworks on Victoria Day and Canada Day. You'll also find more year-round accommodations at spartan **Southgate Motor Inn** (www.thesouthgate.com) and **Park Vista Chalets** (www.parkvistachalets.ca), and summertime diversions such as minigolf, go-carts, and, on a rainy day, **Poor Michael's Bookshop** (May to October), a fantastic little nook run by Brandon musician Murray Evans. Poor Michael's has vintage paperbacks, a good selection of new Manitoba literature, and decent organic coffee.

Fifteen km south of Wasagaming, the slightly larger town of Erickson (highways 10 and 45) is the best place to load up on groceries on your final approach to the park. A statue of a Viking ship pays tribute to the community's Scandinavian heritage. From **Erickson**, head west on Highway 45 to reach the Baldy Lake, Deep Lake, and Moose Lake entrances to Riding Mountain. The first town along the way, **Sandy Lake** (Highway 45 at PR 250), operates a **Ukrainian Heritage Museum** with an outdoor bread-baking facility throughout the summer. Admission is by donation.

Continuing west, **Oakburn** (Highway 45 and PR 577) marks the turnoff to Baldy Lake, where you can access the middle of Riding Mountain's Central Trail. If you have time for a diversion on the short drive north, turn right at PR 566 just past the town of **Olha** and head six km east until you come to two rustic A-frames covered in straw. These are recreations of the buddas used as shelters by Ukrainian pioneers at the beginning of the twentieth century.

Still farther west, **Rossburn** (Highway 45 and PR 264) is your exit point if you're heading to Riding Mountain's Deep Lake entrance. Six km east of the town, there are excellent, newly built cabins with outdoor hot tubs at year-round resort **Woodland Hills** (www.woodlandhillsmb.ca), where the British émigré owners groom sixteen km of classic ski trails right on the property.

West of Rossburn, Highway 45 dips into the scenic Birdtail Creek Valley at **Waywayseecappo First Nation** (pop. 1,200) before continuing west to **Angusville** (Highway 45 and PR 476), the gateway to Riding Mountain's Moose Lake entrance. Angusville's **Heritage Hall**, which sports a trio of Byzantine domes, is worth a quick driveby.

MUST SEE: Assiniboine and Shell River Valley
Glacial meltwaters carved out these wide spillways, now home to Lake of the Prairies and the Asessippi Ski Area.

Assiniboine River Valley

In southern Manitoba, the meandering Assiniboine River isn't much to look at. But west of Riding Mountain, the river flows through a majestic valley that's roughly two km wide and 100 metres deep. Like most of the province's features, this valley was carved by a torrent of glacial meltwater around 10,500 years ago. Today, the ancient spillway's slopes make for excellent mountain biking, passable downhill skiing and fishing and boating on **Lake of the Prairies**, a narrow body of water created in 1968 when the Assiniboine was dammed near the mouth of the Shell River.

The main route along the most dramatic stretch of this valley is Highway 83, which runs loosely parallel to the river for fifty-odd km between the agricultural centres of Russell and Roblin.

Charles Shilliday

Rolling terrain in the Assiniboine River Valley.

Russell

The gateway to the Assiniboine River Valley, **Russell** (pop. 1,587) is a convenient pit stop at the confluence of highways 16, 45, and 83. As the westernmost Manitoba community of any size on the Yellowhead Highway, the town has a **Travel Manitoba information centre** (Highway 16 at 83, May to September), and more than its share of places to crash, most notably the bland but clean **Russell Inn** (Highway 16, www.russellinn.com) and **Boulton Manor Suites** (322 Memorial, www.mts.net/~tweetwl). The latter is a bed-and-breakfast in an 1894 mansion once owned by Charles Boulton, who fought for the Canadian government against Louis Riel in both the Red River Rebellion of 1869 and the North-West Rebellion of 1885 in Saskatchewan.

Asessippi Provincial Park

Lake of the Prairies is Manitoba's modest equivalent of Utah's infamous Lake Powell. Created by dams, both are narrow, artificial bodies of water that attract boaters and anglers but lack the look, feel, and ecology of genuine natural areas.

Most of the development along Lake of the Prairies is concentrated in **Asessippi Provincial Park**, a twenty-three-square-km recreation area encompassing the bottom of the lake, Shellmouth Dam, and the lower part of the steep Shell River Valley – another glacial spillway.

From early December to the first weekend in April, there are twenty-one downhill-ski and snowboard runs on the Shell at

Asessippi Ski Area attracts not just snowboarders and skiers, but also downhill cyclists and river tubers in the summer months.

Parkland Daytrips

Beginning at Winnipeg.

1. Rush through Riding Mountain

Time to go: Victoria Day to Labour Day.

Prerequisites: Basic fitness for one steepish uphill hike, and good time-management skills.

Highlights: Some of the best facets of Riding Mountain National Park – including the Gorge Creek Trail, the town of Wasagaming, and the Lake Audy bison pen – crammed into one day.

The goods: Get up early. From Portage Avenue, drive west on the Trans-Canada past Portage la Prairie. Turn north on Highway 16, the Yellowhead. Now, it's time for the real daytrip to begin.

About 20 minutes' drive northwest, exit at Highway 50 and motor due north to the small community of Langruth. Turn left at PR 265 and follow the gravel through Big Grass Marsh, the first Ducks Unlimited wetlands restoration project in North America. When you hit PR 260, head north to PR 261, then west to Highway 5. Carry on north for about ten more minutes to Highway 19, the eastern road into Riding Mountain.

Next, drive west through the rustic East Gate and park your vehicle at the Gorge Creek trailhead. Hike up and down the Manitoba Escarpment along the creek, shuttling a vehicle to the top, if you don't want to walk back down. Then drive up winding Highway 19, looking out for moose along the road, and continue on to Highway 10 and the resort town of Wasagaming.

Motorists in Riding Mountain National Park slow down to watch a black bear cub cross Highway 10. Traffic 'jams' are common in the summer.

Bartley Kives

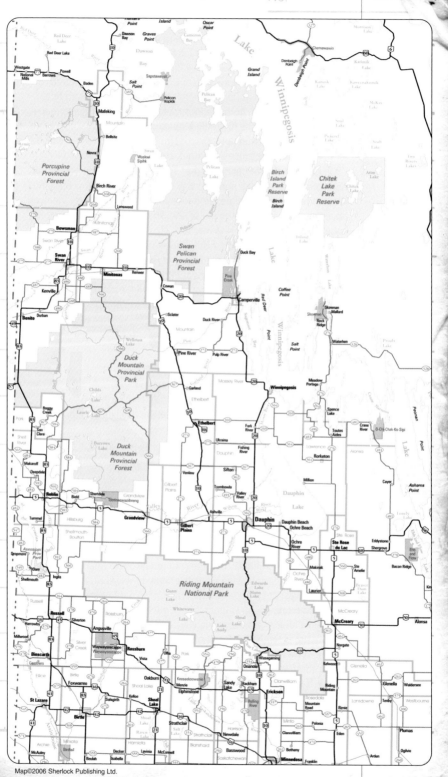

Map©2006 Sherlock Publishing Ltd.

In town, go for a swim at Clear Lake to remove the sweat from the hike. Then bypass Wasagaming's many touristy gift shops – unless you like touristy gift shops – for the Riding Mountain Visitor Centre. Once you've learned all you can learn, drive south on Highway 10 to Onanole and stop in at Poor Michael's for a coffee to go. From here, drive west on PR 262, north on PR 270, then west on PR 354 to reach the Lake Audy entrance to Riding Mountain National Park. Drive north into the bison enclosure and look out for the herd – but don't stray too far from your car, because the critters are quite aggressive.

On the east side of the enclosure, another road will take you to the north side of Clear Lake and Highway 10, which you'll follow back into Wasagaming a second time. Stop for a meal at T. R. McKoys – or if you have the time, on board the cruise ship The Martese – and then drive south out of the park on Highway 10.

Past the town of Erickson, exit Highway 10 at PR 357 and drive east through the hamlet of Mountain Road to Highway 5. Drive north for barely a kilometre, then turn right at PR 352 and follow the Arden Ridge southeast to the settlement of Arden and, eventually, Highway 16. From here, it's a ninety-minute drive back to Winnipeg via Highway 16 and the Trans-Canada.

Driving time: About six hours.

Total time commitment: A full day.

Fees: $6 per person to enter Riding Mountain.

2. Lowlands to Highlands, One-Way

Time to go: June and July – you'll need all the daylight you can get for this one.

Prerequisites: A love of geography, the ability to enjoy long drives along lonely roads, and a packed lunch.

Highlights: The postcard-worthy limestone cliffs of Steep Rock, the remote shores of three Manitoba Great Lakes, a quick visit to Dauphin, the easy climb Manitoba's highest peak, and – if you still have daylight and any energy – a pre-dusk visit to Thunder Hill and the Swan River Valley.

The goods: As early in the day as you can stand, head northwest from the Perimeter on Highway 6 to the community of Woodlands. Exit at PR 518 for a short, scenic drive along the shore of West Shoal Lake before you head west at PR 415 and rejoin Highway 6 at the Lake Manitoba Métis community of St. Laurent. Check out the lake before continuing north on a long, progressively lonely drive to Ashern, where you'll need to top up your tank for what's head. Continue north to PR 239 and head west to Steep Rock. Stop for lunch along the limestone cliffs, take a short walk around the lakeshore, then return to your vehicle to double back to Highway 6. Continuing north, check out the pelicans on the Fairford Dam spillway before driving another fifteen minutes up to PR 328, the last left turn for 140 kilometres. Do not miss the turn! This lonely gravel road will take you through the undeveloped lowlands north of Lake Manitoba to the mostly Cree community of Waterhen. At

PR 276, drive south along the isthmus between Lakes Winnipegosis and Manitoba to Manipogo Provincial Park, named after a supposed sea monster nobody's seen for decades. Go for a swim to stretch your limbs, and then continue south to PR 481, another lonely gravel road, which you'll follow west to the northern tip of Dauphin Lake, then Big Fork Highway 20.

Drive south on the 20 for a half-hour until you get to Dauphin, crossing the Valley River Valley along the way. Stop into Nick's Grill for diner sustenance and pay a visit to Fort Dauphin Museum. Then head west on Highway 5 to Grandview, hooking north on PR 366 to Duck Mountain Provincial Park and Baldy Mountain, the highest peak in the province.

Once at Baldy, climb to the top of the observation tower for a wide view of the valley below. If it's getting dark and you're beat, drive north to Blue Lakes and camp for the night. If there's still fuel in your metabolic tank, continue west through the park on PR 367, stop at the Shell River Valley for a short hike, and exit the park on the way to Highway 83.

On Highway 83, drive north along the Saskatchewan border, past the town of Benito to PR 487. Cross the Swan River and then take a gravel road to the left to reach Thunder Hill, which offers wide views of the darkening Swan River valley to the east.

Drive off the hill and take the northern branch of PR 487 east to Highway 83, which will deposit you in Swan River in a few more minutes. If you've made it this far without cursing me and this guidebook, go have a beer. You deserve it.

Driving time: Up to eight hours. Yes, you read that correctly.

Total time commitment: A very full day

Fees: A Manitoba Parks Pass for Manipogo and Duck Mountain.

Steep Rock, arguably the most photographed spot on Lake Manitoba.

Bartley Kives

Asessippi Ski Area and Winter Park (www.asessippi.com), the newest ski facility in Manitoba. Asessippi has two lifts; a snow-tubing area; a half-pipe and terrain parks for snowboards; and a lodge with fast-food franchises and a pub. Lift rates are $35 a day for adults. There's no lodging at the site, so most skiers stay in Russell or at bed-and-breakfasts in nearby Inglis (see below).

The resort also opens up in July and August for **downhill mountain biking** and **river tubing** on the Shell. Outfitted with special arms to carry bikes, both ski lifts operate on summer weekends for $15 a day (noon to 5 p.m.). River tubing is offered Friday (5 p.m. to 9 p.m.) and weekends (noon to 8 p.m.) for $10. Tubers have to bring their own lifejackets.

The ski area occupies the southeast corner of the provincial park. From Highway 83, head west on PR 482 for two km and turn right into the Shell River Valley.

Keep following PR 482 west to reach the main portion of Asessippi park at the east end of the Shellmouth Dam. The park has a marina, boat launch, beach, two campgrounds, and three short hiking trails. The 1.6-km **Cherry** and 2.3-km **Aspen** trails are flat, but the three-km (return) **Ancient Valley Trail** involves a short climb up and down the Assiniboine River Valley. You'll probably have the trail to yourself – most people come to this park only to fish for pickerel.

Around Asessippi

East of Asessippi, a particularly scenic stretch of the Trans-Canada Trail follows a bend in the Bear Creek to the hamlet of **Inglis** (PR 366 at PR 592), home to the **Inglis Grain Elevators National Historic Site**, a collection of five immense wooden structures from the early twentieth century. They're worth a passing glance on the way to **St. Elijah Romanian Orthodox Church** (just west of PR 592, five km north of Inglis), a 1903 structure founded by the only Romanian pioneer community in rural Manitoba.

Eight km north of Inglis on Highway 83, there are twenty-five-km of challenging cross-country ski loops at **Rivendell X-Country Ski Trails**, a privately maintained trail system one km west of the highway.

Another four km up Highway 83, turn east to visit the **Frank Skinner Arboretum**, where a nursery, gardens, and a short trail celebrate the life's work of the Dropmore, Man., plant breeder who developed and introduced 150 different hybrids that could withstand the nasty Prairie winter.

Roblin

If you're more comfortable on a road bike than on fat tires, you can ride around most of Lake of the Prairies by taking a 100-km circle tour using PR 482, Highway 83, the Trans-Canada Trail, and a short section of Highway 5. The best nearby launch spot is in the town of **Roblin** (pop. 1,818) at the junction of Highways 83 and 5, where locals rave about Austrian restaurant **The Station** (126 1st Street N.W.), a schnitzel-and-spaetzle house operating out of a 1906 CN station.

Dauphin and Vicinity

The largest community in the Parkland, **Dauphin** (pop. 8,085) is a typical Manitoba tourism paradox. Ukrainian culture is the big draw, but the tree-lined little city doesn't have a single restaurant specializing in perogies, cabbage rolls, or other Carpathian culinary treats.

Originally home to Assiniboine and Cree, Dauphin attracted French explorers, British fur-traders, and eventually Ukrainian settlers to the plains north of Riding Mountain, where the Vermilion, Wilson, and Valley Rivers flow east into Dauphin Lake.

Dauphin's Ukrainian Catholic Church of the Resurrection.

Originally the site of a 1741 trading post, the city of Dauphin sits on the Vermilion River at the confluence of highways 5, 10, and 20, only fifteen km north of Riding Mountain. The main attractions are the Byzantine-domed **Ukrainian Catholic Church of the Resurrection** (1106 1st S.W.), a regional art gallery called **Dr. Vernon Watson Allied Arts Centre** (1104 1st N.W.), the **Dauphin Rail Museum** (101 1st N.W.), and, best of all, **Fort Dauphin Museum** (4th S.W. and Jackson).

The Museum goes well beyond the usual pioneer/North West Company content, with exhibits about pre-European culture and archeological sites throughout the region. The museum is open 9 a.m. to 5 p.m. on weekdays from mid-May to the end of June, and daily the rest of the summer.

If you want to stretch your legs, there's a short (1.4 km) walking trail in the middle of town at **Vermilion Park**. As I alluded to earlier, dining options are a bit of a disappointment – you'll have to befriend some locals to find a Ukrainian meal. If you don't care for franchises or small-town Chinese-American buffets, the best place to nosh appears to be the diner-ish **Nick's Grill** (119 Main, 638-7028).

Selo Ukraina Site

For more Ukrainian culture, drive south from Dauphin on Highway 10 to the north slope of Riding Mountain, where the **Selo Ukraina Site** boasts a Ukrainian pioneer village ($3, summer only) and a massive amphitheatre that serves as the focal point for two large summer festivals. Over the August long weekend, Canada's National Ukrainian Festival (www.cnuf.ca) attracts Slavic musicians and dancers from across Canada. In 2005, weekend passes were $55 for adults.

And during the Canada Day weekend, **Dauphin's Countryfest** (www.countryfest.mb.ca) attracts 10,000 cowboys and urban wannabes to one of the two biggest outdoor music festivals in the province (only the Winnipeg Folk Festival garners bigger crowds). Amazingly, about 80 per cent of the Countryfest audience camps out at the site all weekend – the sea of RVs alone is something to behold.

Recent headliners at the four-day, three-stage event have included Gretchen Wilson, LeAnn Rimes, and Big & Rich. In 2006, weekend passes were $170 for adults.

Around Dauphin

If you didn't get your fill of Ukrainian heritage in Dauphin, a remark-ably well-preserved set of hand-built pioneer dwellings stand on the **Wasyl Negrych Farmstead**, about a half-hour drive to the northwest. Ten log structures and an outdoor oven, all built between 1897 and 1910, were designed to emulate Ukrainian dwellings in the Carpathian Mountains. To reach the site from Dauphin, drive west on Highway 5 to Gilbert Plains, head north on PR 274 for seventeen km, and look out for signs on the east side of the road.

Farther west of Gilbert Plains, Highway 5 continues through the town of **Grandview** – a gateway to Duck Mountain Provincial Park (see below) – before criss-crossing the scenic Valley River Valley on the way to Roblin and eventually Saskatchewan.

East of Dauphin, fishing enthusiasts flock to pickerel-rich **Dauphin Lake**, the smallest of Manitoba's "Great Lakes" at 519 square km. The most-popular access point is **Rainbow Beach Provincial Park**, a campground and boat-launch site twenty km east of Dauphin on Highway 20.

Southeast of Dauphin, on a northeast slope of Riding Mountain Provincial Park, the **Ochre River** is one of the most challenging whitewater routes in the province – but it's only possible to shoot during a very short window after the April snowmelt. The recom-mended paddling sections extend twenty-five km from the border of Riding Mountain to a takeout on PR 582, south of the town of Ochre River. You'll need to consult a topographical map to find the put-in.

Forty km east of Dauphin, **Ste. Rose du Lac** (pop. 1,047) is the most northerly Francophone town in Manitoba. It's worth a quick stop to see the stone **Ste. Rose Grotto** at Parc Dollard, just north of Highway 5 on the left side of PR 276. In the winter, the same spot marks the start of a short cross-country ski loop around a bend in the Turtle River.

About thirty-five minutes to the north, in the most-northwestern cranny of Lake Manitoba, you'll find the only provincial park named after a mythical sea serpent. **Manipogo Provincial Park** takes its name from a snakelike aquatic creature that supposedly frequented Lake Manitoba in the middle of the twentieth century. Not coinciden-tally, reports about Manipogo peaked around the same time people in BC claimed to see a Loch Ness–like sea monster of their own in Lake Ogopogo. But unlike deep, dark Loch Ness and Lake Ogopogo, Lake Manitoba is very shallow, and thus is unlikely to harbour many secrets. As a result, even cryptozoologists hold little stock in tales about a Manitoban sea creature.

If you visit Manipogo today, you'll find two campgrounds, a beach, a boat launch, and a short hiking trail – but probably no plesiosaurs. The park is located on PR 276, approximately 60 km north of Ste. Rose du Lac.

Duck Mountain Provincial Park

The highest plateau in Manitoba, **Duck Mountain Provincial Park** is a lot like Riding Mountain's runt of a little brother. While the national park enjoys the protection of strict Parks Canada regulations, this smaller tract of densely forested uplands is scarred by ATV tracks and continues to be logged at a rate that makes conservationists cry in their hemp-flavoured organic brewskis.

Almost two thirds of this post-glacial landscape is open to logging, which is a shame, considering Duck Mountain's natural beauty. Dozens of little lakes – many stocked with trout – are really puddles left behind by retreating glaciers, while the hills that cover the 1,424-square-km plateau are comprised of sand and gravel carried up here by ice 12,000 years ago.

Motorized water-craft are banned from many of the pristine glacial lakes of Duck Mountain Provincial Park.

The tallest of the hills is **Baldy Mountain**, the highest point in Manitoba, which rises up from the southeast corner of the park. Peak-baggers seeking to visit the highest point in every Canadian province will be disappointed by the ease of access to the 831-metre summit: All you have to do is get out of your car and walk a couple of paces.

But the rest of us can appreciate the view. An observation tower provides an even higher vantage point to see the aptly named Valley River Valley to the south.

You can reach the Baldy Mountain parking lot from PR 366, the only north-south route through the park. PR 367 is the sole east-west artery. The two converge near the **Blue Lakes**, popular scuba sites for divers training at altitude. Between East and West Blue Lake, there's a campground, a townsite, and two day-hiking trails. The 5.5-km **Blue Lakes Trail** is a decent little workout, while the one-km **Shining Stone Trail** is just a leg-stretcher.

To the east of the Blue Lakes, the **Wapiti Trail** is a 4.5-km loop near the junction of PR 366 and 367, while there's another camp-ground and beach farther east at Singuish Lake. To the west of Blue Lakes, there's a twenty-three-km, ATV-scarred hike-and-bike trail system at **Mooseberry Lakes**; a built-up area, a campground, and a short hiking/ski loops at **Child's Lake**; and a scenic, 4.5-km loop trail at the **Shell River Valley** in the southwest corner of the park.

MUST SEE:
Baldy Mountain
Manitoba's high-est point...such as it is, with the unspoiled Duck Mountain glacial lakes all around it.

Heading north from Blue Lakes on PR 366, novice canoeists can get their feet wet on the **Chain Lakes** and **Beaver Lake** paddling loops, but the short distances involved make these flatwater routes pointless to anyone but families with small kids. There are also decent day hikes at the **Spray Lake Trail** (5.5 km return) and a good view from the 1.2-km **Copernicus Hill Trail**.

Just to the north, **Wellman Lake** is the largest built-up area in the park, with a campground, a beach, year-round accommodations, and the 3.8-km **Glad Lake cross-country ski trail**, which, in summer, doubles as hiking access to Copernicus Hill.

The Swan River Region

Almost five hours by car from Winnipeg, the Swan River Valley occupies a flat break in the Manitoba Escarpment between Duck Mountain, to the south, and the steep Porcupine Hills to the northwest. This plain is one of the least-visited parts of the province, as southern-Manitoban motorists driving north to Thompson, The Pas, or Churchill usually bypass this area by taking the faster, relatively featureless highways 6 and 60.

The valley is the northernmost agricultural area in Manitoba, parallel in latitude to the northern Interlake and the Canadian Shield wilderness north of Atikaki Provincial Park. As such, it marks the transition between the tourist-oriented parkland and the lonelier, scruffier towns of Manitoba's North.

A pastoral scene in Swan River Valley.

Charles Shilliday

Swan River

Relatively sleepy given its size, the agricultural town of Swan River (pop. 4,032) can be used as a base of operations for exploring the surrounding area. The town has the requisite **pioneer museum** (one km north on Highway 10, May to September), 10 hotels and B&Bs, and one restaurant worth visiting: **Spirit Woman Pottery** (223 5th Avenue North), a pottery studio/café in a 1901 church. An attached gift shop sells crafts by local artists.

Wendy Wilson/Prairie Pathfinders

Thunder Hill

One of the prettiest spots in Manitoba, **Thunder Hill** rises up north of the Swan River Valley, right next to the Saskatchewan border. Archeological evidence suggests that humans have visited this bump in the valley for 9,000 years. Its current name is a modification of the Cree term for Thunderbird Mountain.

To reach the hill as you approach the Swan River Valley from the south, drive

A view of the Swan River Valley from Thunder Hill.

north to PR 487, exiting just north of Benito. Continuing north, cross the Swan River, then turn left at a gravel road that heads northwest. Make another left to access the **Thunder Hill Ski Area**. There's a nice viewpoint at the ski chalet, while sixteen downhill runs are open to skiers in the winter and mountain bikers in the summer.

Porcupine Hills Provincial Forest

Due north of Swan River, **the Porcupine Hills** are home to the second-highest peak in Manitoba, Hart Mountain, at 821 metres above sea level. From Highway 10, the hills rise up on the eastern horizon and continue well into Saskatchewan.

Logging is the main activity in these highlands, but Manitoba Conservation runs three seasonal campgrounds in the hills. **Whitefish Lake** is located in the southwest corner of the park, at the end of PR 279, which branches off Highway 10 about 16 km north of Swan River. Farther north, campgrounds at **Bell Lake** and **North Steeprock Lake** are located on PR 365, which snakes up into the hills just north of Birch River.

There's also one long hike up the Manitoba Escarpment that may be tackled on foot or on a mountain bike. The ten-km (one-way) **Bellsite Trail** follows an old logging road into the hills from a trailhead off Highway 10, about one km north of the town of Bellsite.

Kettle Stones Provincial Park

One of the weirder places in Manitoba, **Kettle Stones Provincial Park** is a four-square-km island of grassland and mixed forest surrounded by the more-dense Jack pine, spruce, and aspen stands of Swan-Pelican Provincial Forest. The main attractions are kettle stones, massive sandstone boulders glued together by dissolved calcium carbonate from ancient seashells. These rare geological formations, sacred to the local Cree, emerged about 8,500 years ago, when wave action on post-glacial Lake Agassiz broke up the surrounding sediments.

Kettle stones ranging between fifty centimetres and five metres in diameter stand out like eerie monuments within this small park, located about seventy km northeast of Swan River. Getting there, however, is a nightmare: Even locals get lost on the way, so it's a good idea to travel with a local guide.

If you're hell-bent on making the trip on your own, the following directions may or may not actually get you there: From Swan River, take Highway 10 east to PR 268, then follow the road north 20.8 km to an unmarked gravel road (if you reach Lenswood, you've gone too far). Turn right and follow a terrible dirt track east for about twenty-five km. Do not attempt this drive in a regular passenger car or van. An off-road 4x4 truck should do the trick, but take a topographical map and compass, just in case. It's easy to get lost, as there are many other dirt tracks in the area.

Once again, this place is not easy to reach, so driver beware.

Lake Winnipegosis Salt Flats

North of the Porcupine Hills, Highway 10 follows the shore of Dawson Bay and Overflowing Bay, the westernmost corners of Lake Winnipegosis. Just north of the 53rd parallel, on the east side of the road, the **Lake Winnipegosis Salt Flats Ecological Preserve** protects an unusual area of pink, orange, and brown saline flats that are home to salt-tolerant plants, and, in late summer, thick mats of colourful microbial growth. Visitors to the site are asked to tread extremely lightly.

A similar site on the southwestern corner of Sagemace Bay, northwest of the town of Winnipegosis, was heavily mined for its salt in the early Victorian era.

Camping Ethics

It's safe to assume many travellers will spend some time outdoors when they visit Manitoba. But while almost every human being has a profound respect for nature, few people agree on the best way to enjoy it – one person's solitude can be another person's redneck bonfire.

In the interest of protecting natural areas and making wilderness trips more enjoyable, the Leave No Trace Centre for Outdoor Ethics, in Boulder, Col., has formulated an excellent series of camping guidelines. The following camping guidelines have been reprinted with permission from Leave No Trace. For more information or materials, please visit www.lnt.org or call (303) 442-8222.

1. Plan Ahead and Prepare

- Know the regulations and special concerns for the area you'll visit.
- Prepare for extreme weather, hazards, and emergencies.
- Schedule your trip to avoid times of high use.
- Visit in small groups. Split larger parties into groups of four to six.
- Repackage food to minimize waste.
- Use a map and compass to eliminate the use of marking paint, rock cairns, or flagging.

2. Travel and Camp on Durable Surfaces

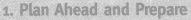

- Durable surfaces include established trails and campsites, rock, gravel, dry grasses, or snow.
- Protect riparian areas by camping at least sixty-five metres from lakes and streams.
- Good campsites are found, not made. Altering a site is not necessary.
- In popular areas: concentrate use on existing trails and campsites; walk single-file in the middle of the trail, even when it's wet or muddy; keep campsites small; and focus activity in areas where vegetation is absent.
- In pristine areas: disperse use to prevent the creation of campsites and trails; avoid places where effects on the ecosystem are just beginning.

Jason Sorby

As annoying as the job may be, you must hang your food and garbage in bear country, if no lock box is available.

3. Dispose of Waste Properly

- Pack it in, pack it out; inspect your campsite and rest areas for trash or spilled foods. Pack out all trash, leftover food, and litter.
- Deposit solid human waste in catholes dug ten to fifteen centimetres deep, at least sixty-five metres from water, camp, and trails. Cover and disguise the cathole when finished.
- Pack out toilet paper and hygiene products.
- To wash yourself or your dishes, carry water sixty-five metres away from streams or lakes and use small amounts of biodegradable soap. Scatter strained dishwater.

4. Leave What You Find

- Preserve the past: examine, but do not touch, cultural or historic structures and artifacts.
- Leave rocks, plants, and other natural objects as you find them.
- Avoid introducing or transporting non-native species.
- Do not build structures or furniture, and don't dig trenches.

5. Minimize Effects of Campfires

- Campfires can cause lasting consequences to the backcountry. Use a lightweight stove for cooking, and enjoy a candle lantern for light.
- Where fires are permitted, use established fire rings, fire pans, or mound fires.
- Keep fires small. Only use sticks from the ground that can be broken by hand.
- Burn all wood and coals to ash, put out campfires completely, then scatter cool ashes.

6. Respect Wildlife

- Observe wildlife from a distance. Do not follow or approach them.
- Never feed animals. Feeding wildlife damages their health, alters natural behaviours, and exposes them to predators and other dangers.
- Protect wildlife and your food by storing rations and trash securely.
- Control pets at all times, or leave them at home.
- Avoid wildlife during sensitive times: mating, nesting, raising young, or winter.

7. Be Considerate of Other Visitors

- Respect other visitors and protect the quality of their experience.
- Be courteous. Yield to other users on the trail.
- Step to the downhill side of the trail when encountering pack stock.
- Take breaks and camp away from trails and other visitors.
- Let nature's sounds prevail. Avoid loud voices and noises.

Despite its image as a Prairie province, more than half of Manitoba is a rugged landscape that's never grown so much as a stalk of wheat. The rocky Canadian Shield covers most of northern Manitoba, with the exception of a strip of tundra along Hudson Bay and the swampy limestone lowlands around Cedar Lake and the northwest side of Lake Winnipeg.

Cree and Dene hunted and fished in this vast area for hundreds, if not thousands, of years before the first European explorers travelled down from Hudson Bay in the seventeenth century. Fur traders followed in the next decades, and trapping took off, but most northern First Nations clung to hunter-gatherer lifestyles until the twentieth century. The last truly nomadic people in the region, the Sayisi Dene, were forcibly removed from their traditional caribou-hunting lands in 1956. Though some indigenous people continue to hunt, fish, and trap, northern Manitoba's economy is now based on mining, logging, and hydroelectric power. There are few road-accessible communities, but the towns with industry are relatively large – Thompson, Flin Flon, and The Pas are Manitoba's third-, ninth-, and eleventh-largest cities, despite the fact that northern Manitoba's population density is extremely low.

There are only four major highways in the region: Highway 6, up from the Interlake to Thompson; Highway 10 to The Pas and Flin Flon; and the 39 and 60, both of which connect the two north-south routes. Narrower roads lead to the mining towns of Snow Lake, Sherridon, and Lynn Lake, hydroelectric centre Gillam, and Norway House Cree Nation, at the north end of Lake Winnipeg. All the other northern communities are only served by rail, floatplane, or ice road, including sixteen economically depressed and extremely isolated First Nations.

Up until the 1980s, tourists visiting the North came primarily to hunt or fish. But lower-impact activities, such as wilderness travel and wildlife-watching, are on the rise, especially in Churchill, the Hudson Bay port town built next to the largest concentration of polar bears in the world.

Obviously, anyone visiting The North is coming for more than a daytrip. It takes 7.5 hours to drive from Winnipeg to Flin Flon or

Opposite: Polar bears are the main tourist draw up in Churchill, but the unusual outpost also boasts beluga whales, migratory birds, wildflowers, and spectacular northern lights.

Joe Bryksa/Winnipeg Free Press

Thompson, while getting to Churchill by any means other than airplane will consume more than a day. But if you have the time, there are many fascinating sights up here, including unusual limestone formations at Clearwater and Iskwasum lakes and along the north shore of Lake Winnipeg, two massive waterfalls along the Grass River, inquisitive beluga whales in the Churchill River estuary; and, in almost every town, the unusual, rugged culture unique to Manitoba's north.

Manitoba Lowlands

When Jean Chrétien was Canada's prime minister, Parks Canada was instructed to establish a national park for all thirty-nine "natural areas" in the nation. They had twenty-two covered, and needed seventeen more to go. One of those areas without a representative park was the Manitoba Lowlands, a huge crescent of very flat land that extends up from the US border, across the Central Plains and Interlake, and northwest into Saskatchewan.

Seeing as it didn't make sense to build a park on top of prime agricultural land, biologists, conservationists, and bureaucrats nominated two sparsely populated patches of land along lonely Highway 6 to become Manitoba's third national park. Plans were made, maps were drawn, and announcements were made – and then absolutely nothing happened, as communities near the proposed park decided they didn't want a protected area in their backyards.

The proposed Manitoba Lowlands National Park, which likely would have been given a Cree name, was supposed to cover two sections of Lake Winnipeg's western shoreline above and below the town of Grand Rapids. The park would have protected hundreds of kilometres of pristine shoreline, one of the world's longest freshwater sand spits, stunning limestone cliffs, a unique colour-shifting lake, bat hibernacula, and nesting grounds for bald eagles, white pelicans, and blue herons. The park would also have been the only place in North America where you could find all five of the continent's big ungulates – moose, elk, deer, caribou, and even a herd of reintroduced wood bison.

At the time this guidebook went to print, though, the prospects for the park were growing grimmer by the day. The only Parks Canada official assigned to the Lowlands file had moved to Alberta, and surrounding communities – the town of Grand Rapids and four

First Nations – were either indifferent or outright hostile to the park idea, despite the obvious potential tourism benefits.

Luckily, the natural wonders that were supposed to be protected by this park aren't going anywhere. On a trip north to Thompson or Churchill, there are a handful of attractions accessible by vehicle from Highway 6. Just make sure you have plenty of gas in your tank, as this is the loneliest road in Manitoba – Grand Rapids has the only gas station for 350 km along a stretch of road from St. Martin Junction, in the northern Interlake, to Ponton, at the confluence of Highways 6 and 39.

The limestone cliffs at Sturgeon Gill Point, a feature of the proposed Manitoba Lowlands National Park.

Lowlands Destinations

Driving north from the Interlake, the first Lowlands sight you can visit is **Long Point**, a large peninsula jutting into Lake Winnipeg's wild and wavy northern basin. About two km north of North Twin Creek, at a ninety-degree bend in Highway 6, the gravel Long Point Road provides access to a fishing-boat launch and a rugged beach where there's an excellent chance of seeing bald eagles and herons in summer. If you don't care about birds, don't bother.

About forty km up the road, gas up at Grand Rapids, a hydro-electric town on the spot where the Saskatchewan River empties into Lake Winnipeg. The rapids, of course, have been tamed by the huge **Grand Rapids Generating Station Dam**, which you can visit by taking an access road on the north side of the river. During the summer, there are usually pelicans on the spillway, which doesn't make a bad picnic spot.

About thirty-two km north of Grand Rapids, another gravel road leads east to **Sturgeon Gill Point**, a small fishing marina next to a rocky beach. The beach leads south to a set of limestone cliffs that rival the impressive formations at Steep Rock on Lake Manitoba. The best time to visit is midwinter, when you can walk onto the lake ice to view the cliffs. In the summer, you'll need a canoe and unusually calm water to get the same view. You can also approach the cliffs on foot, but you'll need waterproof boots and tall gaiters to walk around the edge of a marsh that sits between the parking lot and beach.

Another thirty km north, on the west side of Highway 6, pull over at Mosakahiken Cree Nation to view **Little Limestone Lake**, one of the world's most unusual karst lakes. Karst refers to limestone areas with underwater cavities, but Little Limestone has something even more fascinating than caves: the lake changes colour when the air temperature rises or drops, as lime precipitates out of the lake or gets dissolved back into it. Little Limestone Lake can be blue, turquoise, or green, depending on the temperature. Sadly, it sits on top of a nickel deposit coveted by the mining industry. For now, it remains outside the proposed park area.

The Pas

Six hours northwest of Winnipeg, **The Pas** (pronounced "the paw") is actually two communities rolled into one. About 5,800 people live in the paper-mill town on the south side of the Saskatchewan River, while 2,500 more dwell north of the river in Opaskwayak Cree Nation (OCN), easily the most entrepreneurial reserve in northern Manitoba.

As recently as thirty years ago, the two communities didn't trust each other, as racism divided the white and Aboriginal populations. Today, the situation has improved to the point where two of the most important institutions are shared: Pas residents cheer on the **OCN Blizzard** (www.ocnblizzard.com), a perennial contender in the Manitoba Junior Hockey League, while Opaskwayak members are an integral part of **The Pas Trappers Festival** (www.trappersfestival.com), a February shindig featuring dogsled races, ice-fishing competitions, cured meats, smoked fish, and other rustic traditions.

The main tourist attraction is on the OCN side of the river. **Aseneskak Casino** (Highway 10, www.aseneskak.ca), the first Aboriginal-run casino in Manitoba, offers the usual games plus a gift shop selling Aboriginal crafts. OCN also runs the nicest hotel in the area, the **Kikiwak Inn**, and hosts a First Nations cultural festival every August called **Opaskwayak Indian Days**.

On the south side of the river, the **Sam Waller Museum** (306 Fischer, 623-3802) houses natural and regional history exhibits inside a 1916 brick building, which once served as the local courthouse. It's open all year, and only charges $2 admission for adults. Hours are 1 p.m. to 5 p.m. Wednesday, Saturday, and Sunday, and 1 p.m. to 9 p.m. Thursday and Friday.

You'll also find one of the best greasy spoons in the province in The Pas. **Miss The Pas** (158 Edwards, 623-3130) is the kind of place where there are so many pictures and knicknacks on the walls that you don't need to bring a newspaper. The food is good, homespun diner fare.

Clearwater Lake Provincial Park

While The Pas isn't the prettiest town in Manitoba, there's plenty of natural beauty nearby. Immediately north of town, **Clearwater Lake Provincial Park** (Highway 10 at PR 287) is a 590-square-km greenspace dominated by a cold, almost circular, and – as the name suggests – unusually clear body of water teeming with trout.

Fishing is a big deal here. The park also has two campgrounds, both located off PR 287. There's also one excellent short walking trail between the two campgrounds – **Clearwater Caves**, an 800-metre loop around crevices formed by masses of dolomite limestone that broke away from shoreline cliffs. As well, the **Jackfish Creek Fishway** is worth a stop in the early spring to watch northern pike swim upstream to spawn.

MUST SEE:
Pisew and
Kwasitchewan
Falls
Manitoba's two tallest waterfalls, connected by a twenty-two-km hiking trail through the northern boreal forest.

Flin Flon

Bartley Kives

Heading north from The Pas on Highway 10, the flat, swampy Manitoba Lowlands landscape gives way to rugged and rocky Canadian Shield shortly before Flin Flon, a quirky mining town on the Saskatchewan border.

Like The Pas, **Flin Flon** is really two communities living side by side. About 6,300 people live in houses scattered among the granite hills on the Manitoba side of the border, while another 1,800 live in Creighton, Saskatchewan, to the immediate southwest. **The Hudson Bay Mining and Smelting Company**, just west of downtown, dominates the twin communities. The massive open-face pit is not visible from Highway 10, but you can see the main stack from several kilometres away. At 251 metres, it's the tallest free-standing structure in western Canada. To put that in perspective, the Eiffel Tower in Paris stands 320 metres.

Flin Flon takes its name from Flintabbatey Flonatin, a character in a pulp fiction novel found by a prospector. The statue at the entrance to the town was designed by cartoonist Al Capp of *L'il Abner* fame.

Between 1930 and 1992, HBM&S removed about 63 million tonnes of mostly zinc and copper ore from the open-face pit and two main shafts, including one extending more than a kilometre below the surface. Today, most of the ore refined at the plant is shipped in from other northern Manitoba mines. In one abandoned shaft, an underground greenhouse is used to grow organic veggies, medicinal plants, and even a government-approved crop of medicinal marijuana. A couple of Main Street shops sell T-shirts trumpeting Flin Flon's status as Canada's marijuana capital, to the annoyance of many of the locals.

As if a big mine wasn't enough, Flin Flon's topography adds to the hardscrabble feel of the town, as Canadian Shield greenstone is everywhere. Houses and streets are built on the sides of outcroppings, while long wooden boxes are used to insulate above-ground sewer lines – it's simply not economical to drill holes in solid granite just to move human waste around.

A five-kilometre-long walking trail encircles Ross Lake in the heart of Flin Flon.

Wendy Wilson/Prairie Pathfinders

217

Given the steep inclines, it's arguably more fun to walk around Flin Flon than any other Manitoba town. The best route is a five-km trek around **Ross Lake**, an ancient Shield lake in the middle of the community. Park at Mike's Ice N Burger Hut (Island Drive and 3rd Avenue, 687-8600, summer only) and walk counterclockwise around the lake – you'll cross a flat wooden boardwalk, hike up steep cliffs with wooden stairs, and then descend along 3rd Avenue to gloriously greasy fast food.

Other places to check out include the waterfowl sanctuary at **Hapnot Lake** (Bellevue Avenue at Ross Street); modest **Joe Brain Children's Petting Zoo** (Green Street at Balsam Avenue, May to October); and the **Flin Flon Tourist Park** (Highway 10A at the east end of town), where you can pick up regional tourism info or visit the **Station Museum** (June through August, 10 a.m. to 8 p.m.) and nab a sample of copper ore as a free souvenir.

Outside the museum, an oversized statue of Flintabattey Flonatin, designed by L'il Abner cartoonist Al Capp, explains how the town's unusual moniker derives from a character in a pulp novel found by an early prospector.

Around Flin Flon

Just south of Flin Flon, across the Saskatchewan border, the **Flin Flon Ski Club** maintains 27 km of trails that extend down to the northwest arm of Schist Lake. The hilly Shield topography makes for excellent cross-country skiing and decent mountain biking, especially on sections of bare greenstone. To reach the main parking lot from 3rd Avenue, head south on Boam Street and follow Cemetery, Horace, and then an unnamed road south. Trail-use fees are $4 a day.

Southeast of the city, Highway 10 crosses cool, clear Athapapuskow Lake at **Bakers Narrows Provincial Park**, a popular campground with two beaches and an observation tower offering views of Canadian Shield scenery. If you're looking for peace and quiet, there are six unserviced campsites along the lake at the north side of the park, away from all the RVs and rowdies. Immediately across the highway, you can belly up to hearty buffets at **Bakers Narrows Lodge** (www.bakersnarrowslodge.com), a fishing outfitter that also rents out cabins for $200 a night.

Southwest of Creighton, meanwhile, Saskatchewan Highway 167 heads to **Amisk Lake**, a large Canadian Shield lake used as a summer resort by Flin Flon residents. **Denare Beach**, 18 km southwest of Creighton, is a good spot to buy locally processed wild rice, rent a houseboat for lazy trips on Amisk Lake or simply hang at the beach.

From Denare Beach, Highway 167 continues south along the east shore of Amisk Lake, exiting the Canadian Shield on its way past a series of limestone crevices and the put-in for the lower portion of the **Sturgeon-Weir River**.

From here, it's a two-day, relatively easy whitewater paddle to Sturgeon Landing, where you can arrange to have your vehicle shuttled – Manitoba Highway 10 is only 25 km to the east.

Grass River Corridor

The relatively tame **Grass River** was once a valuable and easy-to-paddle link between traplines in north-western Manitoba and trading posts along Hudson Bay. The 450-km-long river, which flows from the Cranberry Lakes southeast of Flin Flon to the Nelson River near Split Lake, is generally free of both the lazy meanders typical of Manitoba Lowlands rivers and the violent rapids associated with the Canadian Shield.

There are far fewer people on the Grass River today than there were in the eighteenth and nine-teenth centuries, which is surprising, considering the two major roads – highways 39 and 6 – that now parallel the route all the way from Cranberry Portage to Thompson.

Driving down the highways, there are interesting historical and natural attractions along the way, including a karst spring inside Grass River Provincial Park, a stunning pictograph site at Tramping Lake, and Manitoba's biggest waterfalls, Pisew and Kwasitchewan Falls.

The Grass River tumbles 14 metres at Kwasitchewan Falls, Manitoba's highest waterfall, accessible via canoe or the twenty-two kilometre Upper Track Hiking Trail.

Canoeists and kayakers can also tackle portions of the route, enjoying surprisingly clear water and well-marked portages. Hap Wilson and Stephanie Aykroyd's *Wilderness Rivers of Manitoba* has a good description of the first 350 km, while **Clearwater Canoe Outfitters** (www.mts.net/~rgallagh/clearwater), an established out-fitter in The Pas, rents out canoes and can arrange transportation by car or rail.

Grass River Provincial Park

The largest road-accessible park in northern Manitoba, **Grass River Provincial Park** protects 2,300 square km of forests, swamps, and lakes in the transition zone between the Manitoba Lowlands and the Canadian Shield. The main attractions are fishing, camping, and canoeing, though wildlife watching is on the upswing. Woodland caribou range all the way through the park and usually choose to calve on tiny, predator-free islands in the middle of the summer. The park also boasts sizable moose, deer, beaver, otter, black bear, heron, pelican, and cormorant populations, as well as smaller numbers of wolves, lynx, martens, fishers, and even wolverines.

Motorists can access the park in four places. At the west end of the park on Highway 10, the town of **Cranberry Portage** offers water access to First Cranberry Lake, and is the only place to load up on supplies like fishing gear and groceries. Heading east on Highway 39, there are campgrounds, beaches, and boat launches at

Simonhouse Lake, Iskwasum Lake, and wavy Reed Lake, the latter the largest obstacle to paddlers continuing on east. The Iskwasum Lake campground also marks the start of the Karst Spring Trail, a 3.2-km hiking loop that passes by one of the weirder sights in the province: A stream that surges out of solid limestone before it drains into the Grass River.

Tramping Lake and Wekusko Falls

If you're fascinated by early Aboriginal history, you have to add Tramping Lake to your life list. The most dramatic set of ancient pictographs in Manitoba appears on a rock face in the northern channel of this narrow lake. The ochre paintings, believed to be thousands of years old, depict birds, mammals, snakes, and humanoid figures. They stretch for metres up the rock face, which is unusual for pictographs, which normally appear only at canoe level.

The only way to see the pictographs is from the water. If you're not paddling down the Grass River, you can rent a canoe or motorboat at Wekusko Falls Lodge (www.wekuskofallslodge.com) on PR 392, which branches off Highway 39 just east of Tramping Lake. Alternatively, there's a boat launch on the south end of Tramping Lake, at the end of a muddy 4X4 track that leads north from Highway 39.

Wekusko Falls, meanwhile, is worth at least a quick visit, as the Grass River drops twelve metres between Tramping and Wekusko lakes. Wekusko Falls Lodge occupies the west side of PR 392, while small Wekusko Falls Provincial Park is on the east. The park's main campground is massive, but there are ten more-secluded walk-in tent sites scattered along the falls, which is nice if you want to get away from the hum of generators.

MUST SEE:
Tramping Lake pictographs
One of the largest assortments of early Aboriginal rock art in Manitoba, accessible via motorboat or canoe from Wekusko Falls.

Pisew Falls, Kwasitchewan Falls, and Paint Lake

No drive up to Thompson is complete without a pit stop at Pisew Falls, a thirteen-metre Grass River waterfall accessible from Highway 6 about forty km northeast of the community of Wabowden. Boardwalks leading right up to the falls offer close-up views of the torrent, as well as the ferns and mosses that thrive off the spray. It's an even more dramatic sight during the winter – even -30°C temperatures can't freeze the flow.

At the opposite end of the parking lot, the twenty-two-km (return) Upper Track Hiking Trail leads to Kwasitchewan Falls, Manitoba's highest at fourteen metres. There are backcountry campsites at the far end of the trail, the nicest sitting above the falls at a gorgeous set of little rapids. It's a fantastic little overnight, albeit with one potential hazard – there are no bear boxes at the campsites, so be prepared to hang your food from a high tree limb.

The Upper Track loop can also be traversed in a single day, provided you're used to hiking on uneven Canadian Shield terrain. The nearest car camping is forty km south at Setting Lake (across

Highway 6 from Wabowden) or fifty km north at Paint Lake Provincial Park (Highway 6 at PR 375), the usual take-out for longer Grass River canoe trips.

Paint Lake Provincial Park also has a marina, two beaches, and a large campground and five canoe-camping sites, plus three cross-country ski loops, an outdoor skating rink, and a toboggan run in the winter. There are year-round accommodations at **Paint Lake Resort** (677-9303).

Thompson

At the end of long, lonely Highway 6, **Thompson** (pop. 13,256) emerges like a surreal vision of civilization amid the wilds of the boreal forest. Manitoba's third-largest city is also one of the newest communities in the province: there was nothing here before 1956, when a massive body of nickel ore was discovered near the Burntwood River. Over the next five years, mining giant Inco created a city from scratch, building a nickel mine, smelter, refinery, and all the amenities needed to serve the humans required to work all the machinery. As a result, Thompson looks a lot like a 1960s suburb plopped into the middle of the wilderness, with an inner commercial core ringed by neatly planned residential streets and then ... well, nothing. Except trees, and a big, huge nickel mine.

MUST SEE: Flin Flon, The Pas, and Thompson Hardscrabble northern logging and mining towns with a still-thriving frontier spirit.

From the air, the open-face portion of the mine looks like an ugly brown scar on a dark-green landscape. From the ground, it's a little less freaky – **free tours of Inco's surface operations** are offered weekdays at 10 a.m. from June through August, and Thursdays at 10:30 a.m. the rest of the year. You must be at least fourteen and prepared to wear a hardhat.

Aside from mining, Thompson also serves as a transportation hub for the rest of northern Manitoba. Scheduled flights and charters from Thompson Municipal Airport (ten km north of Thompson, off PR 391) serve isolated First Nations and remote fishing lodges across the North. The Via Rail Station (Station Road, east of downtown; www.viarail.ca) offers the cheapest means of getting to Churchill – the thirteen-hour ride from Thompson costs as little as $56 each way if you book in advance.

Whatever you do, do not leave your vehicle at the train station! Anything of value inside will be removed during your visit to Churchill. For a small fee, the staff at **McCreedy Campground** (Mystery Lake Road, just north of the Burntwood River) will look after your car and provide shuttle service to the train station.

If you actually have time to see a bit of Thompson, the best diversion is **Thompson Zoo** (275 Thompson Drive North), where the small collection of creatures includes two lynx, Arctic and timber wolves, three species of owls, and assorted farm animals. Admission is free, but donations are appreciated. The zoo is open noon to 8 p.m. June through August, and noon to 5 p.m. the rest of the year.

If real wolves aren't enough, a much-larger *Canis lupus* is painted on to the side of **Highland Towers** (274 Princeton), an apartment building on the east of town. The ten-storey timber-wolf mural, completed in 2005, is a reproduction of a painting by wildlife artist Robert Bateman.

Since this city is only fifty years old, tourists will be spared the drudgery of a pioneer museum in a dusty, old home. Instead, **Heritage North Museum** (162 Princeton, 677-2216) offers a mix of natural and cultural history inside two hand-built log cabins. Hours vary with the seasons.

Annual events in Thompson include the town fair, **Nickel Days**, usually held the fourth weekend in June; and Winterfest, a February rival to the Trappers Festival in The Pas.

Finally, about fifteen minutes north of Thompson on PR 280, non-profit **Mystery Mountain Winter Park** (www.mysterymountain.ca) has eighteen downhill runs, a cross-country ski trail system, and an area for snow-tubing. Lift rates are $27 per day for adults, tubing is $10 per hour, and cross-country ski access is $5.

Churchill

Aside from Winnipeg, and possibly Riding Mountain, Manitoba's premiere destination is **Churchill** (pop. 963), an extremely isolated Hudson Bay port that's become one of the top ecotourism spots in Canada. This end-of-the-railway outpost's embarrassment of natural attractions includes beluga whales, birds, and wildflowers in the summer; polar bears in the fall; and northern lights and caribou in mid-winter. Factor in a bizarre and colourful history that encompasses fur-trade-era naval intrigue, a Depression-era megaproject, Cold War military paranoia, and even a short-lived stint as a rocket launching pad, and you have a weird and wonderful town worthy of a visit any time of year.

A sunset over the Prince of Wales Fort. Sea-kayaking the mouth of the Churchill River is possible, but only with a guide.

Bartley Kives

Churchill's Unusual History

Ecologically speaking, the tundra around Churchill is the newest piece of the province. The Hudson Bay Lowlands only emerged from glacial ice about 8,000 years ago, a full 4,000 years after Turtle Mountain and other parts of southwestern Manitoba. Compressed by a couple of kilometres of ice, the Churchill region has been rebounding upwards at a rate of 1.3 metres every century since the ice disappeared. When the first Aboriginal people moved into the area – no later than 2,900 years ago, according to archeological evidence found at Twin Lakes, southeast of Churchill – the Hudson Bay coastline was located several kilometres south of the current shore. Geographers have found at least 185 former beach ridges between the original coast and the modern waterline.

For at least a millennium, Dene hunters followed herds of barren-lands caribou around the taiga west of Hudson Bay, occasionally coming into conflict with Cree from the south and Inuit from the north. The first European to see the region was British explorer Thomas Button in 1612, followed by Danish sailor Jens Munck in 1619 and inland adventurer Henry Kelsey, who ventured up the Churchill River in 1690.

In 1732, British fur traders began building Prince of Wales Fort on the west side of the river to protect Hudson's Bay Company assets from the French. The massive stone fort, which had twelve-metre-thick walls and forty cannons, was finally finished forty years later. Comically, the French navy didn't show up for another ten years, finally surprising the hapless Brits in 1782. The mighty fort fell without a shot being fired, but the French soon returned the strategically useless property in a peace treaty.

For the next century, British merchants continued to trade with Dene trappers at Churchill, but the end of the fur trade saw the fort slide into obscurity. Luckily for Churchill, the Manitoba, Saskatchewan, and Alberta governments devised an ambitious plan to build a railway across the muskeg to a new Churchill seaport. Grain from western Canadian farms would then be shipped from Churchill to the UK across the shortest transatlantic shipping route yet.

The rickety Hudson Bay Railway was completed in 1929, when a new port, grain elevator, and town were built on the east side of the Churchill River. But since the shipping lanes were only ice-free three months a year, the port would never become very profitable.

Still, the town got lucky again, as Cold War tensions led the Canadian and American military to build air and naval bases at Churchill to keep an eye out for invading Soviets. A binational aerospace effort even led to the creation of a rocket-launching range in 1956. By 1965, the town's population had swollen to almost 7,000. Unfortunately, advances in radar technology made the airbase obsolete, and the military bases closed down and were soon dismantled. The town's population had shrunk to 1,600 by 1970, and has slowly been declining ever since.

Churchill
Polar bears in the
fall, rare birds in
the spring, and
beluga whales in
the summer at one
of Canada's top
ecotourism desti-
nations.

Adding to the town's misery was the most shameful event in the modern history of Manitoba: the forced relocation of the Sayisi Dene. In 1956, the Canadian government airlifted the nomadic people from its traditional caribou-hunting grounds near Duck Lake in north-central Manitoba and settled them on the outskirts of Churchill. Ostensibly, they were moved to protect the caribou. It was a horrible mistake with disastrous consequences.

Accustomed to living off the land, the 1,100-member band suddenly found itself with no food, shelter, or means of support. Alcoholism, violence, and sexual abuse became norms in the exiled community, which endured a miserable seventeen-year stay in Churchill. A third of their numbers died from suicide, murder, disease, and misadventure.

The Sayisi Dene were finally returned to their traditional lands in 1973, when the survivors set up a new settlement at Tadoule Lake. With the benefit of hindsight, the entire sad episode is considered an act of cultural genocide. It's recounted in *Night Spirits*, a moving non-fiction account by Dene author Ila Bussidor.

On a less-sombre note, Churchill's fortunes have improved since the end of the '70s with the advent of polar-bear-watching tours. Today, ecotourism brings in tens of thousands of visitors a year, outshining even the port as the driving force of the local economy.

Getting to Churchill

Unless you own an icebreaker, the only way to Churchill is by air or rail, with neither option being cheap or easy. There are no roads across the muskeg to Hudson Bay, though Manitoba and Nunavut have talked about one day building a permanent road from Gillam up to Churchill, and eventually along the west coast of Hudson Bay to the high Arctic.

In the meantime, return flights from Winnipeg to Churchill on Calm Air (www.calmair.com) and Kivalliq Air (www.kivalliqair.com) start at $690 and $900, respectively. During the summer and peak polar bear-watching season, there are flights six days a week. The 1,000-km plane ride takes about two hours. In contrast, a Via Rail (www.viarail.ca) trip from Winnipeg takes thirty-six hours each way along a circuitous route that actually curves west into Saskatchewan before heading northwest. The cheapest return ticket is $335. To save money – and time – the best way to reach Churchill from Winnipeg is to drive up to Thompson, park your vehicle at McCreedy Campground (see the *Thompson* section), and then take the thirteen-hour, $56 (one-way) Via Rail trip north across the muskeg.

Regardless of whether you travel by plane or train, make sure the tours and accommodations you desire aren't booked up before your visit. If that sounds too complicated – and money is not an issue – you can book a combination flight/motel/ecotourism package through companies such as **Churchill Nature Tours** (www.churchillnaturetours.com), **Frontiers North Adventures** (www.frontiersnorth.com), or **Churchill Wild** (www.churchillwild.com) and save yourself the logistical headache.

Bartley Kives

Churchill Ecotourism

So what makes Churchill such a desirable place to watch wildlife? Mostly, it's a fluke of geography. Just east of the town, about 1,200 **polar bears** spend the summer lazing about the tundra in protected Wapusk National Park, home to largest concentration of denning sites in the world. The bears can't hunt for seals, their main food source, without ice on Hudson Bay. So every fall, they head to the one place where the bay freezes up earliest – the Churchill area, where fresh water from the Churchill River dilutes the seawater.

On any given day in late October and early November, dozens of polar bears are usually visible on the tundra to the immediate east of the town. For decades, the human residents used to bemoan the presence of these ferocious and extremely intelligent carnivores that occasionally wander into the community in search of an easy meal. Too often, aggressive bears were killed for being too curious. But in 1979, following another period of economic stagnation, some locals finally got the bright idea to offer tours of the surrounding tundra and show off the massive creatures to the world. They use oversized vehicles with massive, bog-eating wheels and windows well above the (usual) reach of polar bears.

Today, two tour companies have the exclusive right to offer trips around the tundra between Churchill and the northwest border of Wapusk: **Tundra Buggy Tours** (www.tundrabuggy.com) and **Great White Bear Tours** (www.greatwhitebeartours.com). You'll pay in the hundreds for a day of polar bear watching – and thousands for a package tour. To many people, the chance to watch the world's most dangerous land predator is a once-in-a-lifetime experience. And along with bears, you're likely to see Arctic foxes, Arctic hares, and ptarmigans out on the tundra. But don't come expecting a wilderness experience, as you'll be sharing your ride with several dozen other tourists. As well, the bears appear to be quite used to the vehicles – some of the critters even try to drink the wastewater that leaks from portable tundra lodges, which are just buggies linked together and equipped with beds and kitchens.

Above: A view of Prince of Wales Fort from Cape Merry, just west of Churchill.
Left: An Arctic fox.

Of course, it's possible to see polar bears in the wild without paying big bucks for a tundra vehicle tour, but unlikely if you don't plan to rent a car. Travelling on foot would be insane during polar bear season, though any bears that venture too close to Churchill are captured by Manitoba Conservation officers and locked up in a "bear jail" east of town until the ice freezes, or the opportunity arises to move them by helicopter. The cheapest tourists used to pay cabbies to drive them to the town dump – also known as "the polar bear diner" – and wait for scavenging bears to arrive. But the dump was closed in 2005, much to the chagrin of locals who believe their kitchens will be the bears' next target.

While bears are the main draw in Churchill, the summer congregation of **beluga whales** at the mouth of the Churchill River can be more rewarding. In July and early August, about 3,000 of the four-metre-long whales feed on small fish called capelin in the partly saline estuary, with grey whale calves swimming circles around their bright-white mothers in an amazing displays of aquatic grace.

Most tourists see the whales on a tour boat or on Zodiacs operated by **Sea North Tours** (www.seanorthtours.com), which also offers tours of Prince of Wales Fort on the west side of the river. You're guaranteed to see whales this way, but anyone who's slightly fit should also try **Kayak Churchill** (www.kayakchurchill.com), which offers guided paddles into the rivermouth. There are few experiences more profound than being surrounding by a pod of these highly intelligent mammals as they chirp like birds, vent their blowholes, and, if you're really lucky, playfully nudge your kayak. The downside is that some day-paddles may not result in whale encounters.

Other summertime sights around Churchill include spectacular blooms of **wildflowers** from June through August, and fantastic **birding** from mid-April into July. Churchill is one of the top birdwatching spots in North America, with loons, tundra swans, eiders, mergansers, and gyrfalcons among the most sought-after species. Some of the top birding spots include upriver in the Churchill River estuary; Bird Cove, east of town; and Akudlik Marsh to the southeast (see *Around Churchill*, below). Unfortunately, there's no safe way to wander on foot for any distance, as encounters with stealthy and silent polar bears are possible at any time of year. The only safe way to go for a hike at any time of year is with **Adventure Walking Tours** (675-2147). Guide Paul Ratson, a knowledgeable naturalist, carries a bear banger, just in case.

Tours of the Churchill area by dogsled, snowmobile, helicopter, and Bombardier – a tank-like covered snowmobile – may also be arranged. For a complete list of options, visit the **Tourist Information Centre** located across from the Via Rail station.

The Churchill Townsite

When you live in a place where the neighbours are capable of killing and eating you, you tend to develop a weird personality. That's part of the allure of Churchill, the only town in Canada where gun-toting escorts take kids trick-or-treating on Halloween, and police ignore ATV drivers who cruise down the main drag with shotguns strapped to their back.

From a very young age, Churchillians are taught to fear and respect polar bears, one of the few creatures actually known to prey on people, if given the chance. During polar bear season, the townsfolk are incredibly wary – they take cabs to travel even short distances at night and don't even poke their noses outside their homes until they're sure no bears are lurking in the area.

Their vigilance has been rewarded with a remarkable statistic: No human has been killed by a polar bear since 1983, when a hapless drunk tempted fate by wandering into a burned-out building to relieve himself. Bears will snack on humans even though we don't have enough fat to really interest them (they much prefer a tasty meal of rich seal blubber).

In daylight, the Churchill townsite is generally safe to negotiate, especially during the long summer days. Attractions in the compact town include interpretive displays at the **Parks Canada Visitor Reception Centre** in the Via Rail Station; incredible Inuit art at the **Eskimo Museum**; Aboriginal art of all stripes for sale at **Northern Images**; and handmade crafts at **Arctic Trading Company**. It's also fun to jump around the rocks on the Hudson Bay coast behind the sprawling **Town Centre Complex**, but even here, polar bears can be a danger.

The nicest-looking places to grab a meal in Churchill are the **Lazy Bear Café**, a gorgeous wooden room in the Lazy Bear Lodge, and the less-well-lit **Trader's Table**. Located at opposite ends of Kelsey Boulevard, they both serve Arctic char, and sometimes caribou, at tourist-trap prices. More-economical meals can be found at the cafeteria-like **Gypsy's Bakery**, where you can get great sandwiches, fries, superior baked goods, and great provisions such as imported cheeses and hard Italian sausage. Given the prices elsewhere, most tourists consider this place a godsend.

Churchill hotels tend to be expensive and disappointing, as only **Lazy Bear Lodge** (www.lazybearlodge.com) has some aesthetics going for it. B&Bs are a more affordable option. The accommodations database at www.travelmanitoba.com has the basic lowdown.

If you fancy a drink, Churchill bars can be a little gritty, but locals know the value of the tourism industry and tend to leave visitors in peace. The **Seaport Hotel** has the largest bar, but the atmosphere is funkier at the **Churchill Legion**. If you can get a Churchillian talking, you'll be entertained for hours – there isn't a person in town who doesn't have some kind of tale to spin about a close encounter with a bear.

The wreck of the *MV Ithaca*, grounded in the shallows of Hudson Bay east of Churchill. Thanks to polar bears, it's unsafe to visit without an armed escort.

Bartley Kives

Around Churchill

To explore the area around the Churchill townsite, you'll have to rent a car or hire a cab for the day. It simply is not safe to walk around in polar bear country. But if you are spending several days in town, it's fun to go driving around on your own, packing a pair of binoculars to watch birds and scan for polar bears. You should also take an air horn, for the unlikely event that a little blast of noise will deter any polar bear that sneaks up on you.

West of town, the monstrous grain elevator at the **Port of Churchill** dominates the landscape, rising up from the tundra like an otherworldly monolith. Tours can take you to upper floors, where there are amazing views of the coast. Farther west, **Cape Merry** offers a view of the mouth of the Churchill River and of Prince of Wales Fort across the strait. You'll need to hire a boat if you want to get across and see the impressive but slowly disintegrating stone structure.

Driving east of Churchill along the Hudson Bay coast, sights include the remains of cargo plane **Miss Piggy**, which crashed in 1979 on an approach to Churchill Airport, and the rusted-out hulk of the *MV Ithaca*, a British steamship that ran aground west of Bird Cove during a storm in 1960. At low tide, you can walk right up to the wreck and inspect the interior – but only if you have an armed escort, and even then, the locals may chide you for your risk-taking behaviour. Nearby **Bird Cove** is a good birding spot, while the next point to the east makes for an excellent shoreline walk, but again, only with an armed escort.

Continuing east, the former **Churchill Rocket Research Range** is now a national historic site, though there isn't much to see besides an old metal silo. The site is now home to the **Churchill Northern Studies Centre** (www.churchillmb.net/~cnsc), a base for biologists, archeologists, and other researchers. The centre also offers week-long educational vacations for ordinary tourists. Packages range from $850 for birding and wildflower tours to $2,000 for polar-bear excursions. The centre is twenty-five km east of the Churchill townsite.

Southeast of CNSC, the road continues on to a small cottage area at **Twin Lakes**, where archeologists discovered 2,900-year-old remains of pre-Dorset culture fishing camps. Again, you need to take special care walking around here.

Driving south from Churchill, you'll pass by **Akudlik Marsh**, where serious birders try to spot the rare Ross's Gull, and continue to the former site of **Dene Village**. When the Sayisi Dene were moved to Churchill, they were first deposited on the banks of the Churchill River, and later put up in houses next to a graveyard – ignoring a cultural taboo against visiting gravesites – and were finally put up in this suburb, where all the plate-glass windows were soon smashed and the people descended into madness. All that's left today are the concrete foundations of the old homes and a grim plaque that remembers the dead and pointedly uses the term genocide.

If you continue south, you'll eventually reach **Goose Creek**, a fishing spot and birding area ten km up the Churchill River. Farther

Bartley Kives

The rocks along Hudson Bay, immediately north of Churchill's town centre complex. Due to a process known as isostatic rebound, the shore is rising at a rate of several centimetres a century.

south of Churchill, accessible only by train and a short ride on a Bombardier, **Wat'chee Lodge** (www.watcheelodge.mb.ca) offers the most-secluded wildlife-watching opportunities in the Churchill area. Parks Canada has begun experimenting with camping tours inside Wapusk National Park, where tourists stay inside the perimeter of an electric fence. But until you hear otherwise, the polar bear denning areas are off-limits to anyone but researchers, in the interest of protecting both bears and tourists.

Northern Manitoba Wilderness Rivers

Although this guidebook makes no pretense of functioning as a wilderness traveller's handbook, there are two river trips in northern Manitoba worth mentioning.

In the seventeenth and eighteenth centuries, the **Hayes River** was the busiest highway in the north, used to transport goods between the Red River Settlement and York Factory at Hudson Bay in flat-bottomed York boats. Today, the river has retained its wild character, as Manitoba Hydro has chosen to dam up other rivers. It takes experienced whitewater paddlers three weeks to a month to traverse all 600 km between Norway House and York Factory, where the remains of fur storehouses still stand.

The more-remote **Seal River**, which runs from Tadoule Lake to Hudson Bay, demands even better whitewater, route-finding, and survival skills. A guide is recommended for the 300-km, three-week jaunt.

Toward the end of both trips, Hudson Bay tides and polar bears present additional dangers. Guided Hayes trips can be arranged through **Northern Soul Wilderness Adventures** (www.northernsoul.ca) and **Wilderness Spirit** (www.wilderness spirit.com), two respected Winnipeg ecotourism companies.

Hayes River
This Canadian heritage river follows the historic fur-trade route between Lake Winnipeg and York Factory, on Hudson Bay.

Acknowledgements and Thanks

The basic structure of this book is a shameless rip-off of the excellent *Lonely Planet* formula, minus most of the hotel and restaurant info that usually winds up out-of-date by the time you purchase your copy, anyway.

Many facts, figures and dates in the introductory chapters of this guidebook were compiled from materials published online by Statistics Canada, Travel Manitoba, Manitoba Conservation, Manitoba Highways, the Manitoba Historical Society, and Environment Canada, as well as most of the guidebooks listed in the *Selected Sources* section.

Overall, this guidebook would not exist without the patience and encouragement of my partner Katarina Kupca and the initiative and hard work of Gregg Shilliday, Adam Levin, Anita Daher, and Jewls Dengl at Great Plains Publications. As well, designer Suzanne Braun deserves an award for making a guidebook attractive to read.

A Lake Winnipeg–sized ocean of gratitude must also be extended to my colleagues and editors at the *Winnipeg Free Press*, particularly Paul Pihichyn and Margo Goodhand, for giving me the opportunity and flexibility to write about wilderness travel. I'm also indebted to Jill Wilson and Alison Mayes for allowing me to go AWOL during the fall of 2005 to complete this book.

Katarina Kupca, Suzanne Matczuk, Jason Old, Lynne Skromeda, and Jason Sorby all deserve major props for ferreting out flaws and inconsistencies. More thanks go out to Jon Thordarson for opening up the *Free Press* photo archives and to Charles Shilliday for taking it upon himself to snap many of his own shots.

Other people deserving of kudos are Mireille Lamontagne at Parks Canada; Leone Banks at Prairie Pathfinders, for the 411 on Swan River; Frank Sjoberg at Wilderness Supply, for the extended loan of Ruth Marr's hiking guide; John K. Samson for the free legal; and Susy Levin at Leave No Trace for granting swift permission to reprint her organization's excellent camping ethics. Also helping out with info or advice were Colleen Simard, Karin McSherry, Kim Hope, Dave Bidini, Brad Bird, Rob Williams and Geoff Kirbyson.

Additional thanks belong to my immediate family – Eema, Aba, Cheryl, Ronni, Claire, Zada, Saba, Sam, Donna, Eta, and Stefan – for tolerating my preoccupation during the latter months of 2005.

Finally, anyone who's ever put up with me on the trail or on the road deserves a generous glass of something decent: Jason, Jeff and Lauren, Jason and Kara, Jerrod, Ewan and Marnie, Billy, Lynne, Brian, Geoff, Kevin, Julie and Brad, Phil, Mike, and especially Katarina, my ever-supportive guinea pig.

Thanks, todah, merci, meegwetch, danke, dakuyem, and gracias. I think that just about covers it.

Selected Sources and Further Reading

Go out and buy these books. Ruth Marr's hiking guide is out of print, but the rest should be available in Manitoba bookstores.

Aksomitis, Linda. *Backroad Mapbook: Southern Manitoba*. Burnaby, BC: Backroad Mapbooks, 2005.

Ames, Doris, Peggy Bainard Acheson, Lorne Heshka, et al. *Orchids of Manitoba*. Winnipeg: Native Orchid Conservation Inc., 2005.

Archer, Laurel. *Northern Saskatchewan Canoe Routes*. Erin, Ont.: Boston Mills Press, 2003.

Bezener, Andy, and Ken De Smet. *Manitoba Birds*. Edmonton: Lone Pine, 2000.

Buchanan, John. *Canoeing Manitoba Rivers – Vol. 1 South*. Calgary: Rocky Mountain Books, 1997.

Henderson, Jeff. *Where the York Boats Meet the Ox Carts*. Swan River, Man.: Mixed Forest Research & Advisory Committee, 2002.

Huck, Barbara. *Exploring the Fur Trade Routes of North America*. Winnipeg: Heartland Publications, 2000.

Lake of the Woods Museum. *The Explorer's Guide to Lake of the Woods*. Kenora, Ont.: The Lake of the Woods Museum, 2000.

Lebrecht, Sue. *Trans-Canada Trail Guide: Manitoba*. Kingston, Ont.: Canadian Geographic, 2003.

Manitoba Avian Research Committee. *The Birds of Manitoba*. Winnipeg: Manitoba Naturalists Society, 2003.

Marr, Ruth. *Manitoba Walking and Hiking Guide*. Saskatoon: Fifth House, 1990.

Morton, Marilyn, ed. *Manitoba: Colour Guide*. Halifax: Formac Publishing, 1995.

Senecal, Catherine. *Pelicans to Polar Bears: Wildlife Watching in Manitoba*. Winnipeg: Heartland, 1999.

Prairie Pathfinders. *Manitoba Walks*. Winnipeg: Prairie Pathfinders, 2001.

Stewart, Kenneth W., and Douglas A. Watkinson. *The Freshwater Fishes of Manitoba*. Winnipeg: University of Manitoba Press, 2004.

Stillwell, Bill. Scenic Secrets of Manitoba. Brandon, Man.: Prairie Mountain, 1997.

Welsted, John, John Everitt, and Christoph Stadel, eds. *The Geography of Manitoba – Its Land and its People*. Winnipeg: University of Manitoba Press, 1996.

Wilson, Hap, and Stephanie Aykroyd. *Wilderness Rivers of Manitoba*. Erin, Ont.: Boston Mills Press, 2004.

Index